4

Hiro Mashima

Translated and adapted by William Flanagan
Lettered by North Market Street Graphics

Ballantine Books · New York

A Del Rey Manga/Kodansha Trade Paperback Original

Fairy Tail volume 4 copyright © 2007 by Hiro Mashima
English translation copyright © 2008 by Hiro Mashima

Published in the United States by Del Rey, an imprint of The Random House Publishing Group, a division of Random House, Inc., New York.

DEL REY is a registered trademark and the Del Rey colophon is a trademark of Random House, Inc.

Publication rights arranged through Kodansha Ltd.

First published in Japan in 2007 by Kodansha Ltd., Tokyo

ISBN 978-0-345-50557-6

Printed in the United States of America

www.delreymanga.com

9 8 7 6 5 4 3 2 1

Translator/Adapter—William Flanagan
Lettering—North Market Street Graphics

Contents

Natsu's pose on the cover...
What the heck is he doing...?
Maybe the only reason for it is
that I wanted to draw a hand in
that shape. No matter how much
I wanted to draw it, the fact that
I couldn't draw it well is very
much like me. (laughs)
"That's it! I wanna draw that!!"
There are a whole lot of
examples of that kind of feeling
in this very volume, but the
final drawings never seem to
measure up to my mental image
of them....
I'll keep trying.

—Hiro Mashima

Honorifics Explained

Throughout the Del Rey Manga books, you will find Japanese honorifics left intact in the translations. For those not familiar with how the Japanese use honorifics and, more important, how they differ from American honorifics, we present this brief overview.

Politeness has always been a critical facet of Japanese culture. Ever since the feudal era, when Japan was a highly stratified society, use of honorifics—which can be defined as polite speech that indicates relationship or status—has played an essential role in the Japanese language. When addressing someone in Japanese, an honorific usually takes the form of a suffix attached to one's name (example: "Asuna-san"), is used as a title at the end of one's name, or appears in place of the name itself (example: "Negi-sensei," or simply "Sensei!").

Honorifics can be expressions of respect or endearment. In the context of manga and anime, honorifics give insight into the nature of the relationship between characters. Many English translations leave out these important honorifics and therefore distort the feel of the original Japanese. Because Japanese honorifics contain nuances that English honorifics lack, it is our policy at Del Rey not to translate them. Here, instead, is a guide to some of the honorifics you may encounter in Del Rey Manga.

-**san**: This is the most common honorific and is equivalent to Mr., Miss, Ms., or Mrs. It is the all-purpose honorific and can be used in any situation where politeness is required.

-**sama**: This is one level higher than "-san" and is used to confer great respect.

-**dono**: This comes from the word "tono," which means "lord." It is an even higher level than "-sama" and confers utmost respect.

-kun: This suffix is used at the end of boys' names to express familiarity or endearment. It is also sometimes used by men among friends, or when addressing someone younger or of a lower station.

-chan: This is used to express endearment, mostly toward girls. It is also used for little boys, pets, and even between lovers. It gives a sense of childish cuteness.

Bozu: This is an informal way to refer to a boy, similar to the English terms "kid" and "squirt."

Sempai/ Senpai: This title suggests that the addressee is one's senior in a group or organization. It is most often used in a school setting, where underclassmen refer to their upperclassmen as "sempai." It can also be used in the workplace, such as when a newer employee addresses an employee who has seniority in the company.

Kohai: This is the opposite of "sempai" and is used toward underclassmen in school or newcomers in the workplace. It connotes that the addressee is of a lower station.

Sensei: Literally meaning "one who has come before," this title is used for teachers, doctors, or masters of any profession or art.

-[blank]: This is usually forgotten in these lists, but it is perhaps the most significant difference between Japanese and English. The lack of honorific means that the speaker has permission to address the person in a very intimate way. Usually, only family, spouses, or very close friends have this kind of permission. Known as *yobisute*, it can be gratifying when someone who has earned the intimacy starts to call one by one's name without an honorific. But when that intimacy hasn't been earned, it can be very insulting.

FAIRY TAIL

4

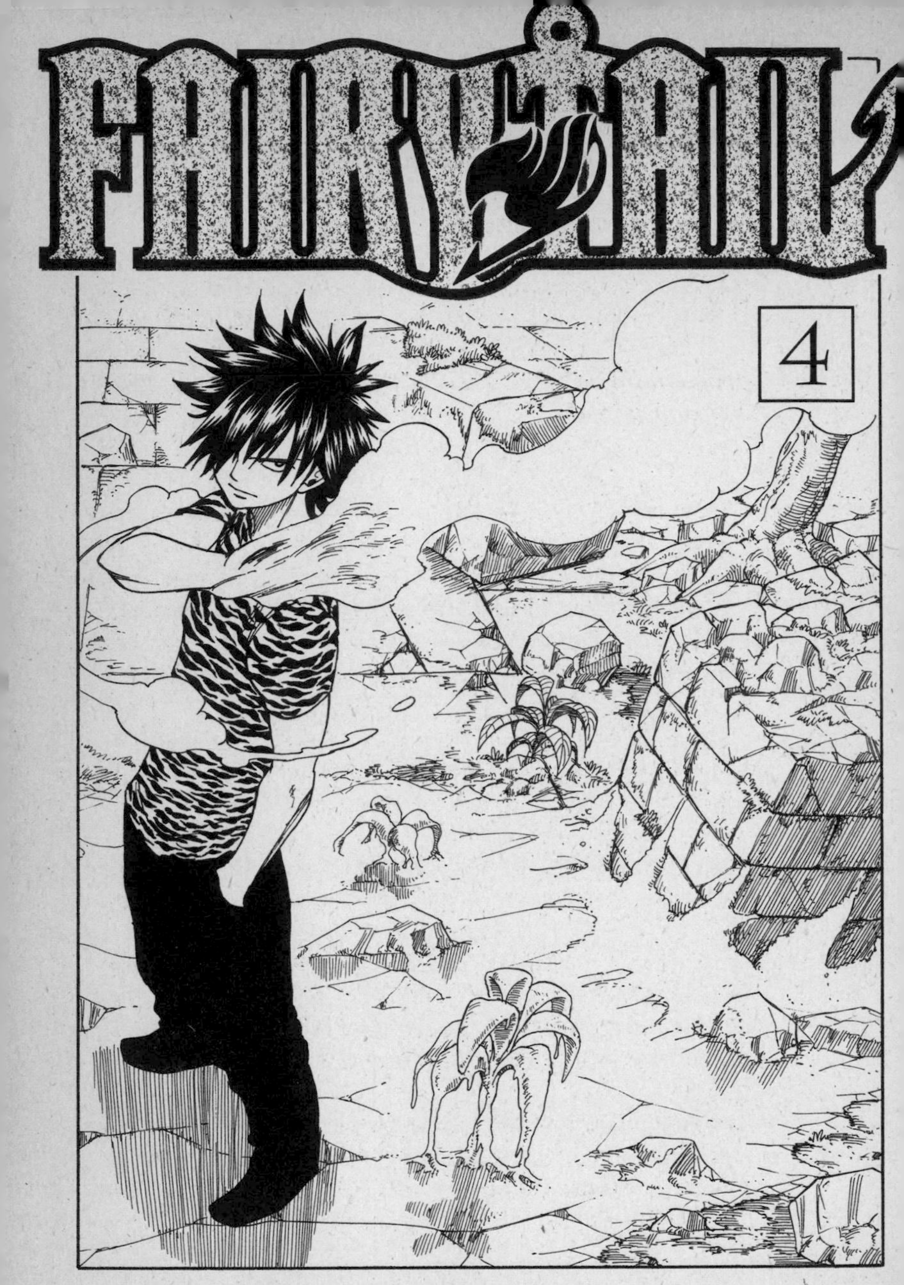

HIRO MASHIMA

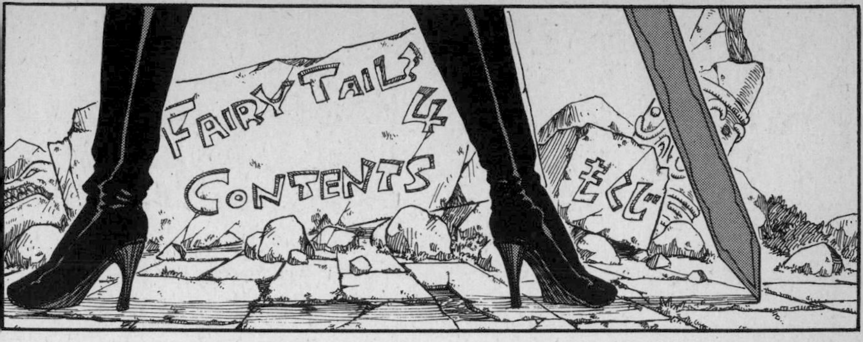
FAIRY TAIL 4
CONTENTS

FAIRY TAIL

Chapter 23:
Crime and Punishment

FAIRY TAIL

Name: Natsu

Age: Unknown

Magic: Dragon Slayer

Dislikes: Moving Vehicles

Likes: Fire

Remarks

Fairy Tail's problem child. His magic allows him to eat fire and envelop himself in fire. It seems to be a very ancient magic. Along with his partner Happy, he is in constant search of the one who raised him, Igneel (a dragon).

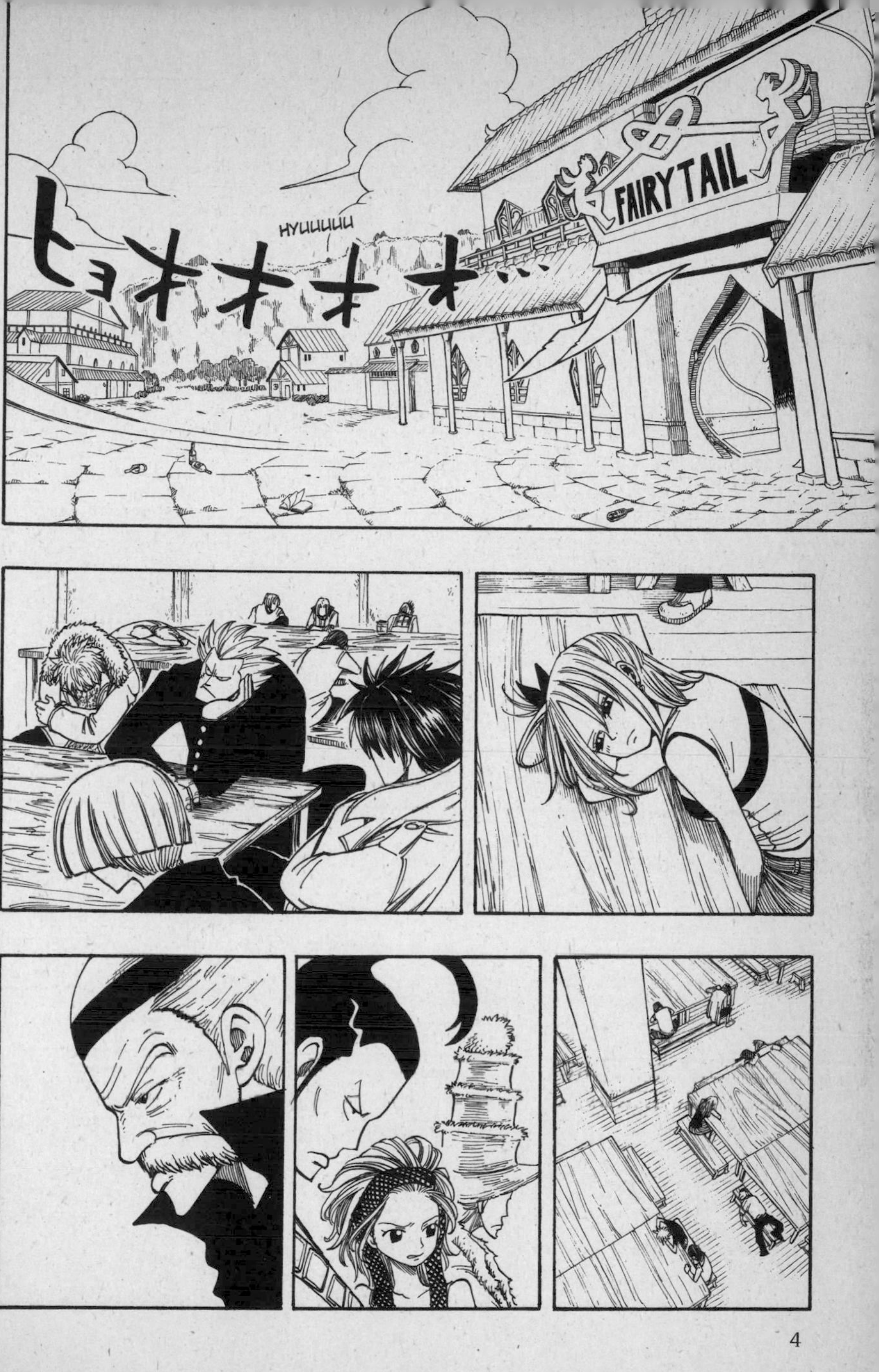
FAIRY TAIL
ヒョォォォォ…
HYUUUUU

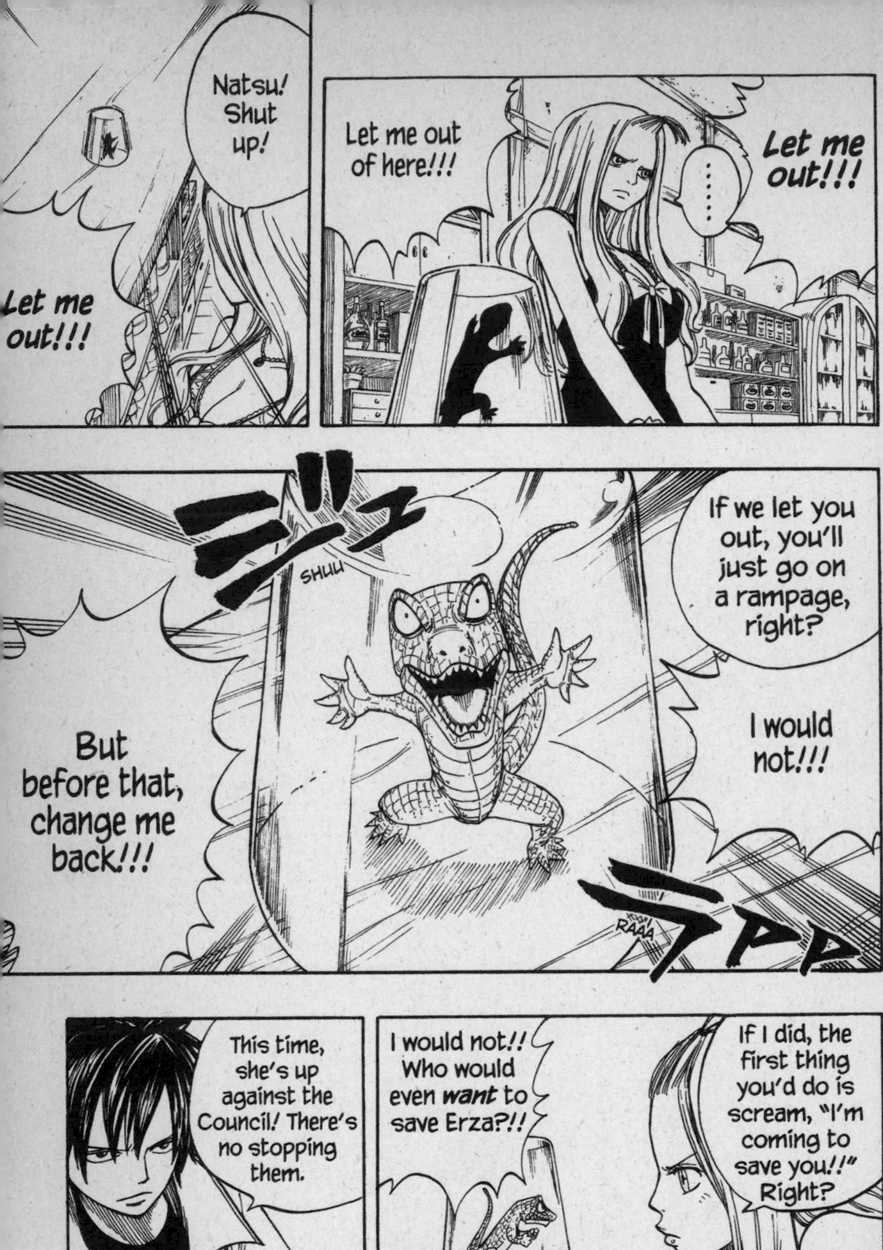
Let me out!!!
......
Let me out of here!!!
Natsu! Shut up!
Let me out!!!
If we let you out, you'll just go on a rampage, right?
ジュ
SHUU
I would not!!!
But before that, change me back!!!
ラアア
RAAA
If I did, the first thing you'd do is scream, "I'm coming to save you!!" Right?
I would not!! Who would even *want* to save Erza?!!
This time, she's up against the Council! There's no stopping them.

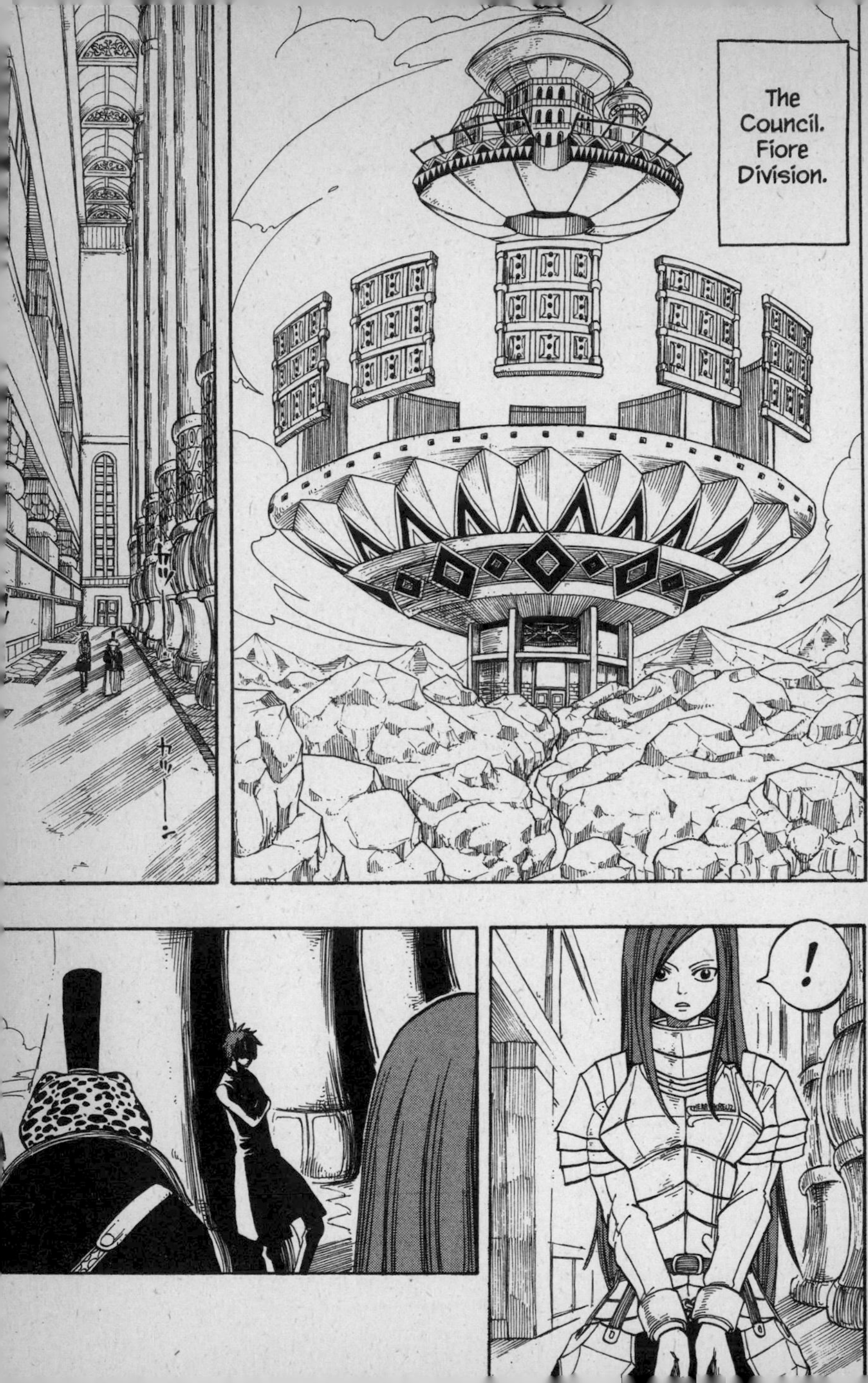
The Council. Fiore Division.
カツー
カツーン
!

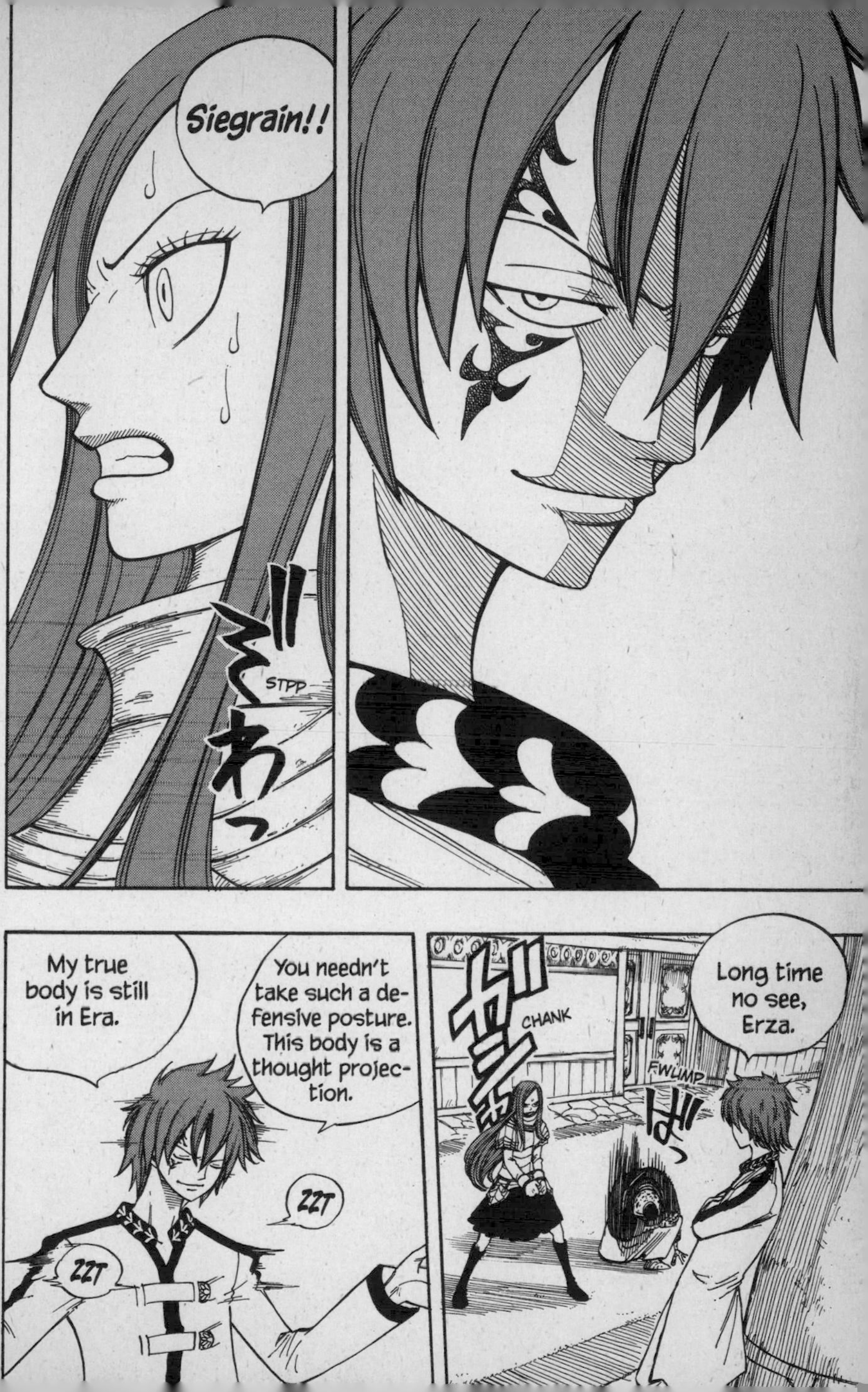
Siegrain!!
STPP
Long time no see, Erza.
CHANK
FWUMP
You needn't take such a defensive posture. This body is a thought projection.
My true body is still in Era.
ZZT
ZZT

10

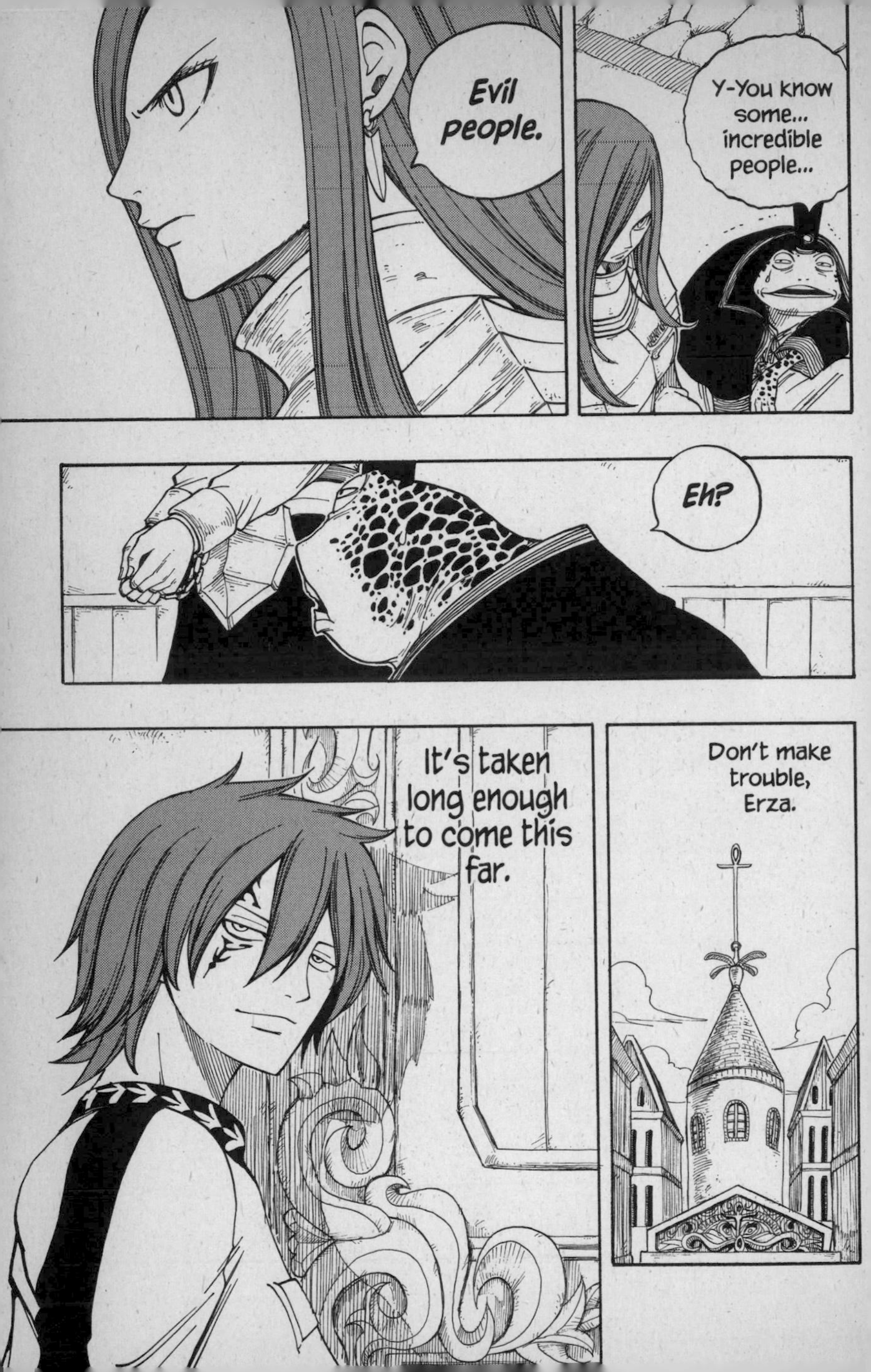
Y-You know some... incredible people...
Evil people.
Eh?
Don't make trouble, Erza.
It's taken long enough to come this far.

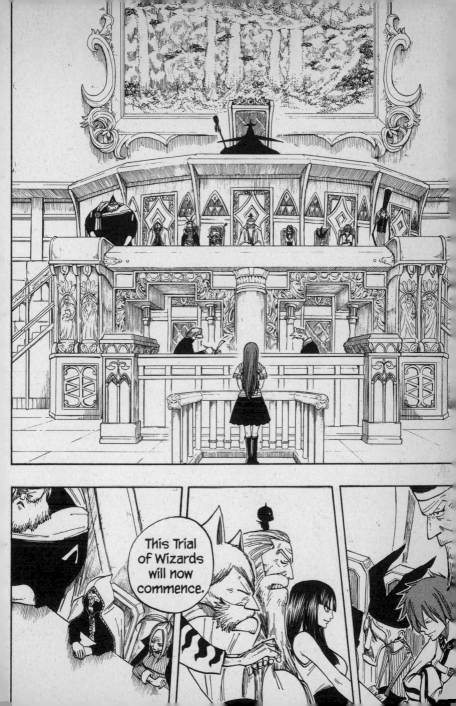

This Trial of Wizards will now commence.

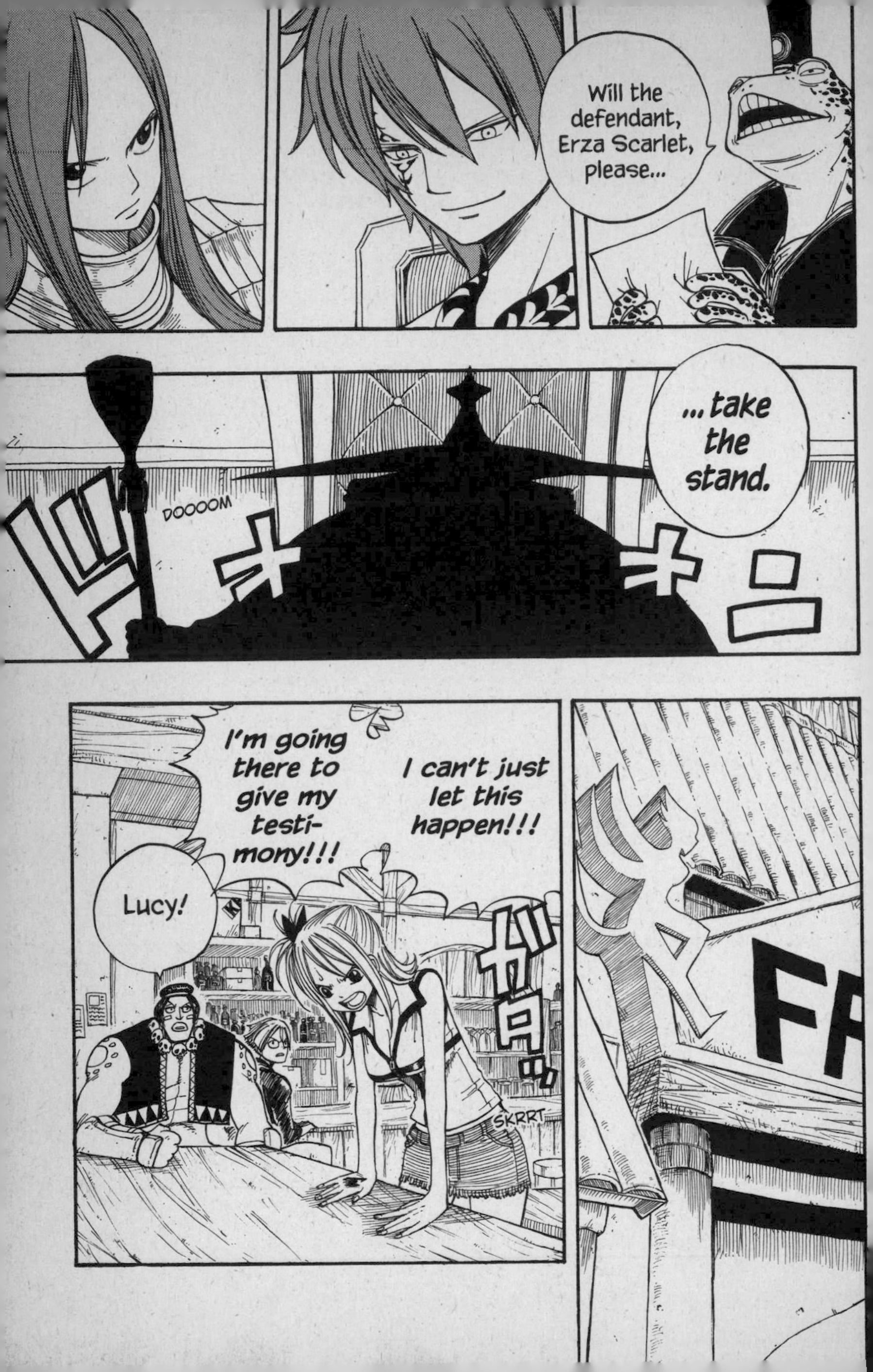
Will the defendant, Erza Scarlet, please...
...take the stand.
DOOOOM
FA
I can't just let this happen!!!
I'm going there to give my testi-mony!!!
Lucy!
SKRRT

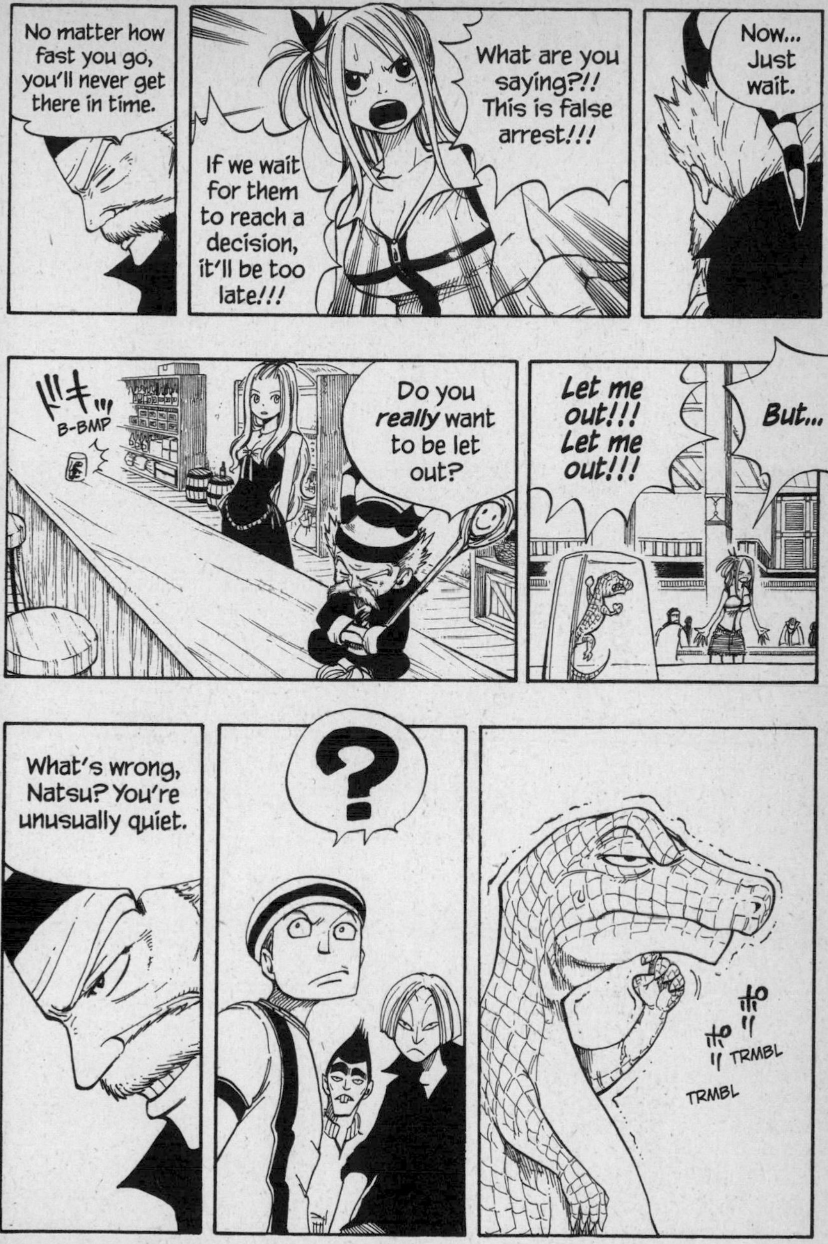
Now... Just wait.
What are you saying?!! This is false arrest!!!
If we wait for them to reach a decision, it'll be too late!!!
No matter how fast you go, you'll never get there in time.
But...
Let me out!!! Let me out!!!
Do you *really* want to be let out?
ドキ
B-BMP
TRMBL
TRMBL
?
What's wrong, Natsu? You're unusually quiet.

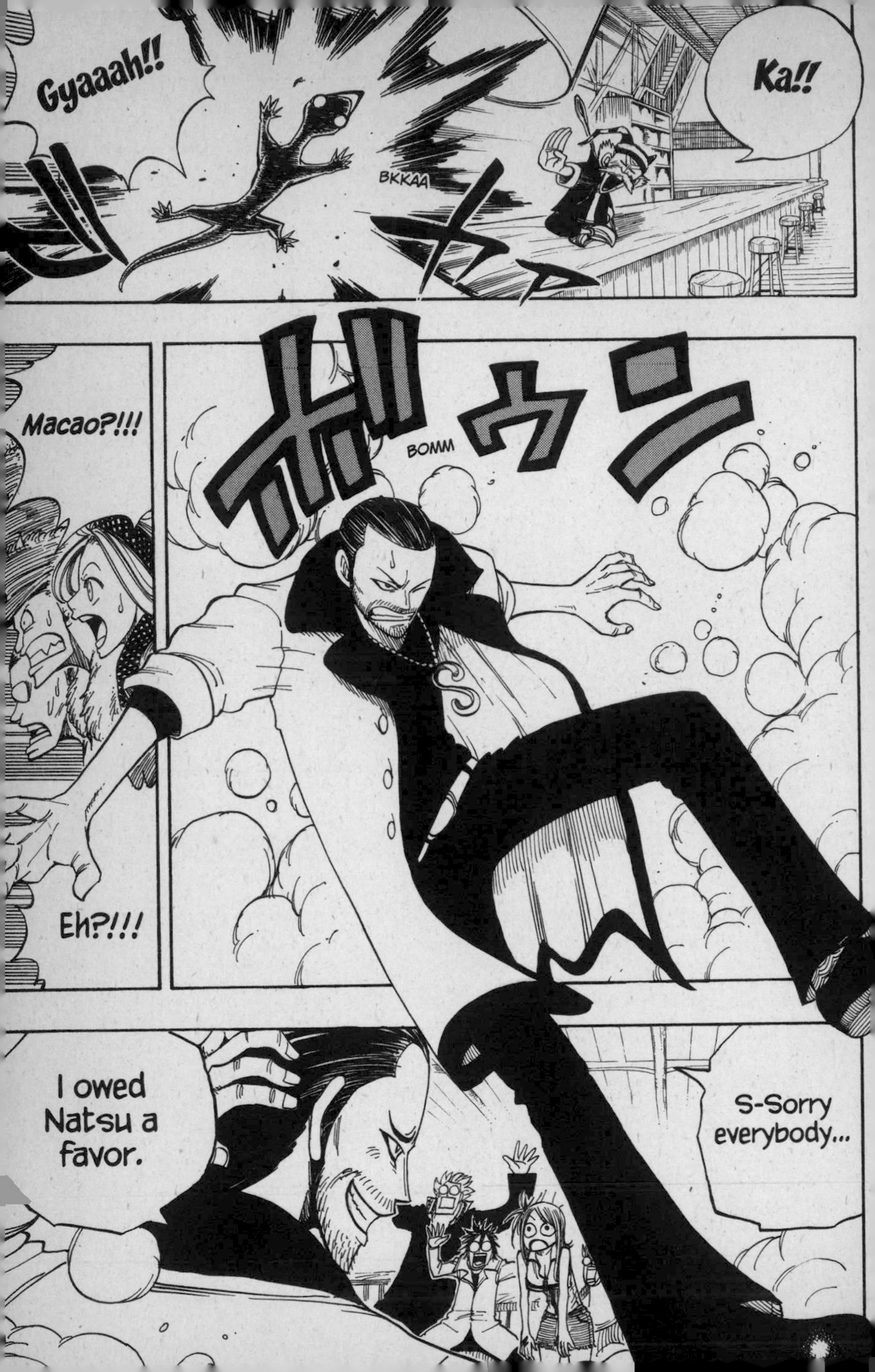
Ka!!
BKKAA
Gyaaah!!
ボウン
BOMM
Macao?!!!
Eh?!!!
S-Sorry everybody...
I owed Natsu a favor.

16

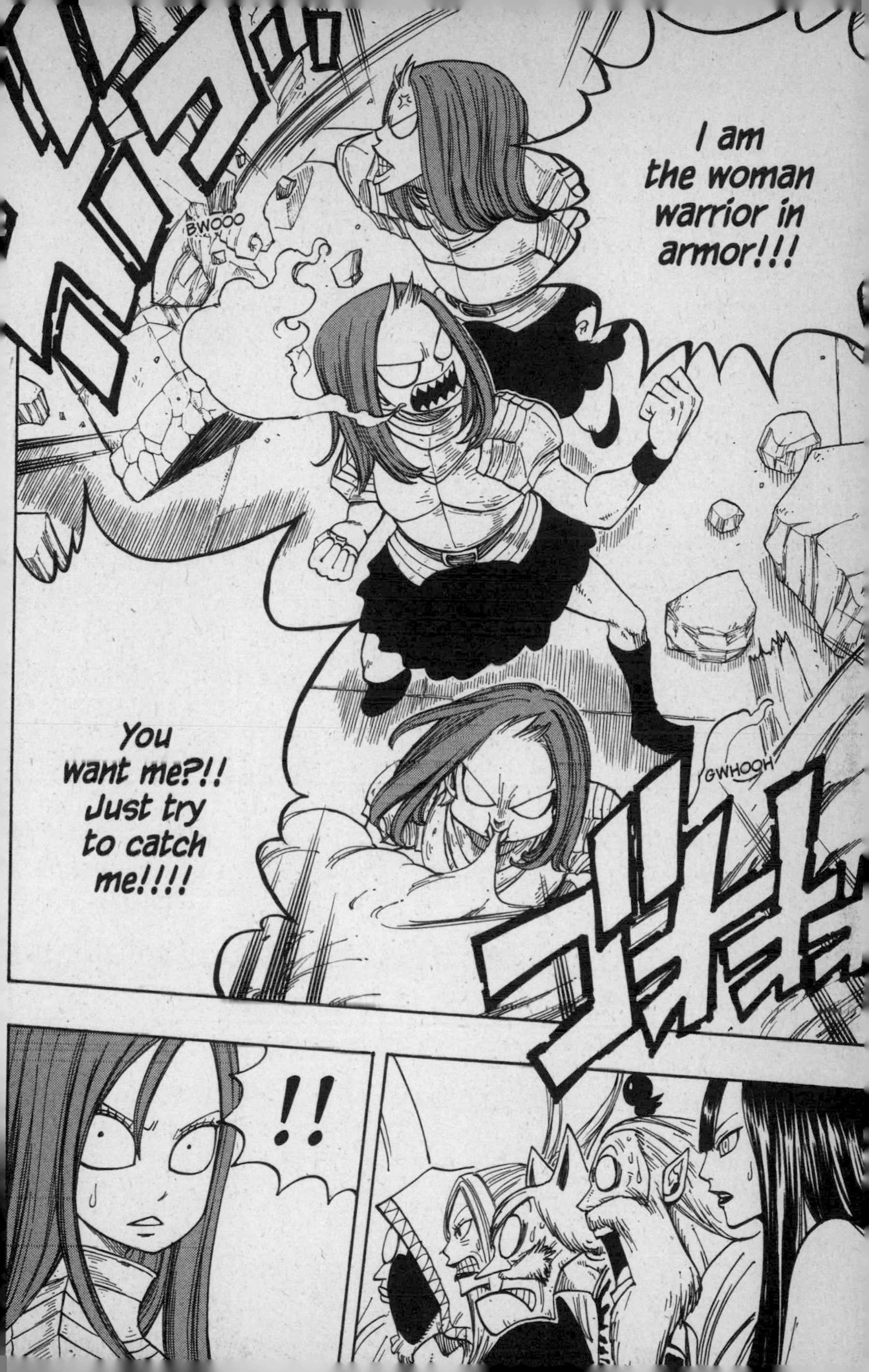

I am the woman warrior in armor!!!
BWOOO
GWHOOH
You want me?!! Just try to catch me!!!!
!!

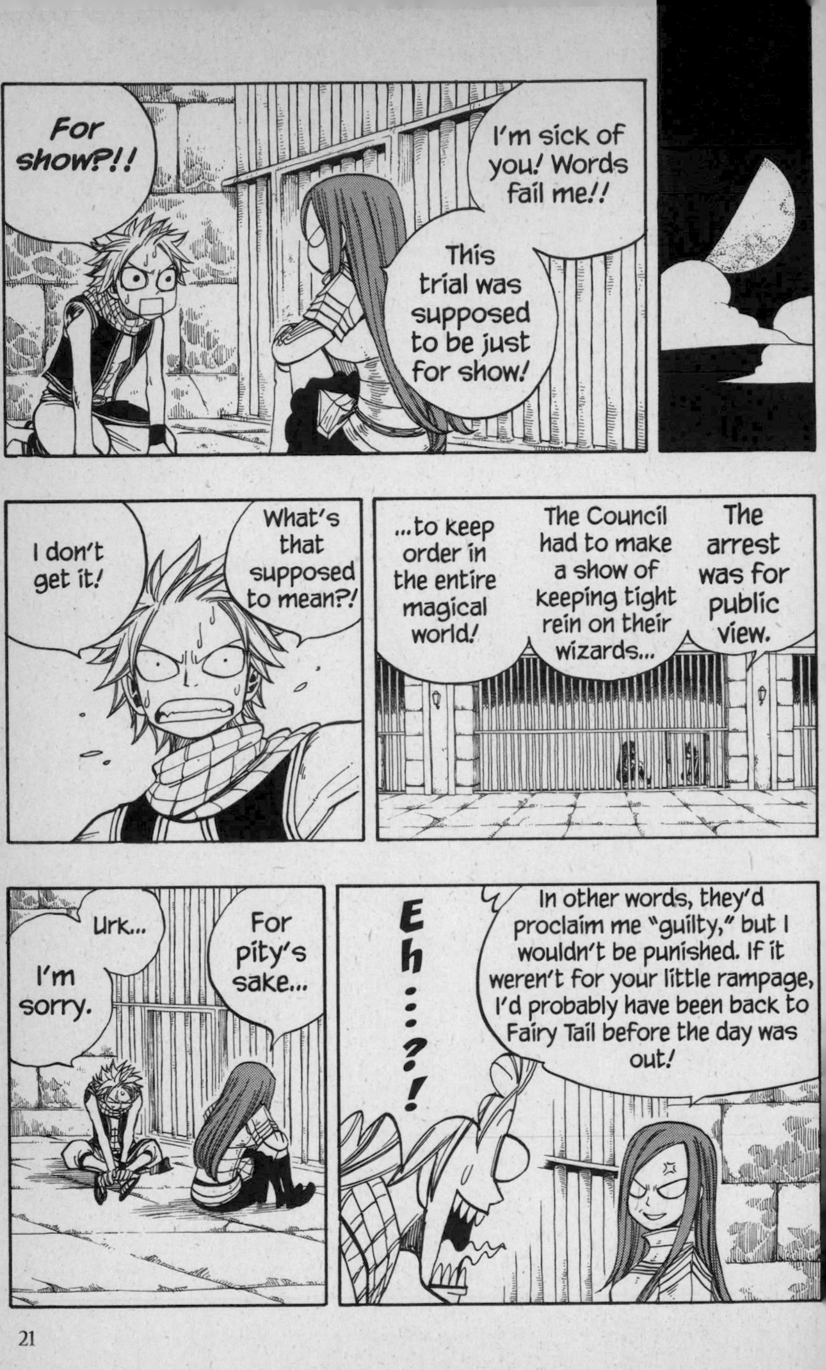
I'm sick of you! Words fail me!!
This trial was supposed to be just for show!
For show?!!
The arrest was for public view.
The Council had to make a show of keeping tight rein on their wizards...
...to keep order in the entire magical world!
What's that supposed to mean?!
I don't get it!
In other words, they'd proclaim me "guilty," but I wouldn't be punished. If it weren't for your little rampage, I'd probably have been back to Fairy Tail before the day was out!
Eh...?!
For pity's sake...
Urk...
I'm sorry.

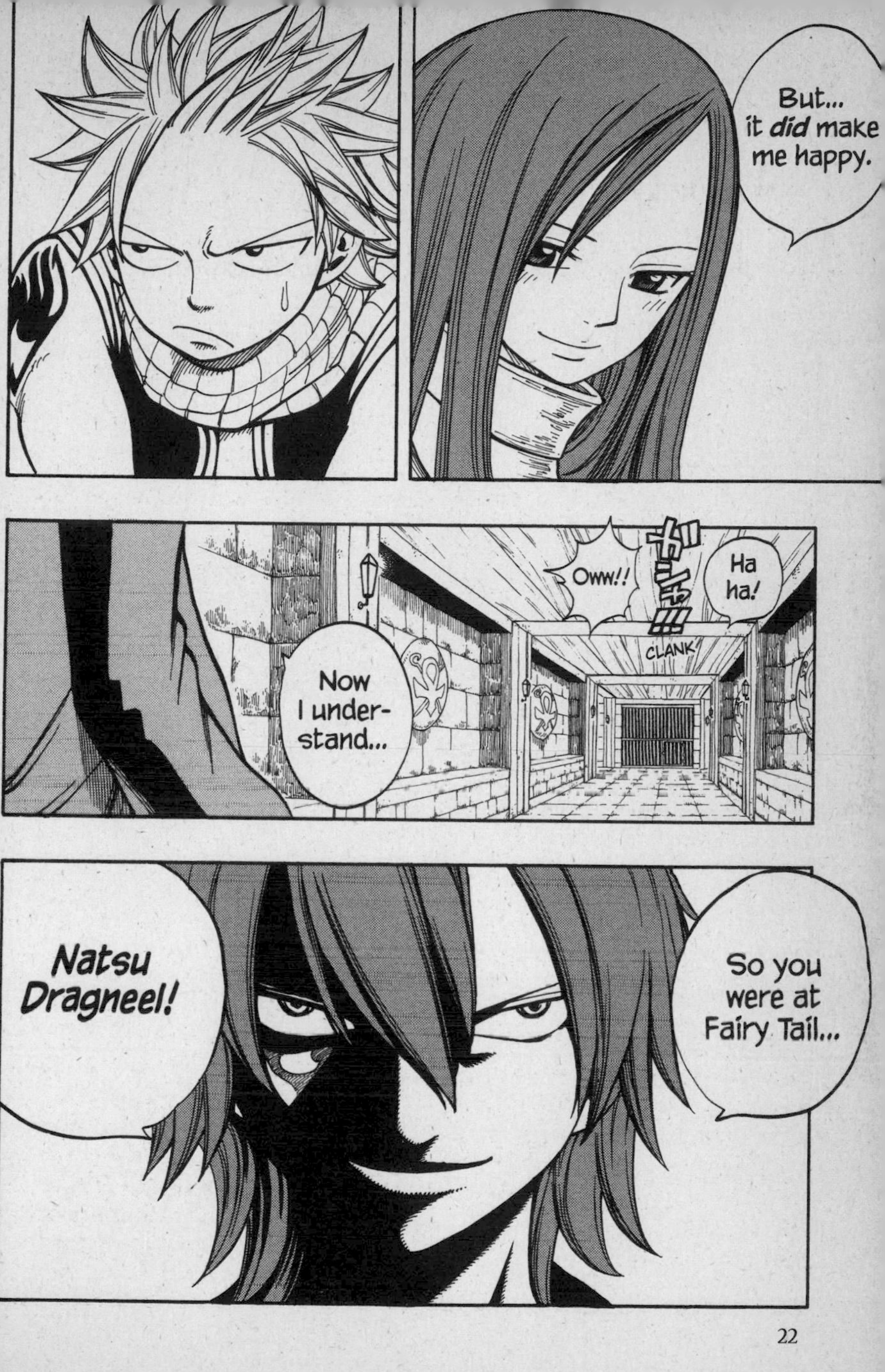
But... it *did* make me happy.
Ha ha!
Oww!!
CLANK
Now I understand...
So you were at Fairy Tail...
Natsu Dragneel!

FAIRY TAIL

Chapter 24: Second Floor

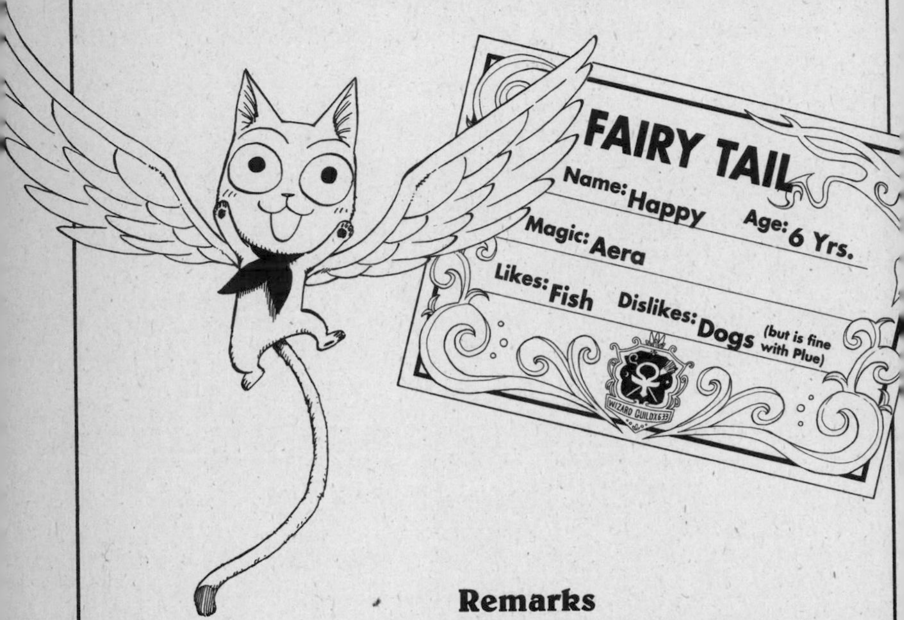
FAIRY TAIL
Name: Happy
Age: 6 Yrs.
Magic: Aera
Likes: Fish
Dislikes: Dogs (but is fine with Plue)
WIZARD GUILD

Remarks

The cat (?) that is always with Natsu. He talks and can use magic, but nobody seems to question him about it. Everyone probably just figures that's just the kind of animal that he is, and lets it go at that. The story of his meeting with Natsu is a tale for another day.

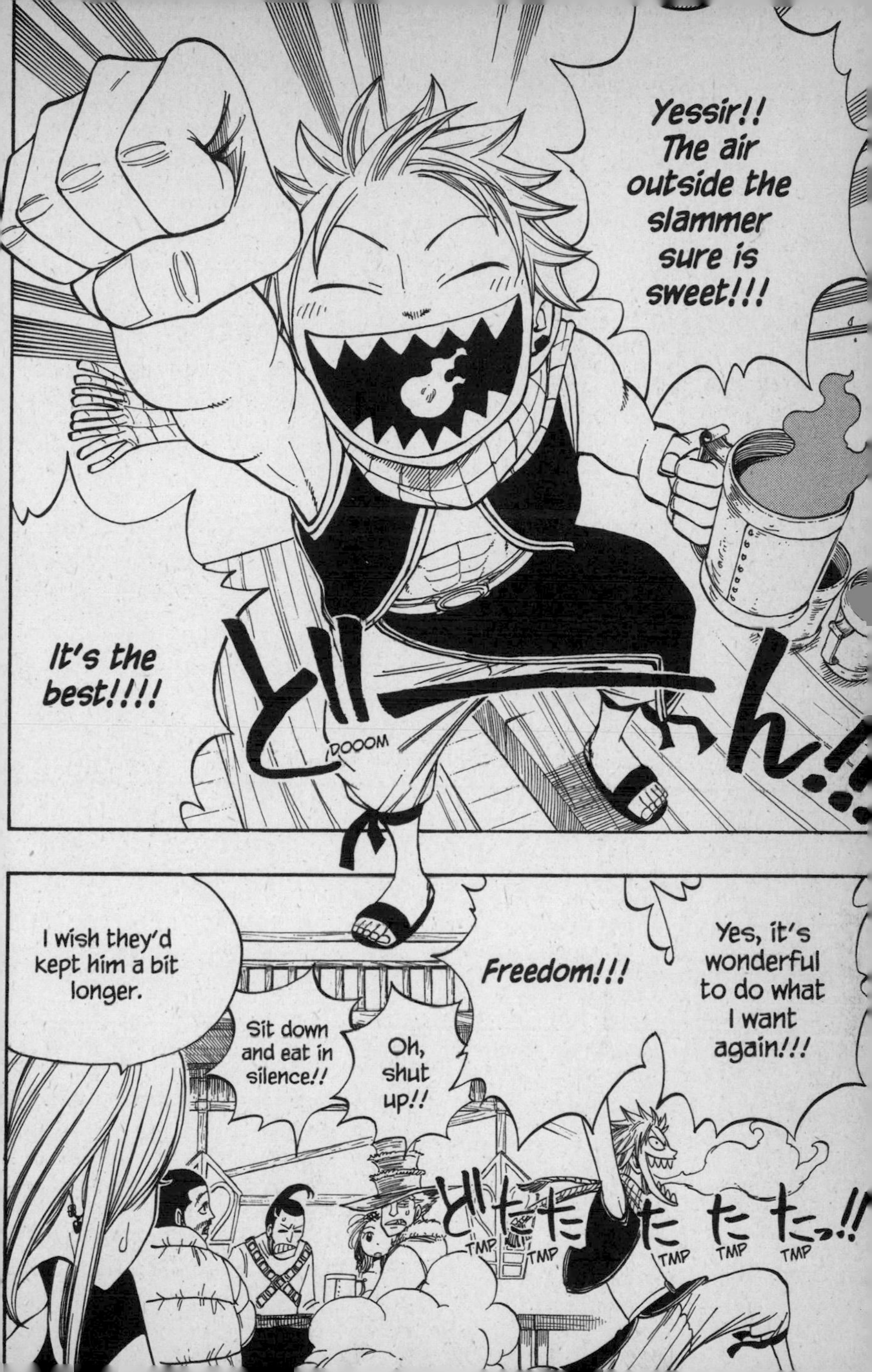
Yessir!! The air outside the slammer sure is sweet!!!
It's the best!!!!
DOOOM
Yes, it's wonderful to do what I want again!!!
Freedom!!!
Oh, shut up!!
Sit down and eat in silence!!
I wish they'd kept him a bit longer.
TMP TMP TMP TMP TMP

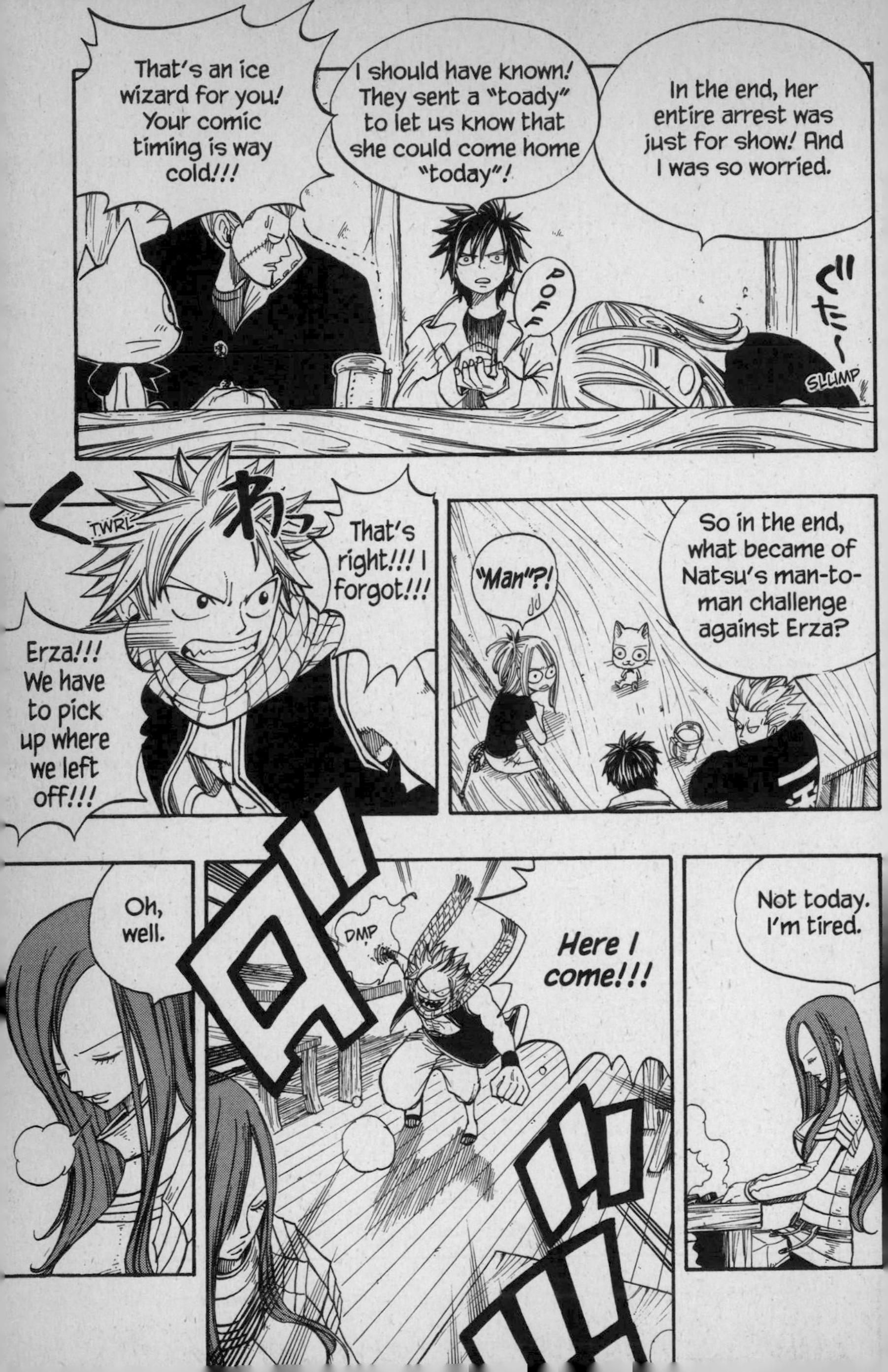
In the end, her entire arrest was just for show! And I was so worried.
SLUMP
POFF
I should have known! They sent a "toady" to let us know that she could come home "today"!
That's an ice wizard for you! Your comic timing is way cold!!!
So in the end, what became of Natsu's man-to-man challenge against Erza?
"Man"?!
That's right!!! I forgot!!!
TWRL
Erza!!! We have to pick up where we left off!!!
Not today. I'm tired.
Here I come!!!
DMP
Oh, well.

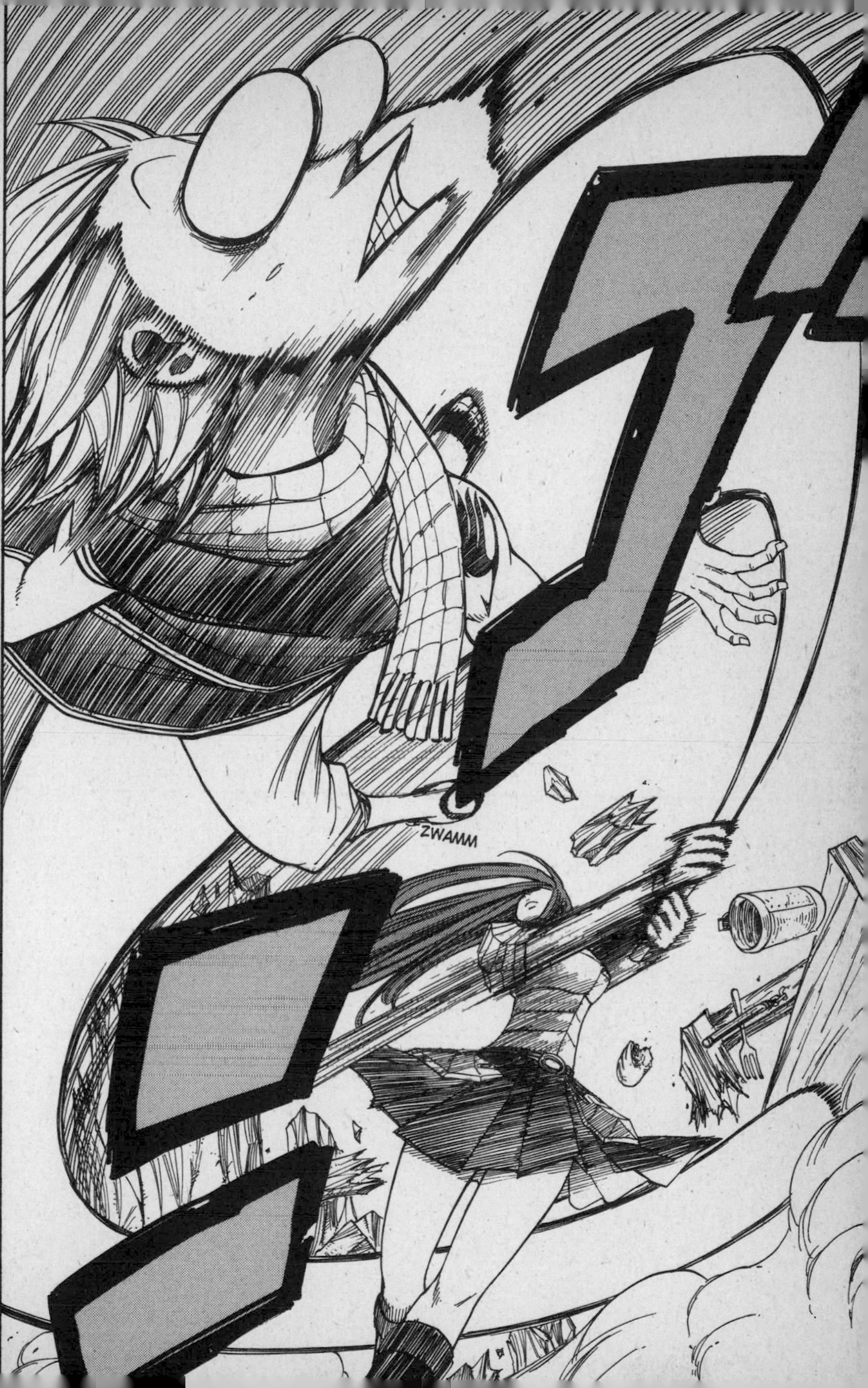
ZWAMM

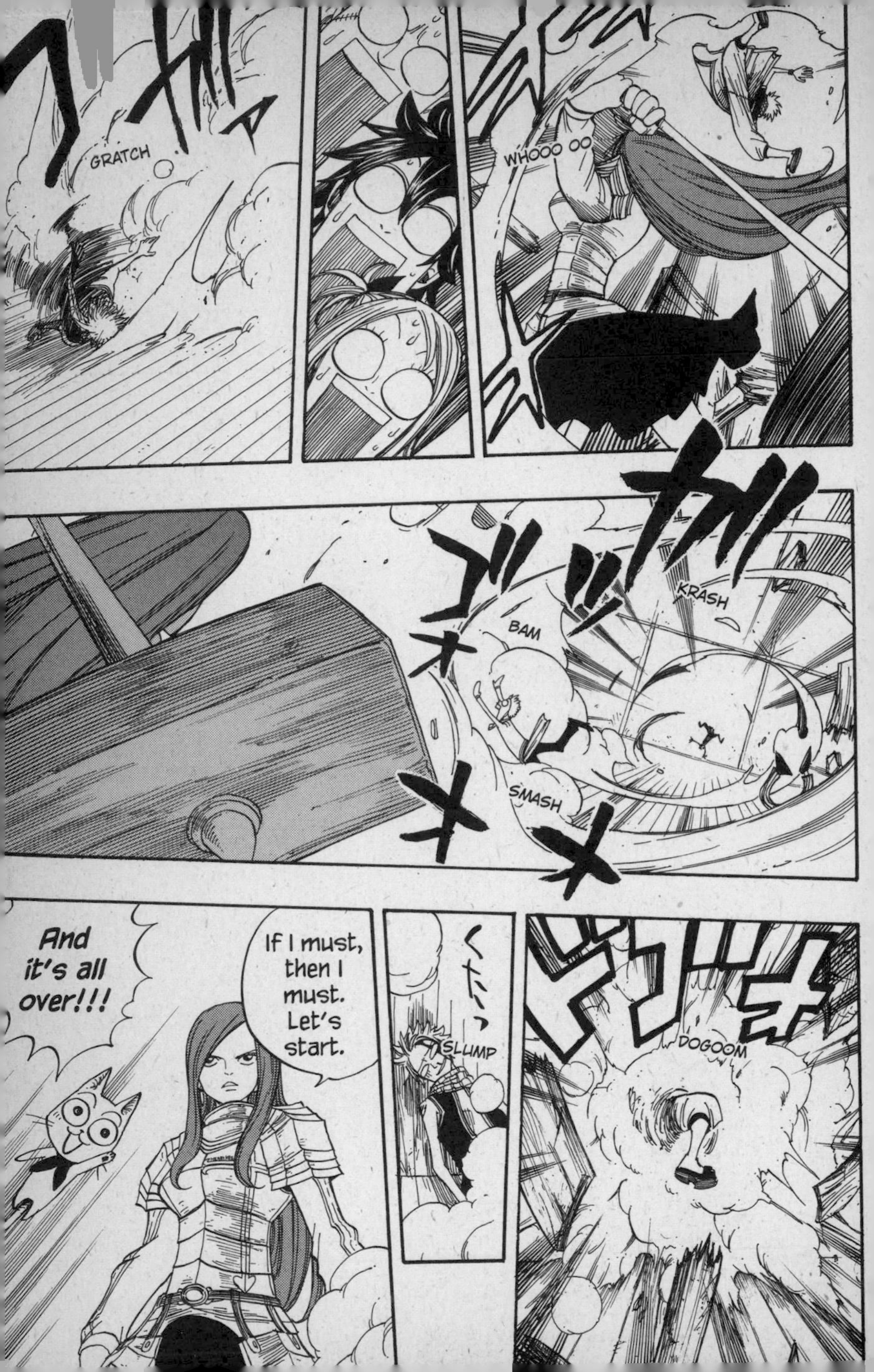
WHOOO OO
GRATCH
KRASH
BAM
SMASH
DOGOOM
SLUMP
If I must, then I must. Let's start.
And it's all over!!!

28

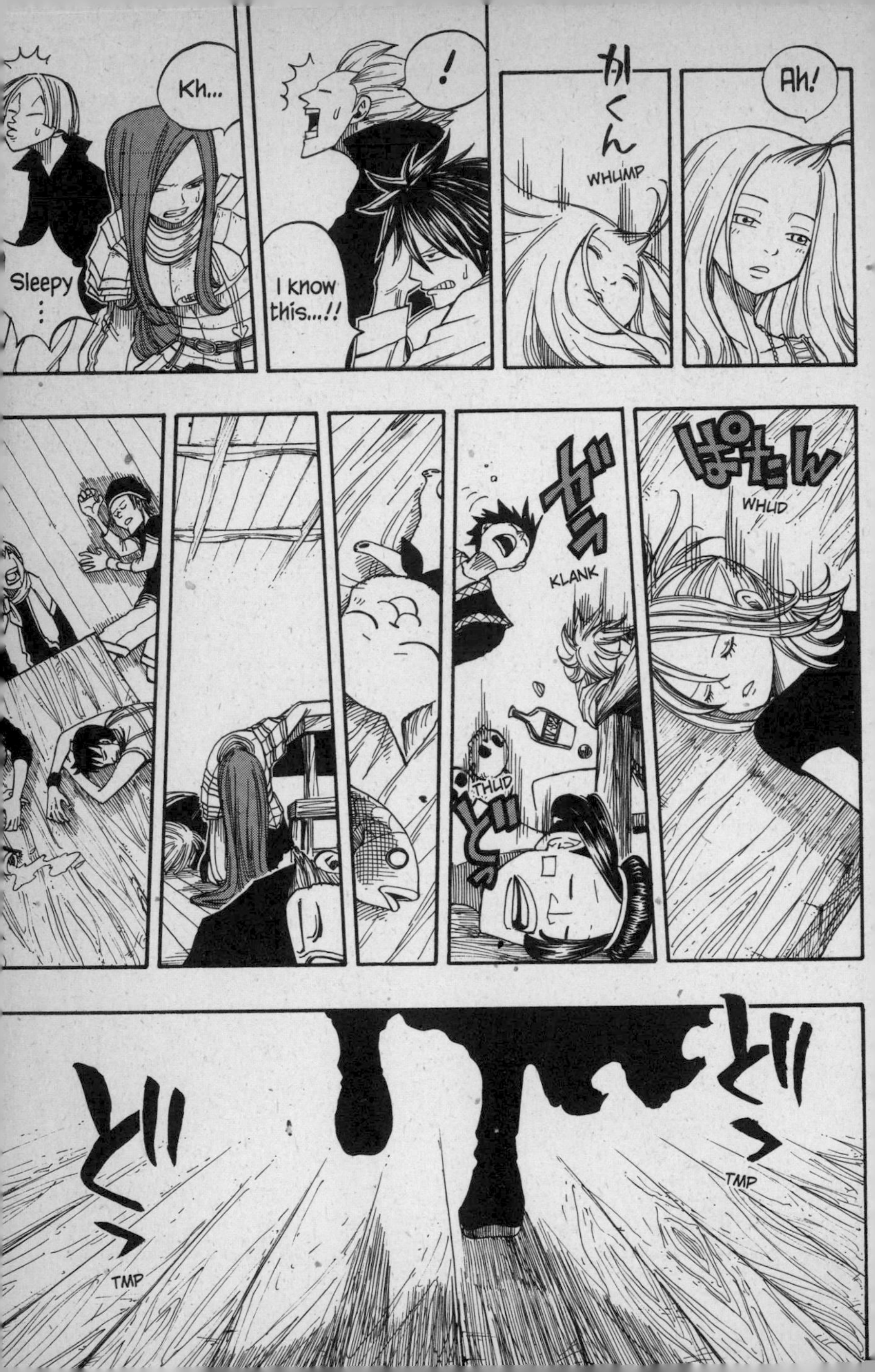
Ah!
かくん
WHUMP
!
I know this...!!
Kh...
Sleepy...
ぽたん
WHUD
ガラ
KLANK
どっ
THUD
どっ
TMP
どっ
TMP

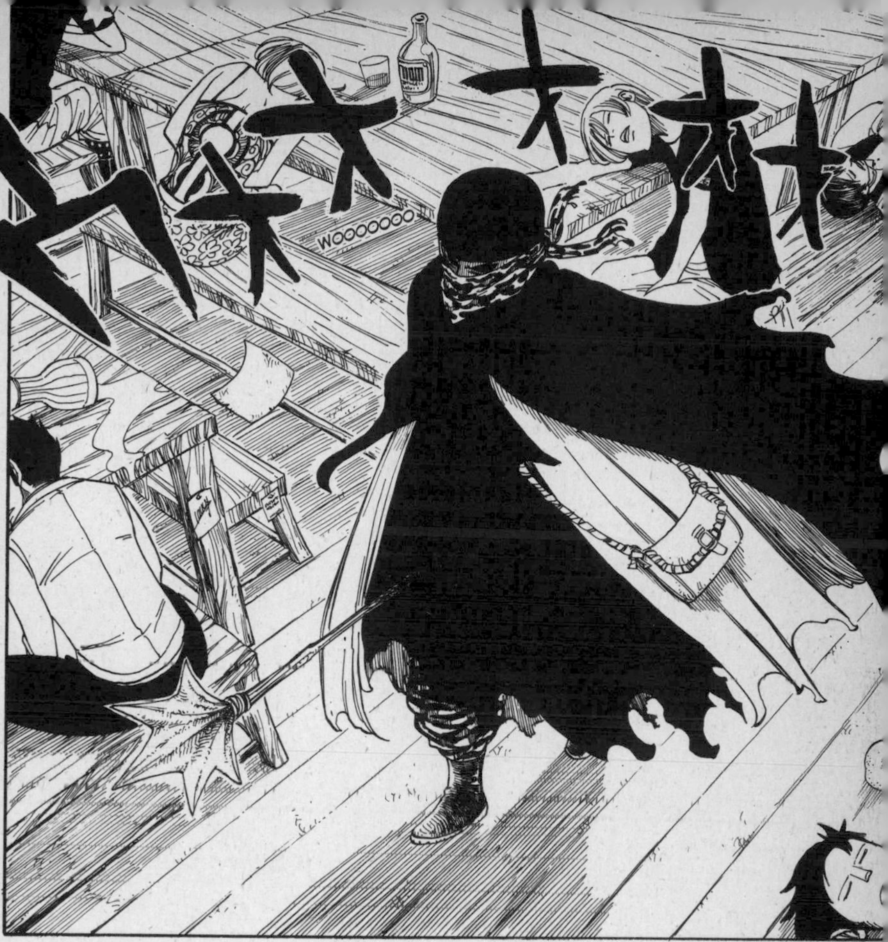
WOOOOOOO

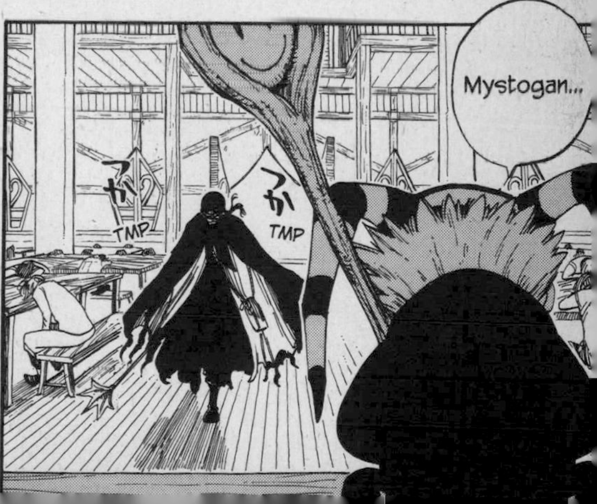
Mystogan...
つか
TMP
つか
TMP

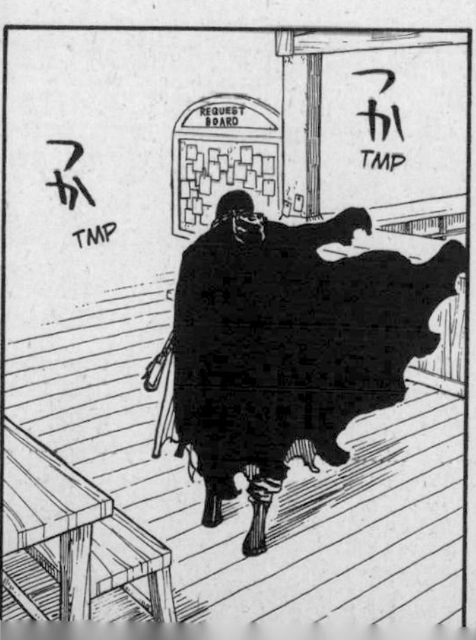
REQUEST BOARD
つか
TMP
つか
TMP

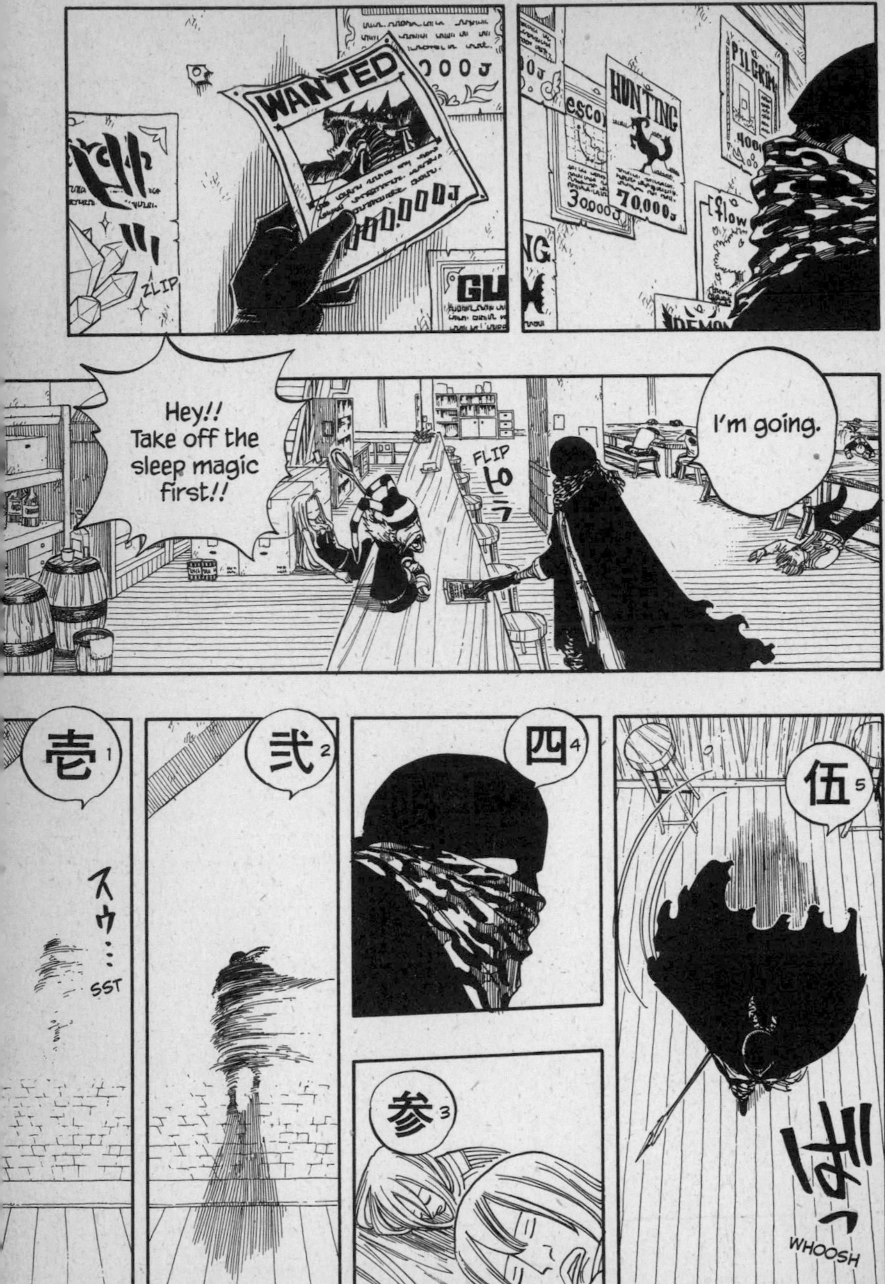

PILGRIM
HUNTING
70,000J
30,000J
flow
WANTED
ZLIP
I'm going.
Hey!! Take off the sleep magic first!!
FLIP ピラ
壱 1
スゥ… SST
弐 2
参 3
四 4
伍 5
ばっ WHOOSH

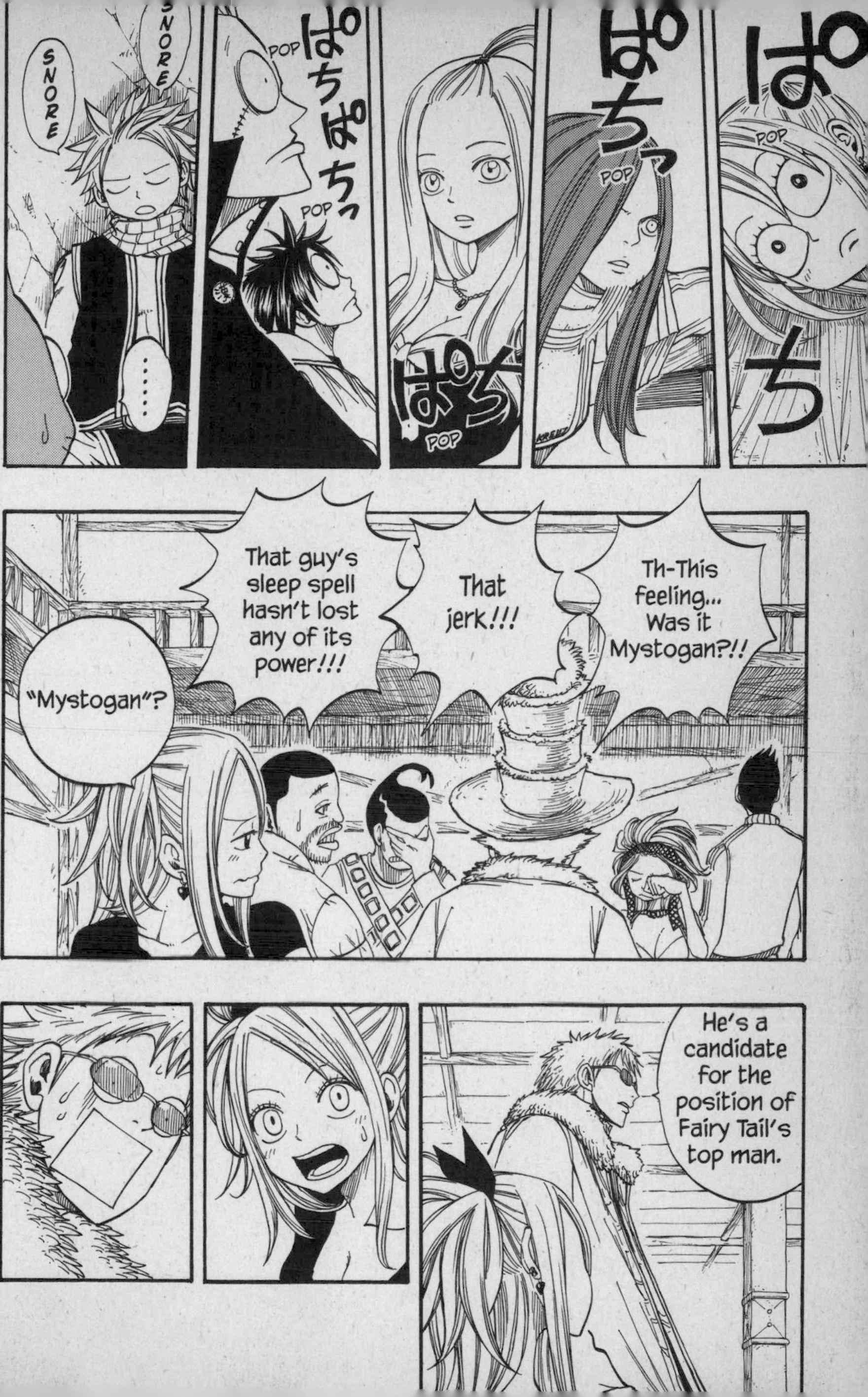
ぱち
POP
ぱちっ
POP
ぱち
POP
ぱちぱちっ
POP
POP
SNORE
SNORE
......
Th-This feeling... Was it Mystogan?!!
That jerk!!!
That guy's sleep spell hasn't lost any of its power!!!
"Mystogan"?
He's a candidate for the position of Fairy Tail's top man.

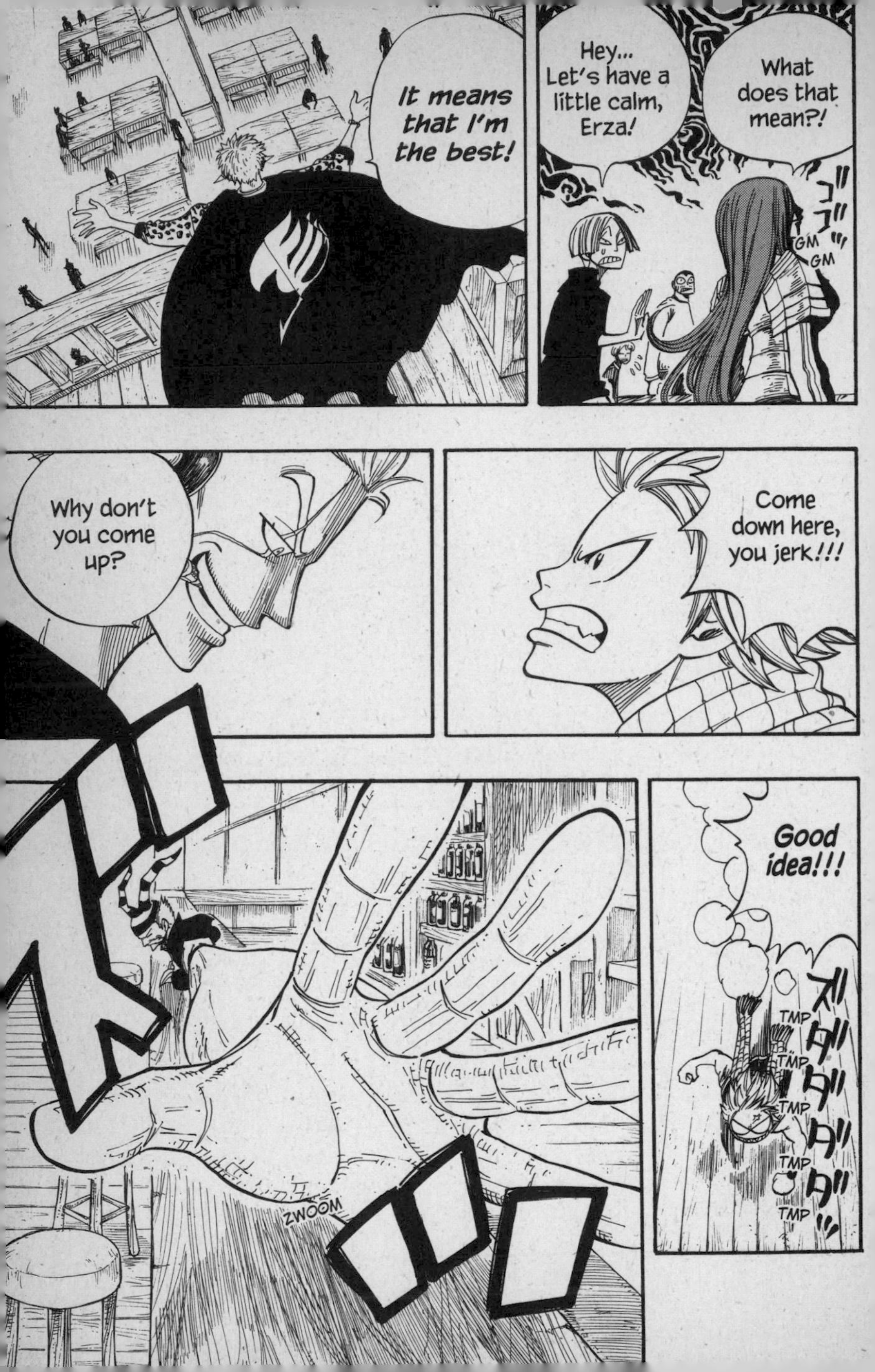
What does that mean?!
Hey... Let's have a little calm, Erza!
GM
GM
It means that I'm the best!
Come down here, you jerk!!!
Why don't you come up?
Good idea!!!
TMP
TMP
TMP
TMP
TMP
ZWOOM

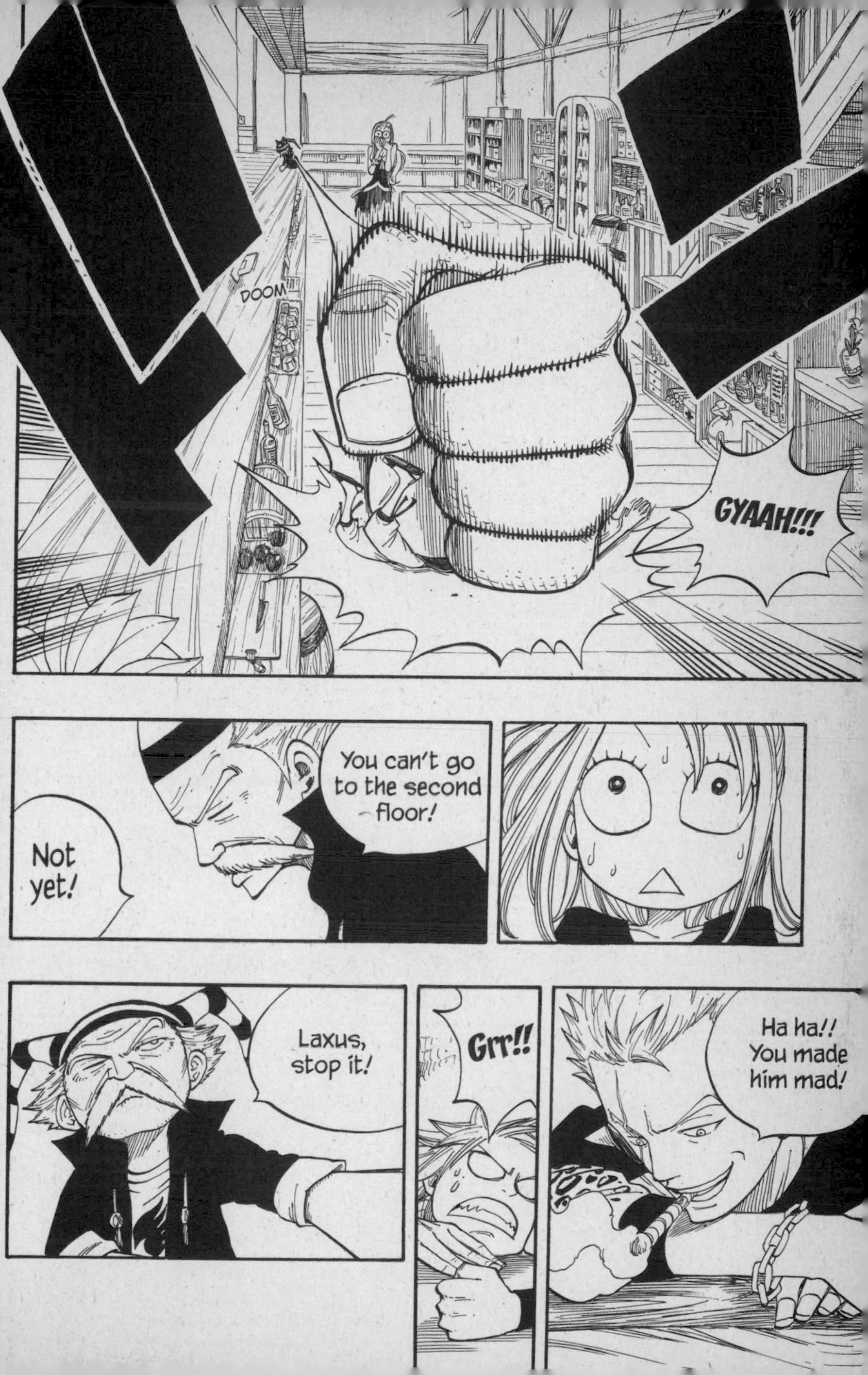
DOOM
GYAAH!!!
You can't go to the second floor!
Not yet!
Ha ha!! You made him mad!
Grr!!
Laxus, stop it!

Those are S-Class requests!

The request board on the first floor doesn't even compare to the one on the second floor in terms of difficulty and hazards.

Pu-puu?!

S-Class?!!

Don't even think of taking S-Class requests. They're the kind of missions you couldn't complete even if you had a number of lives to waste. ♡

I think you're right about that.

The only people who are allowed to take S-Class requests are the wizards the Master has decided can handle them.

Only five people have the right to take those missions. Among them are Erza, Laxus, and Mystogan.

They're the kind of mission where a moment's misjudgment would result in death. But for that reason, the rewards are much higher.

Wow...

38

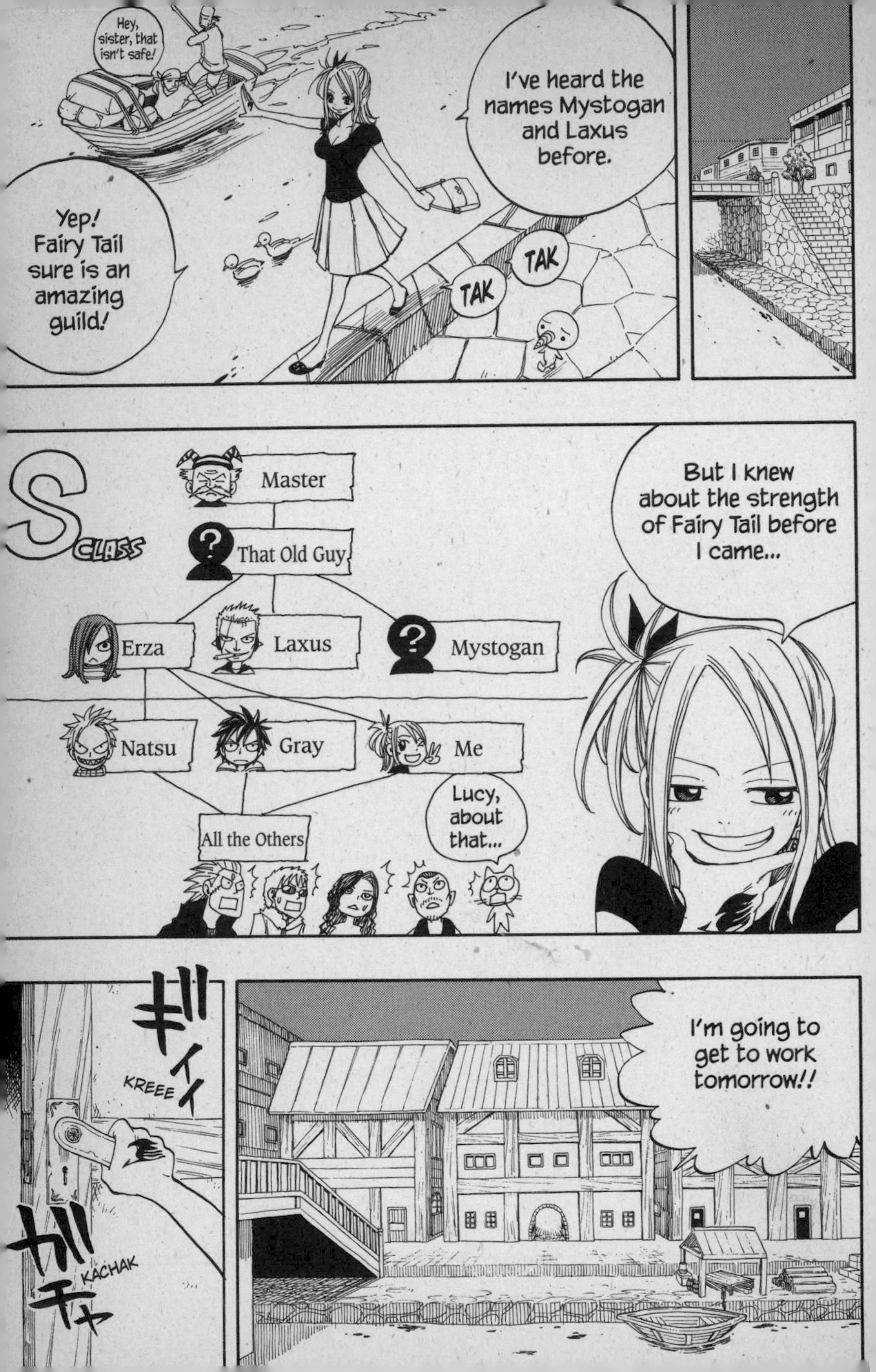
I've heard the names Mystogan and Laxus before.
Hey, sister, that isn't safe!
TAK
TAK
Yep! Fairy Tail sure is an amazing guild!
But I knew about the strength of Fairy Tail before I came...
S CLASS
Master
That Old Guy
Mystogan
Laxus
Erza
Me
Gray
Natsu
All the Others
Lucy, about that...
I'm going to get to work tomorrow!!
ギイ
KREEE
ガチャ
KACHAK

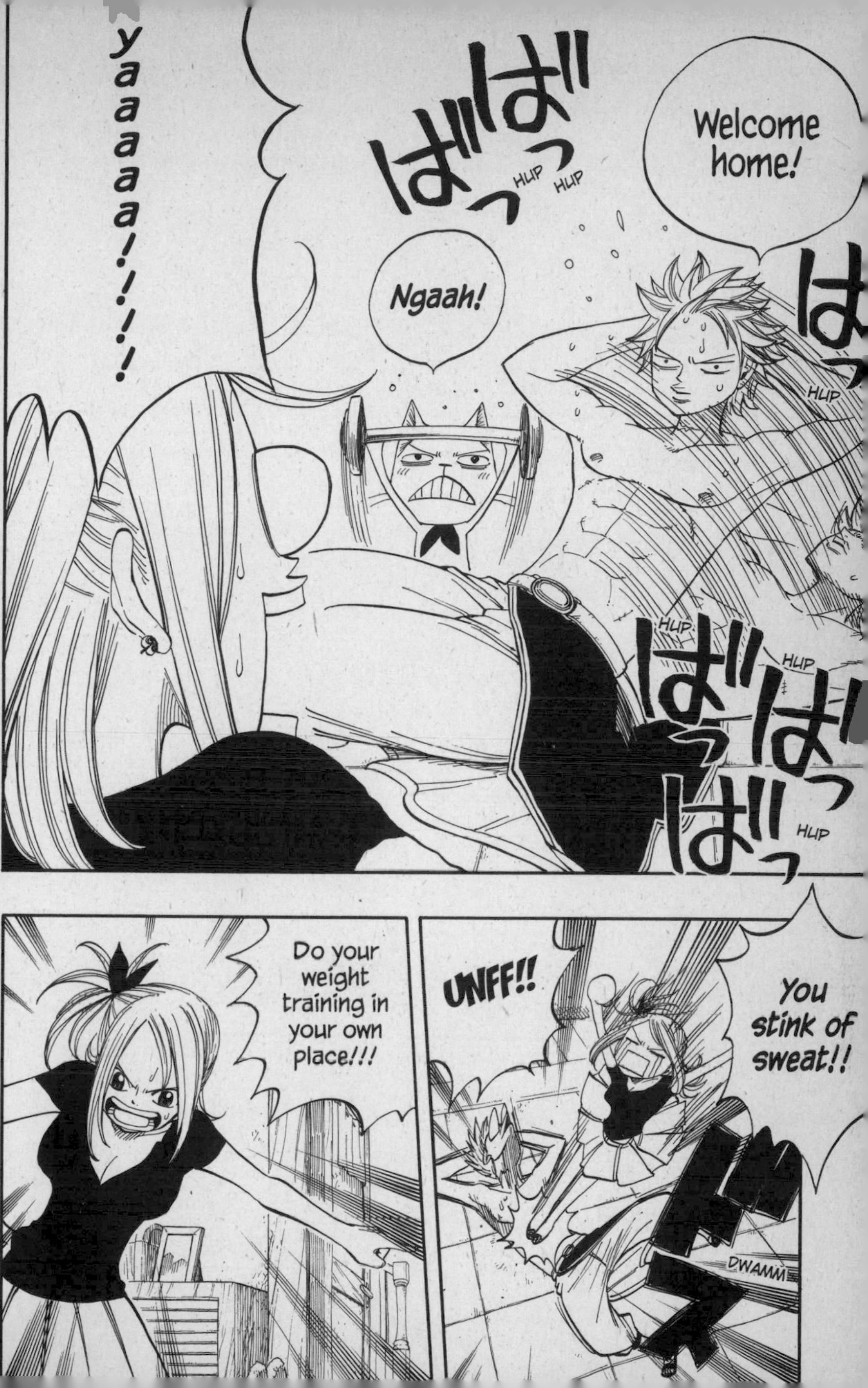
Welcome home!
はっ
HUP
ばっばっ
HUP HUP
Ngaah!
HUP
ばっばっばっ
HUP HUP
yaaaaa!!!!!
You stink of sweat!!
UNFF!!
DWAMM
Do your weight training in your own place!!!

41

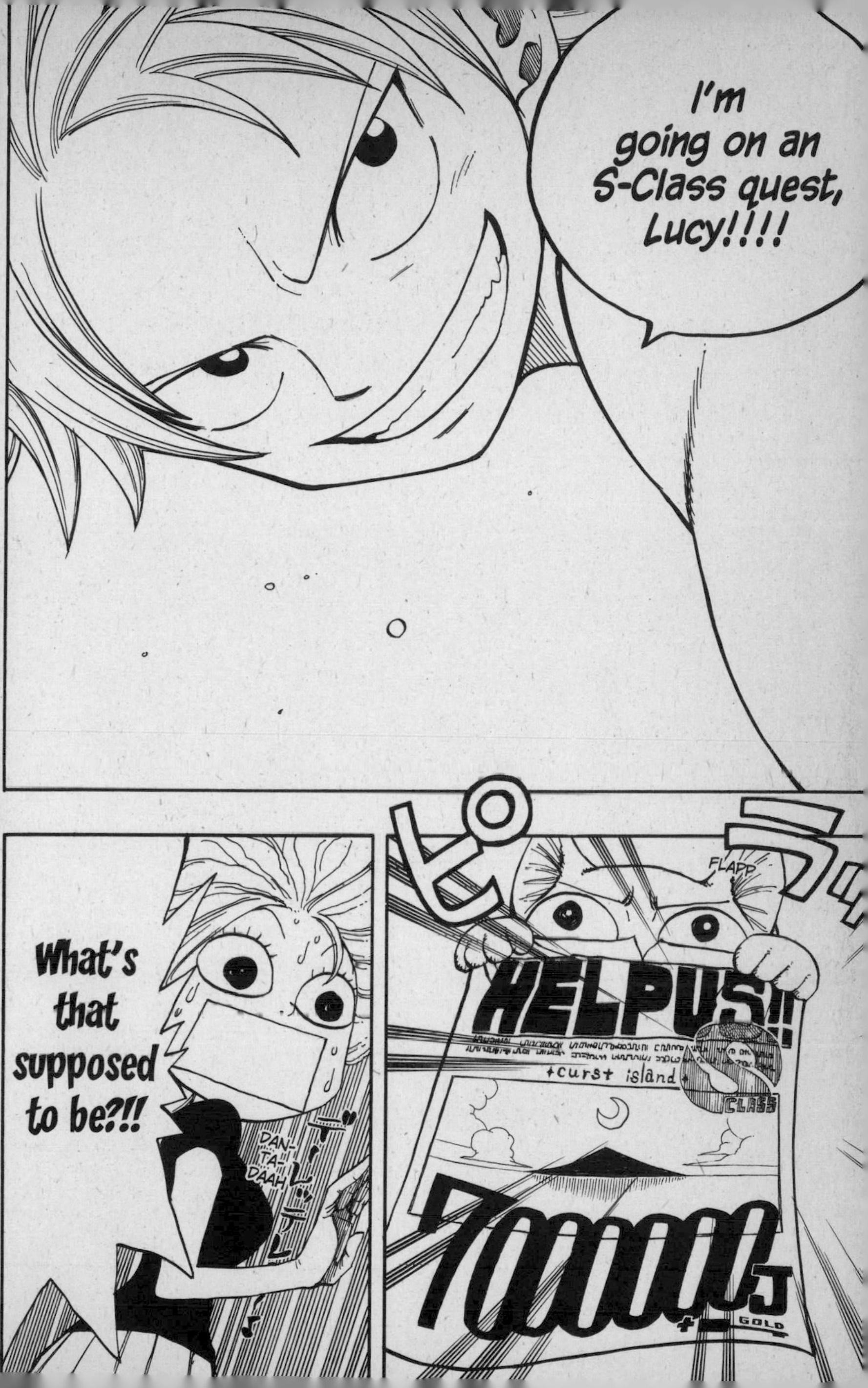
I'm going on an S-Class quest, Lucy!!!!
FLAPP
HELPUS!!
curst island
CLASS
700000J
GOLD
What's that supposed to be?!!
DAN-TA-DAAH

FAIRY TAIL

Chapter 25: The Cursed Island

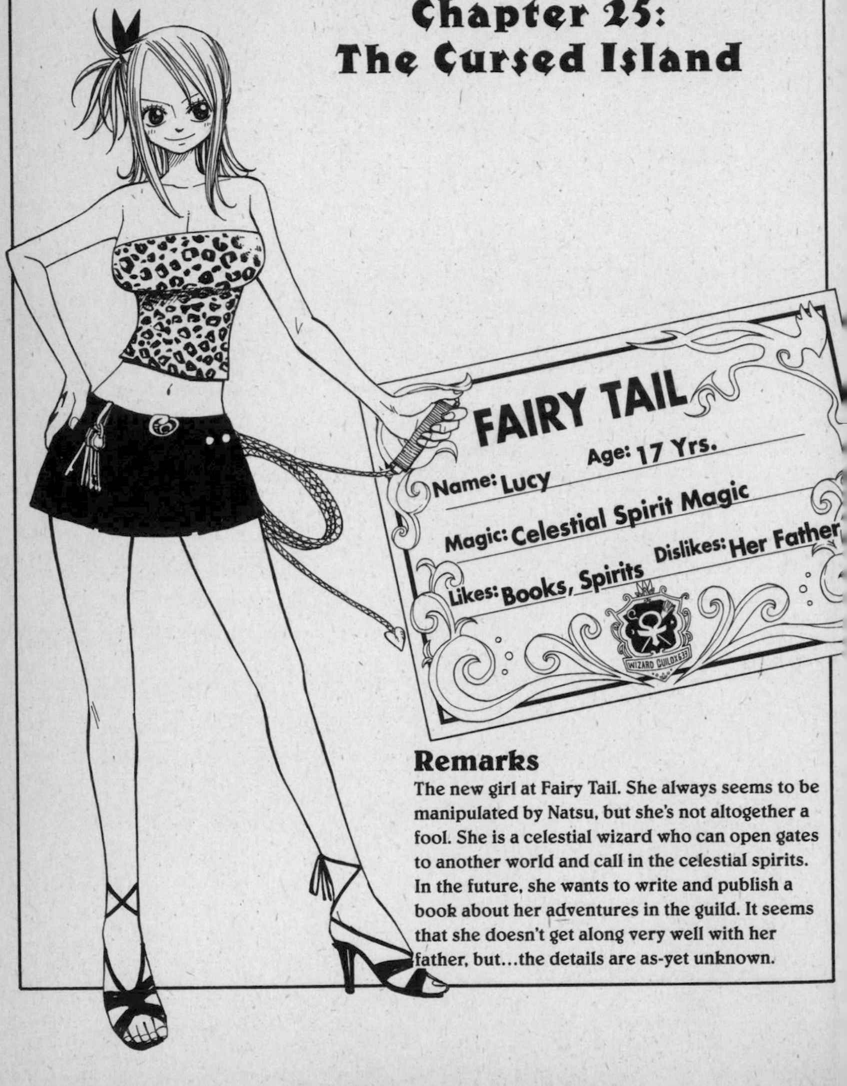
FAIRY TAIL
Name: Lucy
Age: 17 Yrs.
Magic: Celestial Spirit Magic
Likes: Books, Spirits
Dislikes: Her Father

Remarks

The new girl at Fairy Tail. She always seems to be manipulated by Natsu, but she's not altogether a fool. She is a celestial wizard who can open gates to another world and call in the celestial spirits. In the future, she wants to write and publish a book about her adventures in the guild. It seems that she doesn't get along very well with her father, but…the details are as-yet unknown.

What is this supposed to mean?!!

You're not even allowed to be on the second floor!!!

No!! We have no right to take on S-Class missions!!

Even so, it was seven million Jewels!

Anyway, it was our first time, so we picked the cheapest job on the second floor.

WHOOSH

You cat burglar!!!

I went up without permission and picked this up.

FLIP

FWIP

But if we do it successfully, they'd have to admit that we've got the right!

44

45

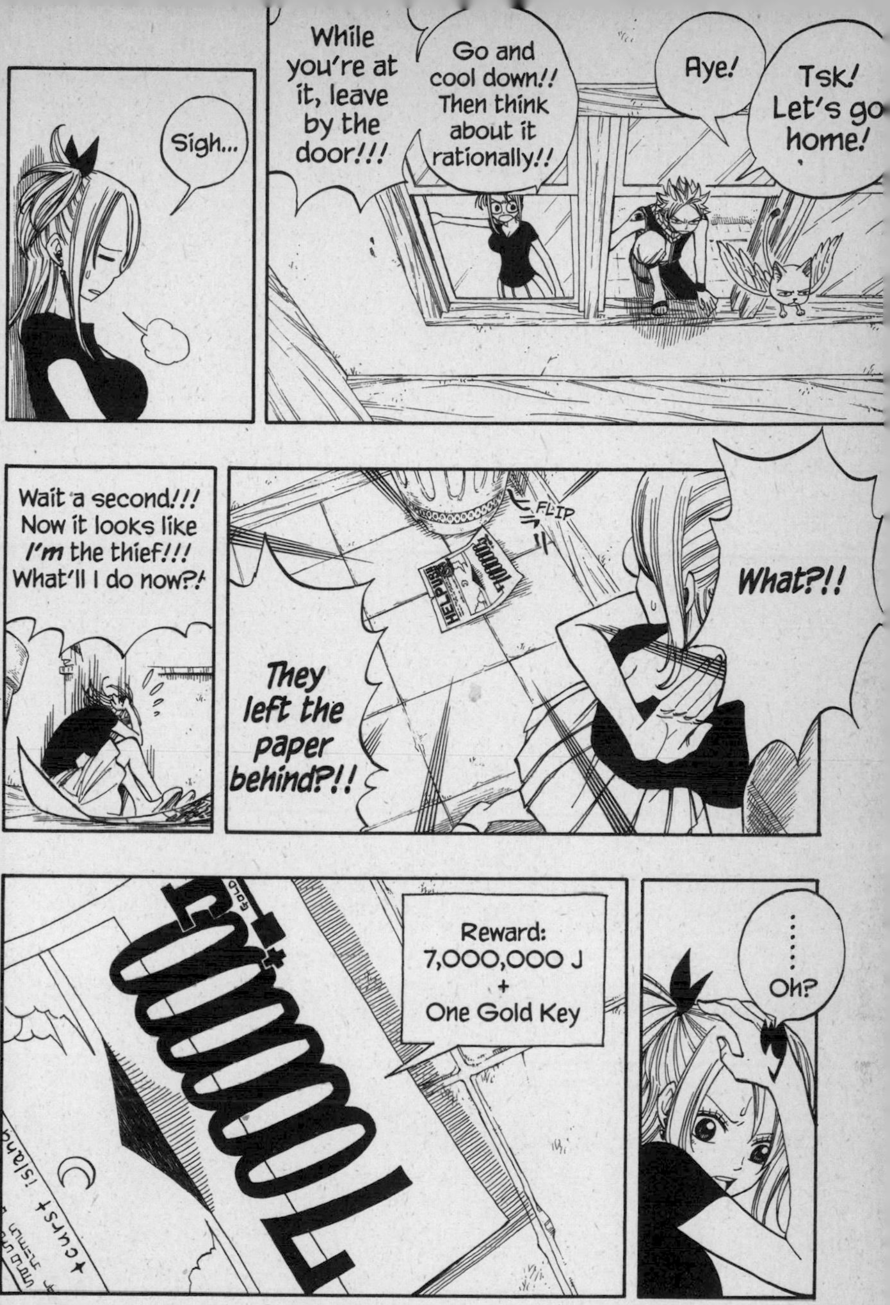
Tsk! Let's go home!
Aye!
Go and cool down!! Then think about it rationally!!
While you're at it, leave by the door!!!
Sigh...
What?!!
FLIP
They left the paper behind?!!
Wait a second!!! Now it looks like *I'm* the thief!!! What'll I do now?!
...... Oh?
Reward: 7,000,000 J + One Gold Key

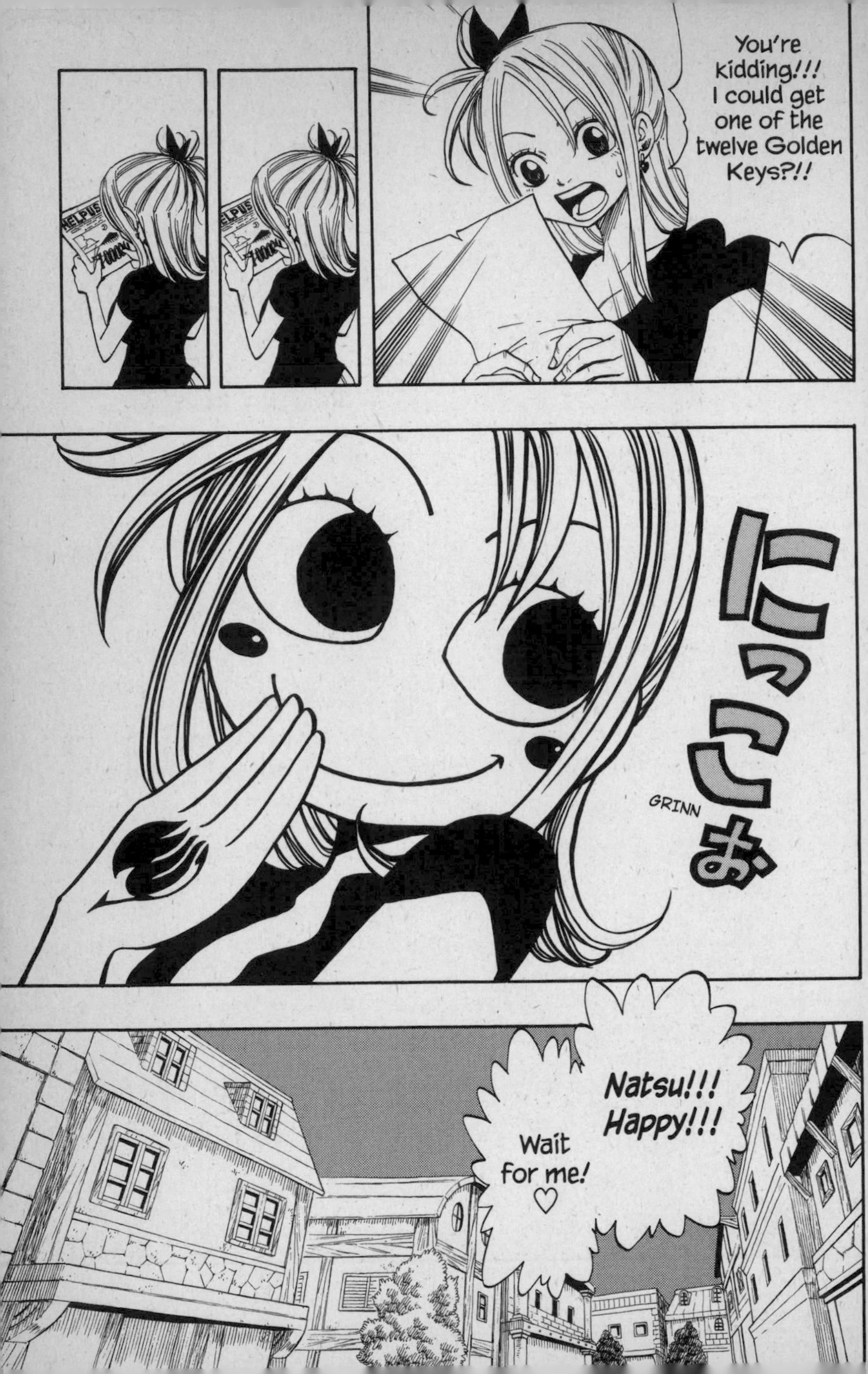
You're kidding!!! I could get one of the twelve Golden Keys?!!
HELPUS
HELPUS
にっこぉ
GRINN
Natsu!!! Happy!!!
Wait for me! ♡

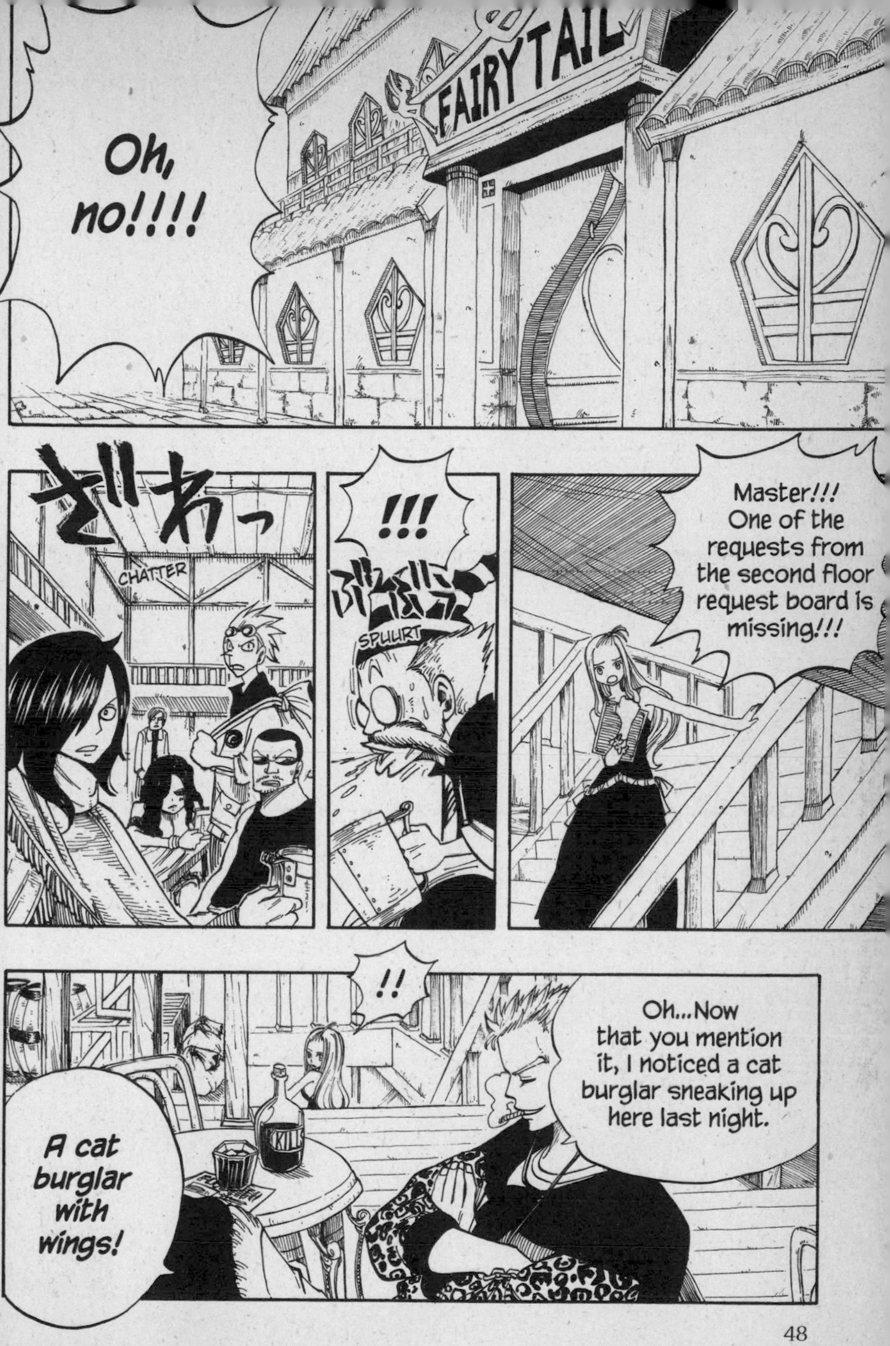
Oh, no!!!!
FAIRY TAIL
Master!!! One of the requests from the second floor request board is missing!!!
!!!
SPUURT
ざわっ
CHATTER
Oh...Now that you mention it, I noticed a cat burglar sneaking up here last night.
!!
A cat burglar with wings!

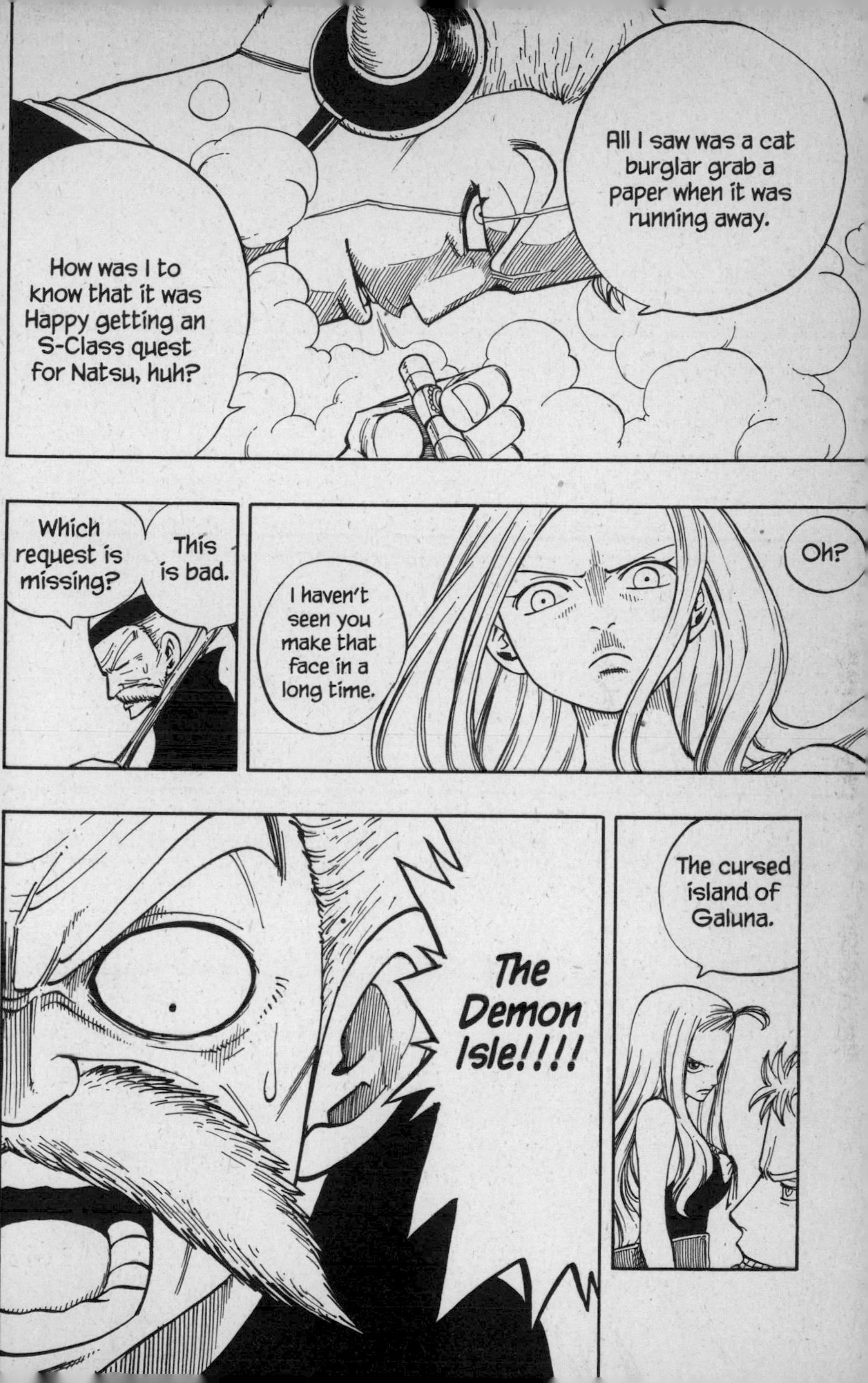
All I saw was a cat burglar grab a paper when it was running away.
How was I to know that it was Happy getting an S-Class quest for Natsu, huh?
Oh?
I haven't seen you make that face in a long time.
This is bad.
Which request is missing?
The cursed island of Galuna.
The Demon Isle!!!!

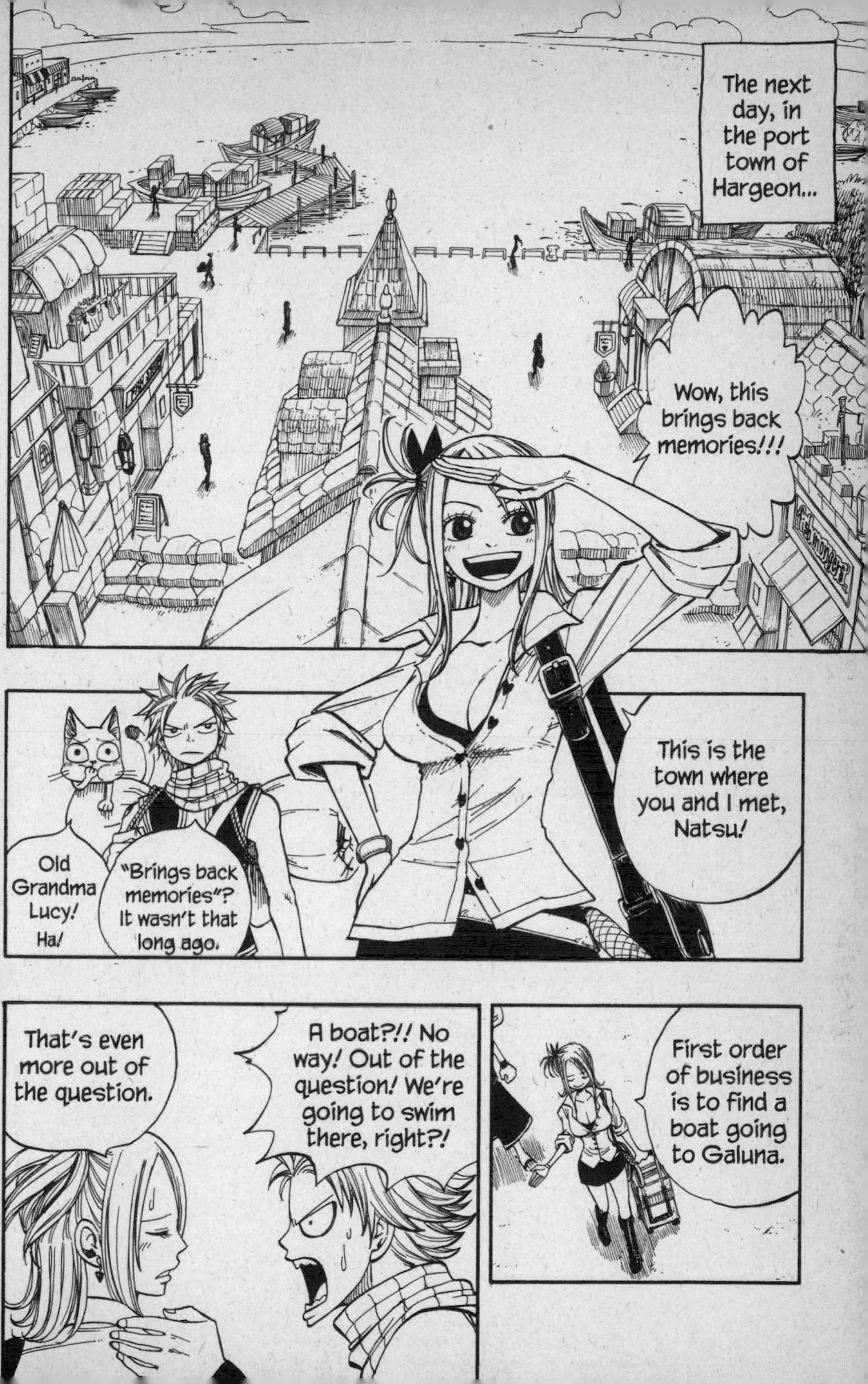
The next day, in the port town of Hargeon...
Wow, this brings back memories!!!
This is the town where you and I met, Natsu!
"Brings back memories"? It wasn't that long ago.
Old Grandma Lucy! Ha!
First order of business is to find a boat going to Galuna.
A boat?!! No way! Out of the question! We're going to swim there, right?!
That's even more out of the question.

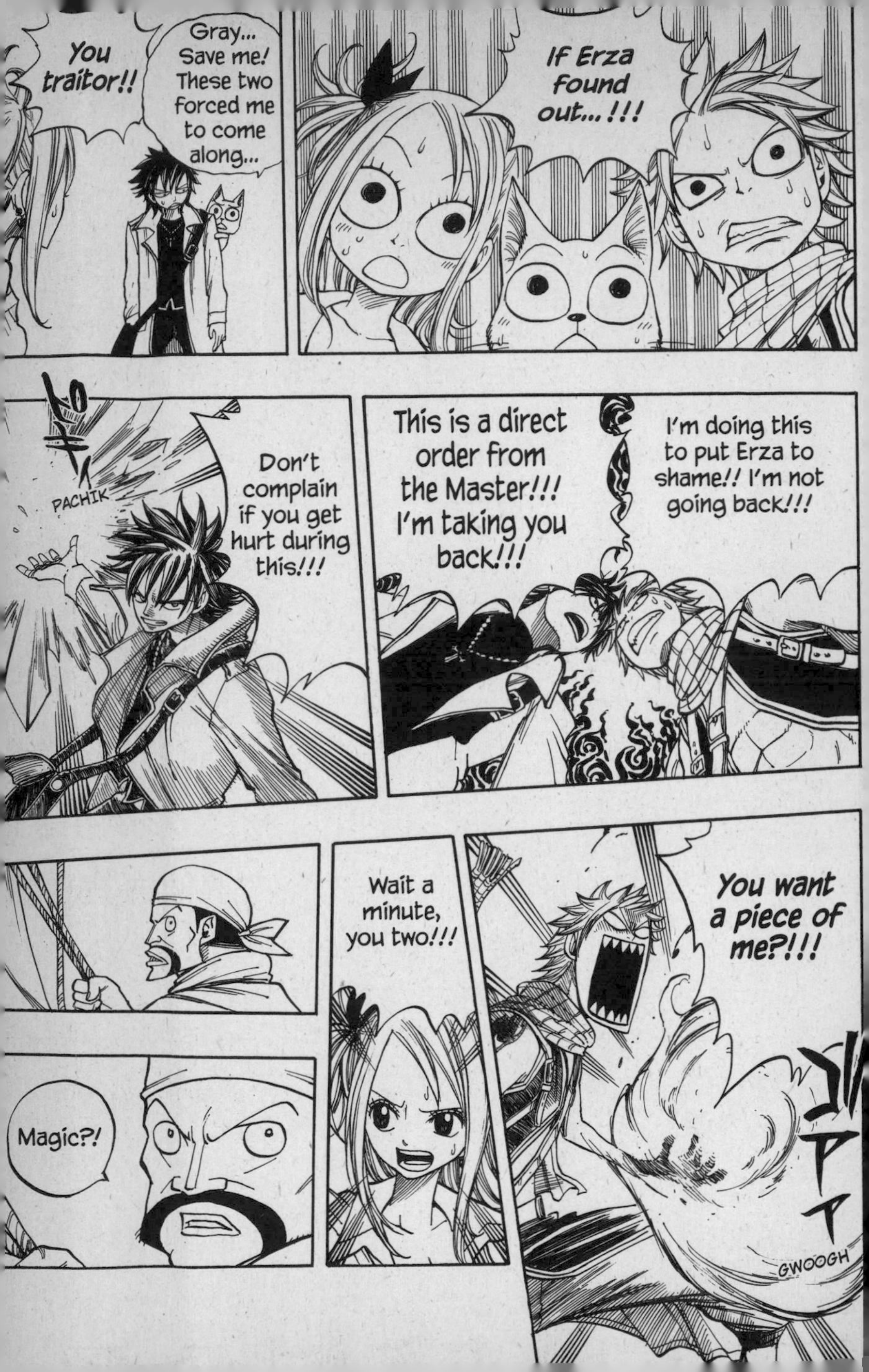
If Erza found out...!!!
Gray... Save me! These two forced me to come along...
You traitor!!
I'm doing this to put Erza to shame!! I'm not going back!!!
This is a direct order from the Master!!! I'm taking you back!!!
Don't complain if you get hurt during this!!!
PACHIK
You want a piece of me?!!!
GWOOGH
Wait a minute, you two!!!
Magic?!

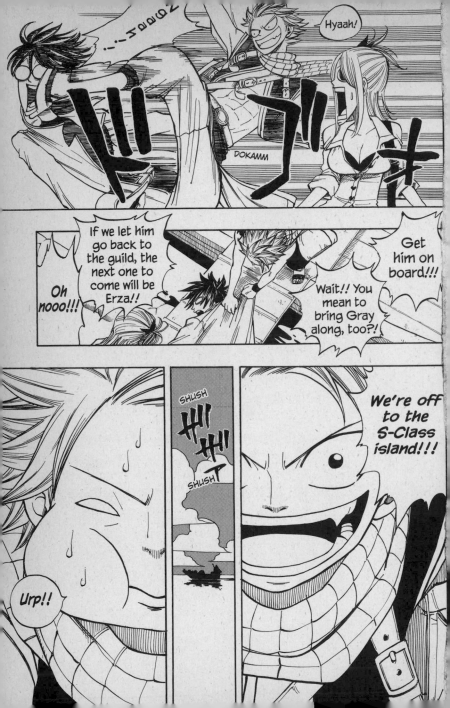

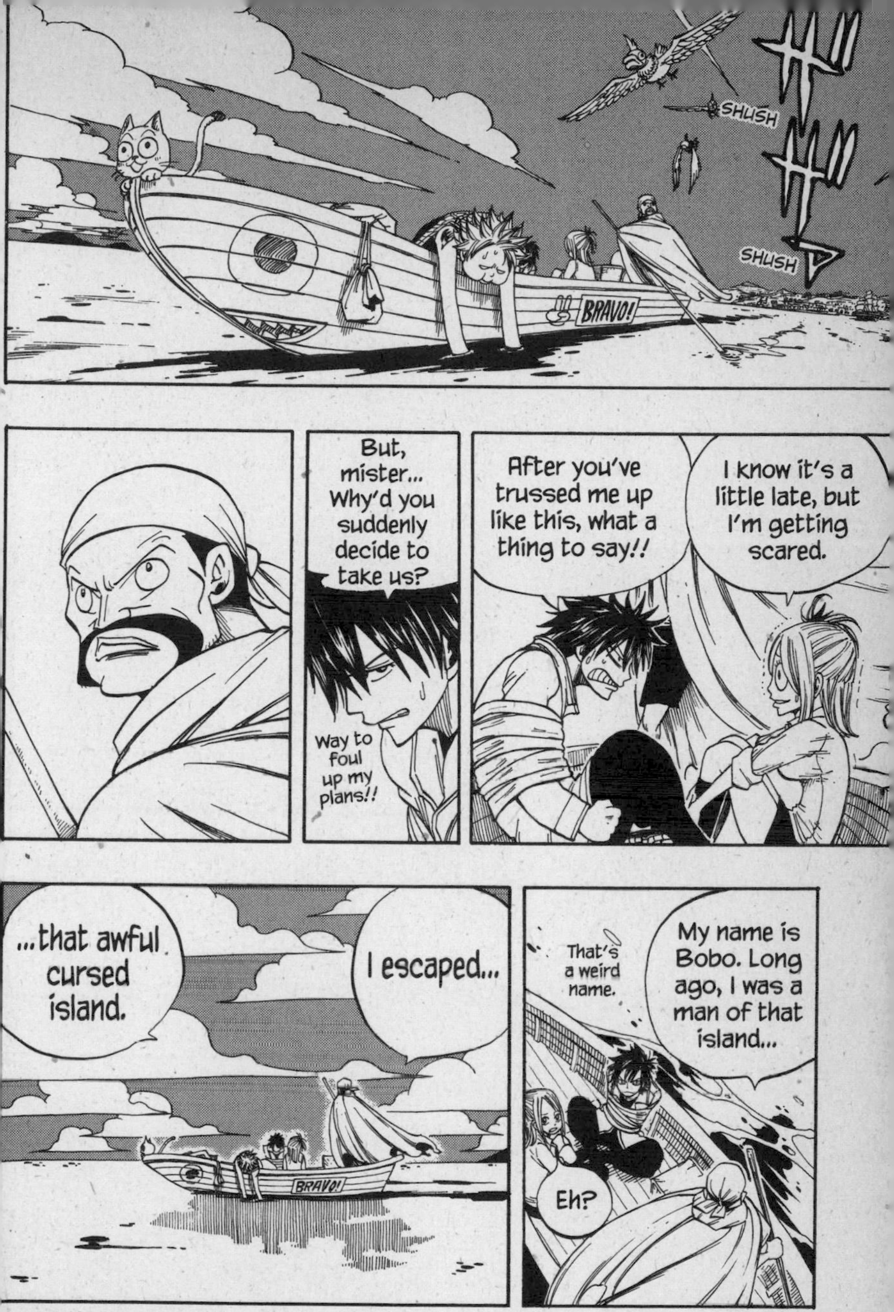
SHUSH
SHUSH
BRAVO!
I know it's a little late, but I'm getting scared.
After you've trussed me up like this, what a thing to say!!
But, mister... Why'd you suddenly decide to take us?
Way to foul up my plans!!
My name is Bobo. Long ago, I was a man of that island...
That's a weird name.
Eh?
I escaped...
...that awful cursed island.
BRAVO!

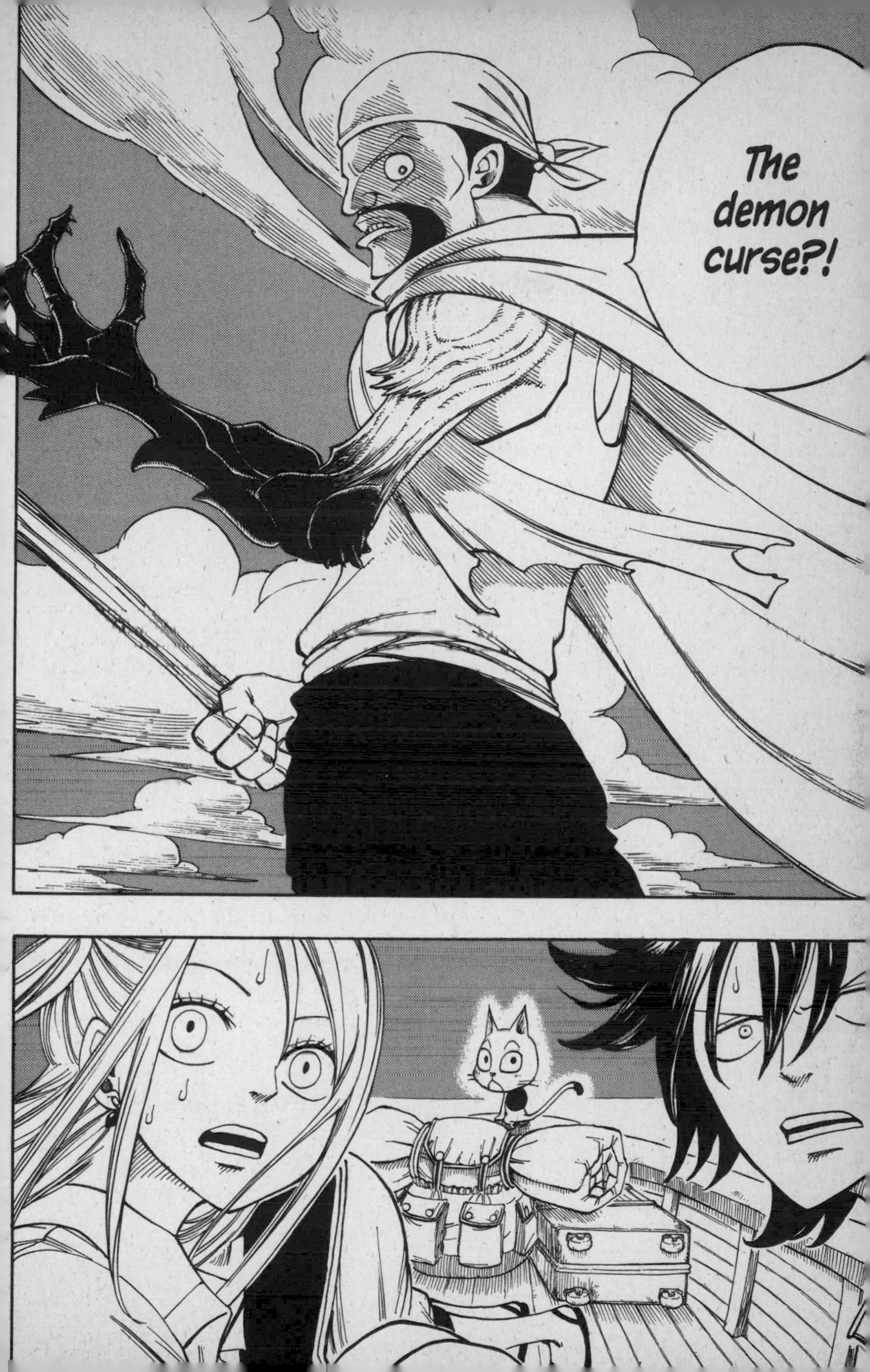
The demon curse?!

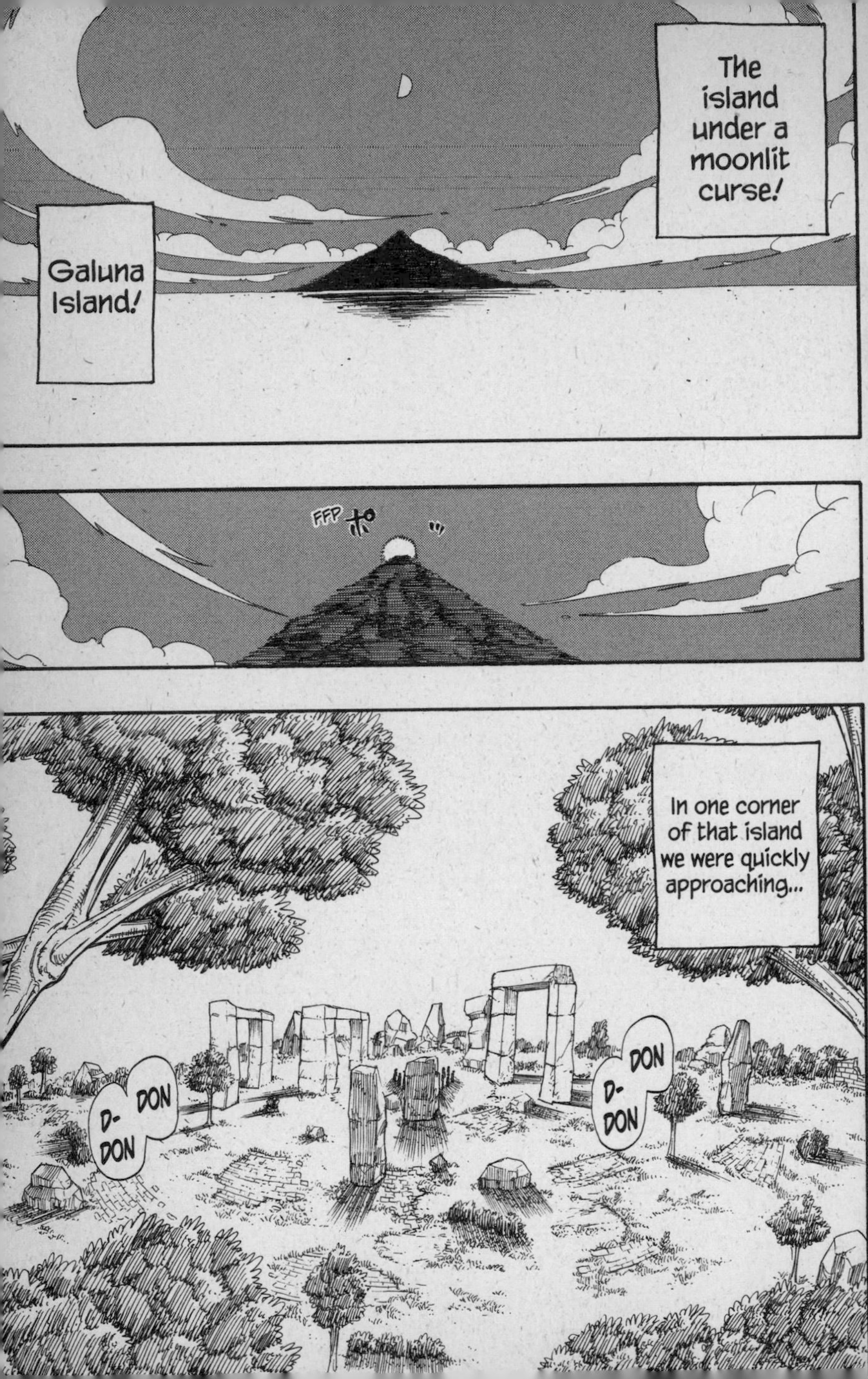
The island under a moonlit curse!
Galuna Island!
FFP
In one corner of that island we were quickly approaching...
DON D-DON
DON D-DON

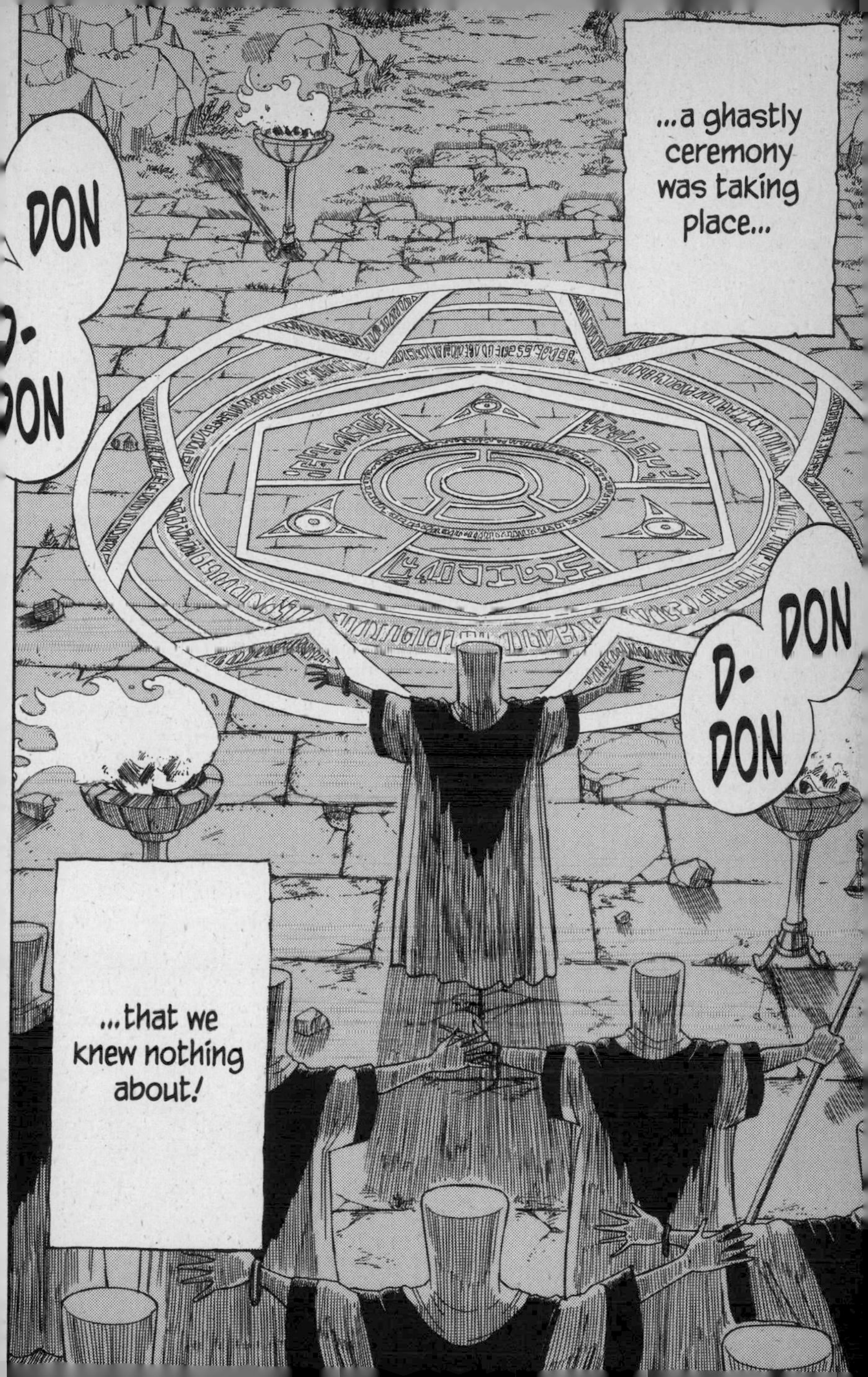
...a ghastly ceremony was taking place...
DON D-DON
DON D-DON
...that we knew nothing about!

Chapter 26: Is the Moon Out Tonight?

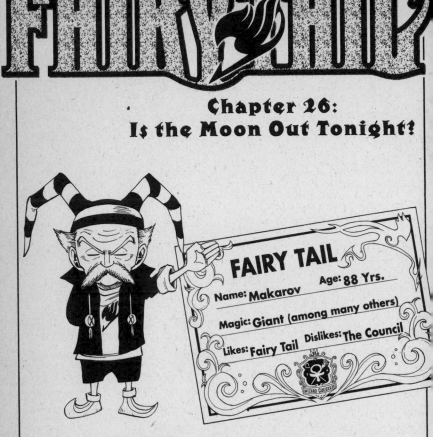

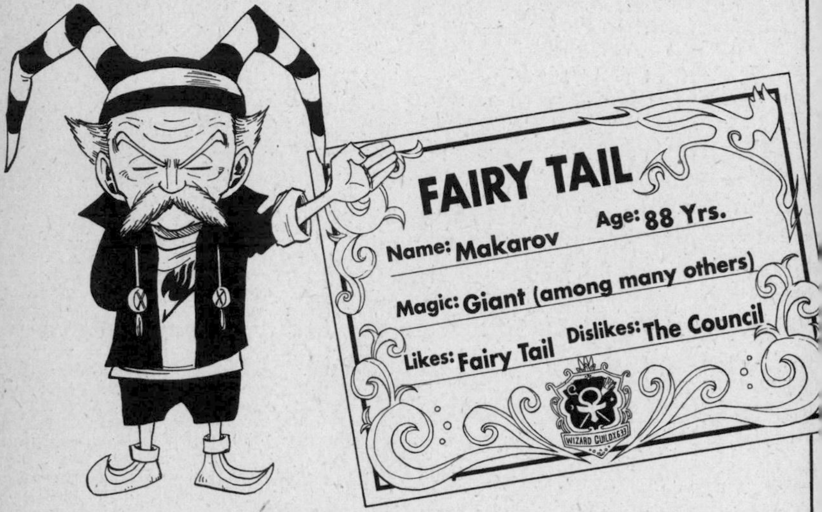
FAIRY TAIL
Name: Makarov
Age: 88 Yrs.
Magic: Giant (among many others)
Likes: Fairy Tail
Dislikes: The Council
WIZARD GUILD

Remarks

The Master of Fairy Tail, a guild that is known to be a gathering of problem wizards. He is thought to possess an immeasurably high level of magic and skills. He is especially skilled at giant magic, the ability to vastly increase one's size, but he also has a general knowledge of fire, ice, and wind magic as well.
He is not known to open up even to people of the guild, so there are sides of his personality that are steeped in mystery.

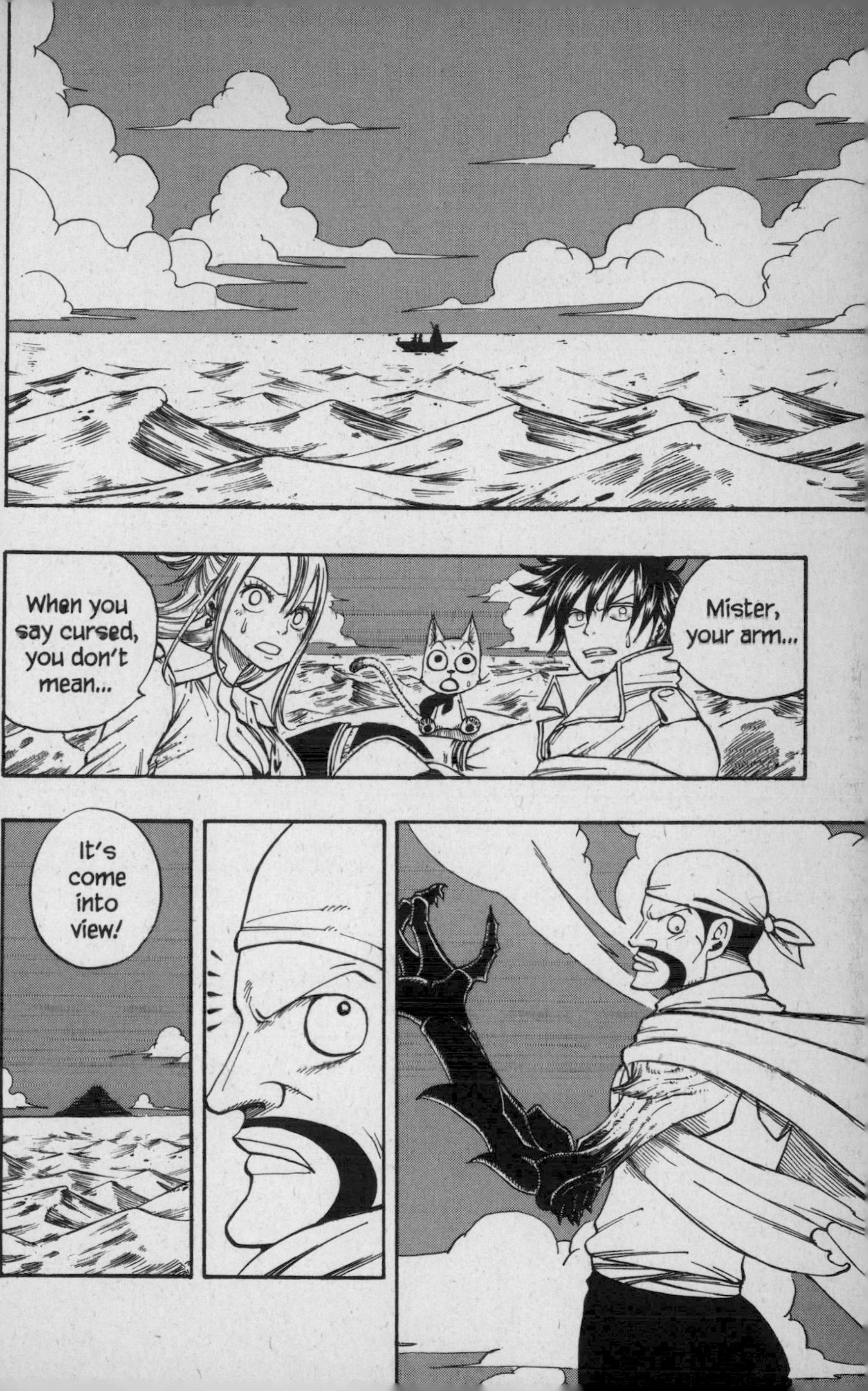
Mister, your arm...
When you say cursed, you don't mean...
It's come into view!

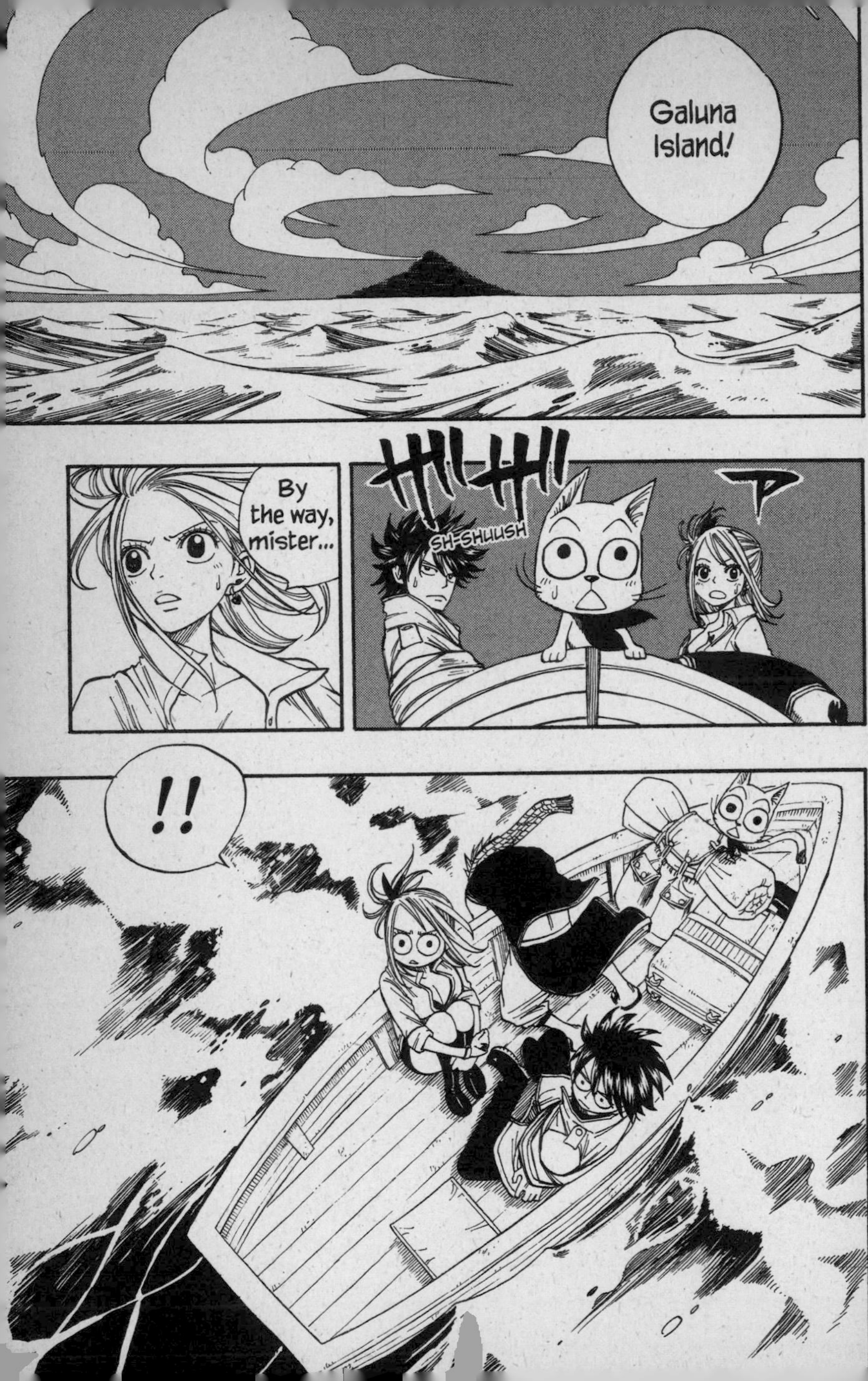
Galuna Island!
SH-SHUUSH
By the way, mister...
!!

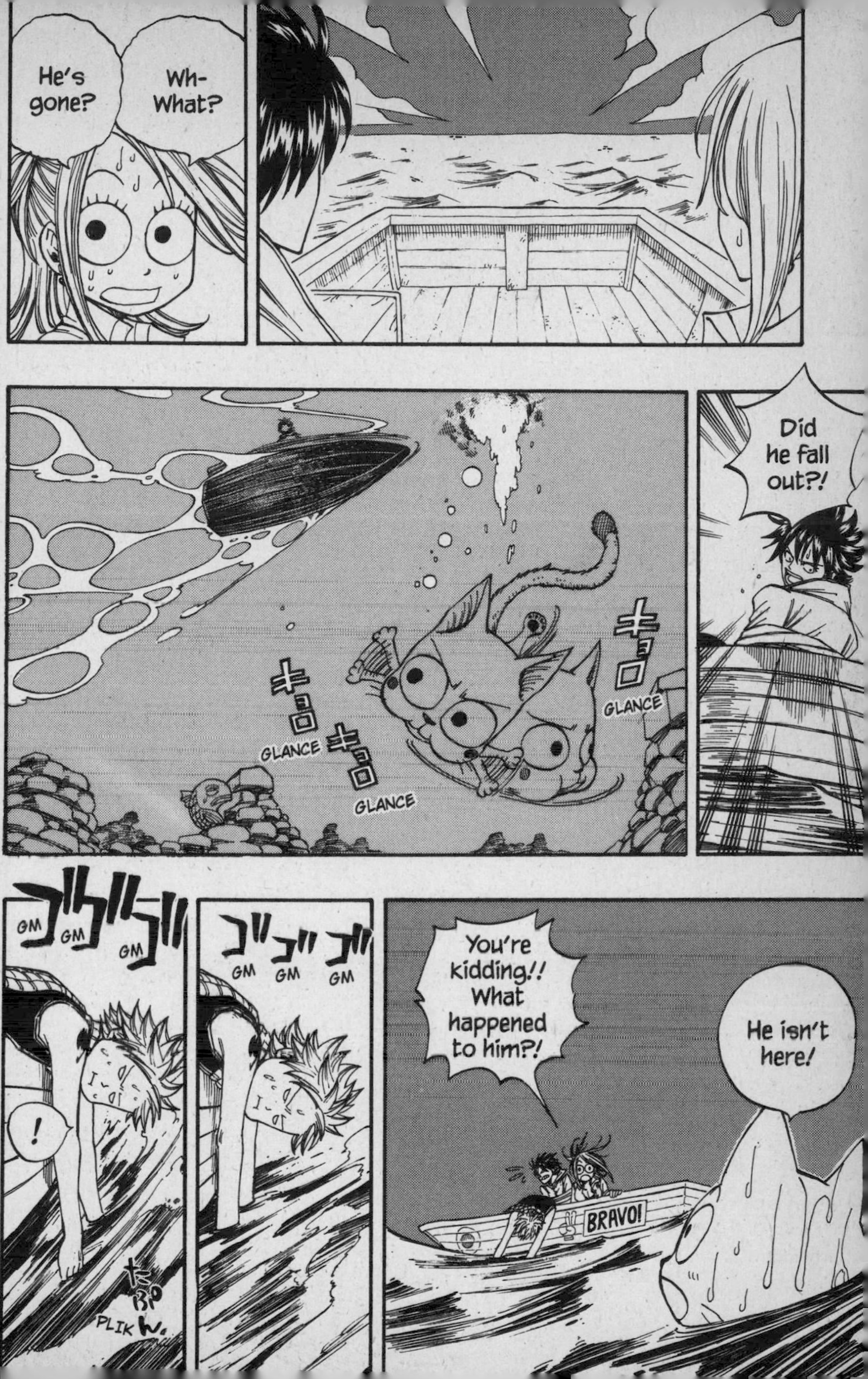

Wh- What?
He's gone?
Did he fall out?!
キョロ
GLANCE
キョロ
GLANCE
キョロ
GLANCE
He isn't here!
You're kidding!! What happened to him?!
BRAVO!
GM GM GM
GM GM GM
!
PLIK

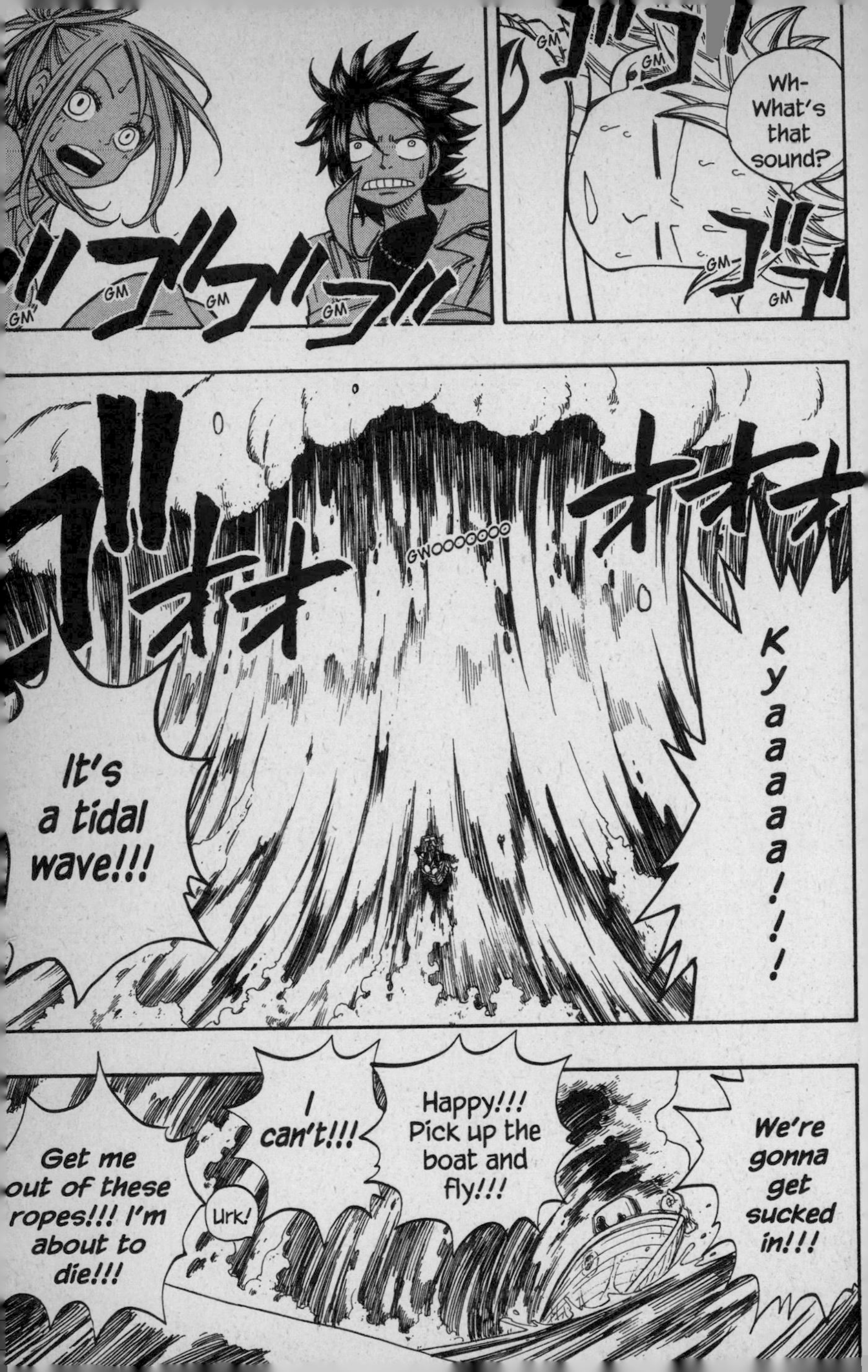
GM
GM
Wh- What's that sound?
GM
GM
GM
GM
GM
GM
GWOOOOOOO
Kyaaaaa!!!
It's a tidal wave!!!
We're gonna get sucked in!!!
Happy!!! Pick up the boat and fly!!!
I can't!!!
Urk!
Get me out of these ropes!!! I'm about to die!!!

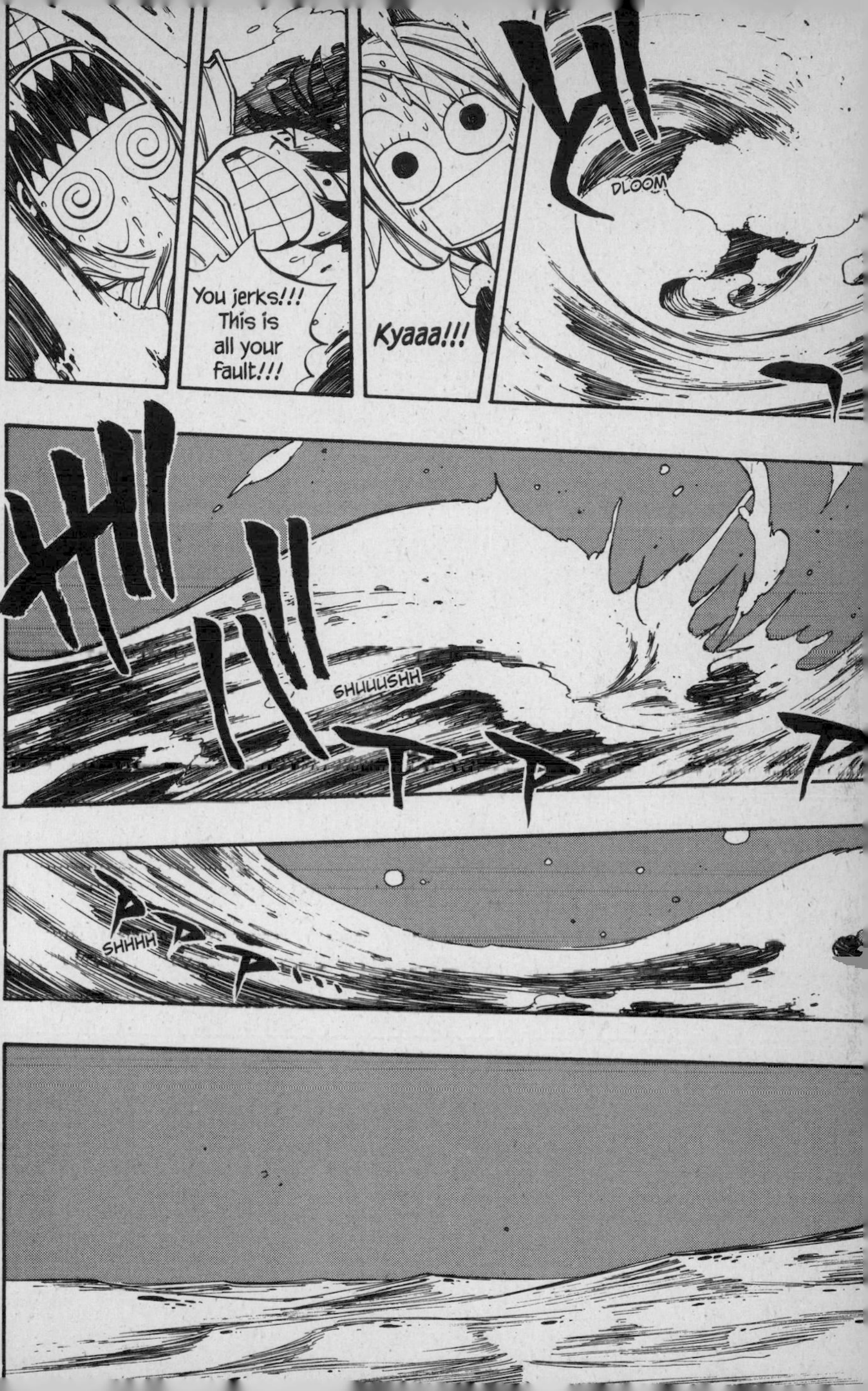
DLOOM
Kyaaa!!!
You jerks!!! This is all your fault!!!
SHUUUSHH
SHHHH

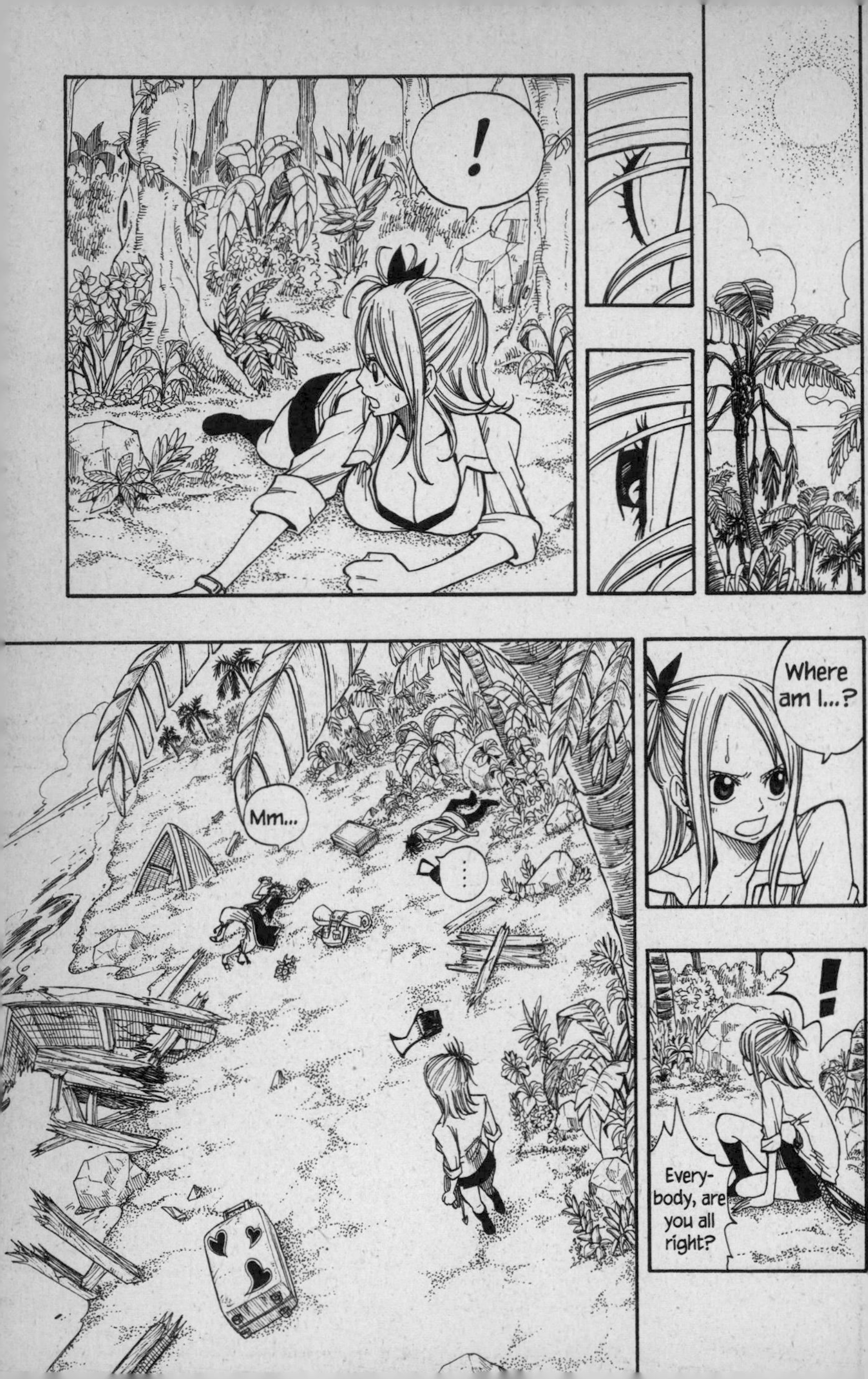
!
Where am I...?
!
Every-body, are you all right?
Mm...
....

......

It seems like the tidal wave pushed us here last night.

Whoa!! Are we here?! Galuna Island?!!

がばっ

GAMPH

From what the request paper said, isn't that the very thing we should be wary of?!!

Aye!!

Who cares?!! Let's go exploring!! Exploring!!!

But I wonder what that was? That guy's arm... Was it the demon curse?

And then the guy disappeared!

Wait a second!

That's where we should go first.

There should be only one village on this island.

And the headman of the village made the request.

70

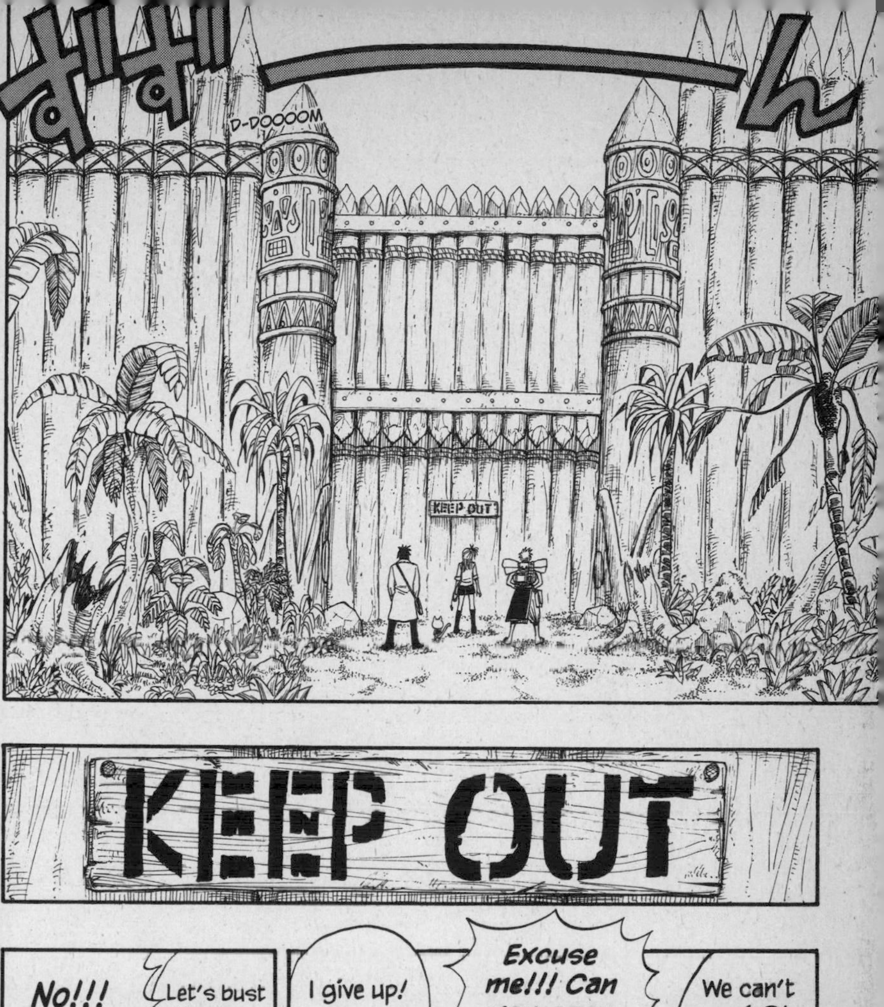
ずずーん
D-DOOOOM
KEEP OUT
KEEP OUT
We can't go in?! What kind of village is this?!
Excuse me!!! Can you open up for a bit?!
I give up!
Let's bust the door down.
No!!!
くわっ
TWRL

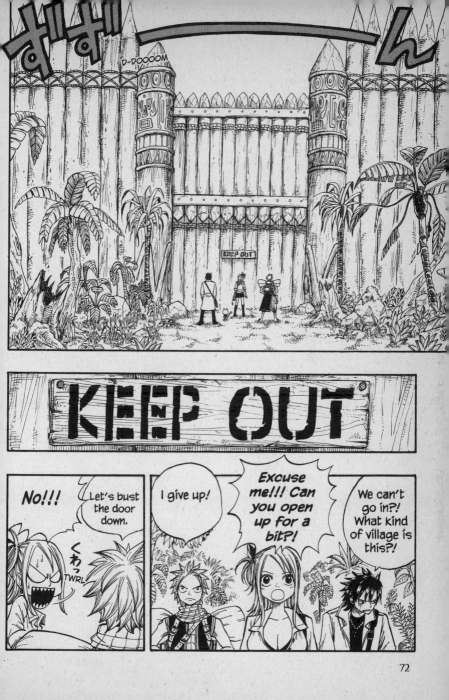

73

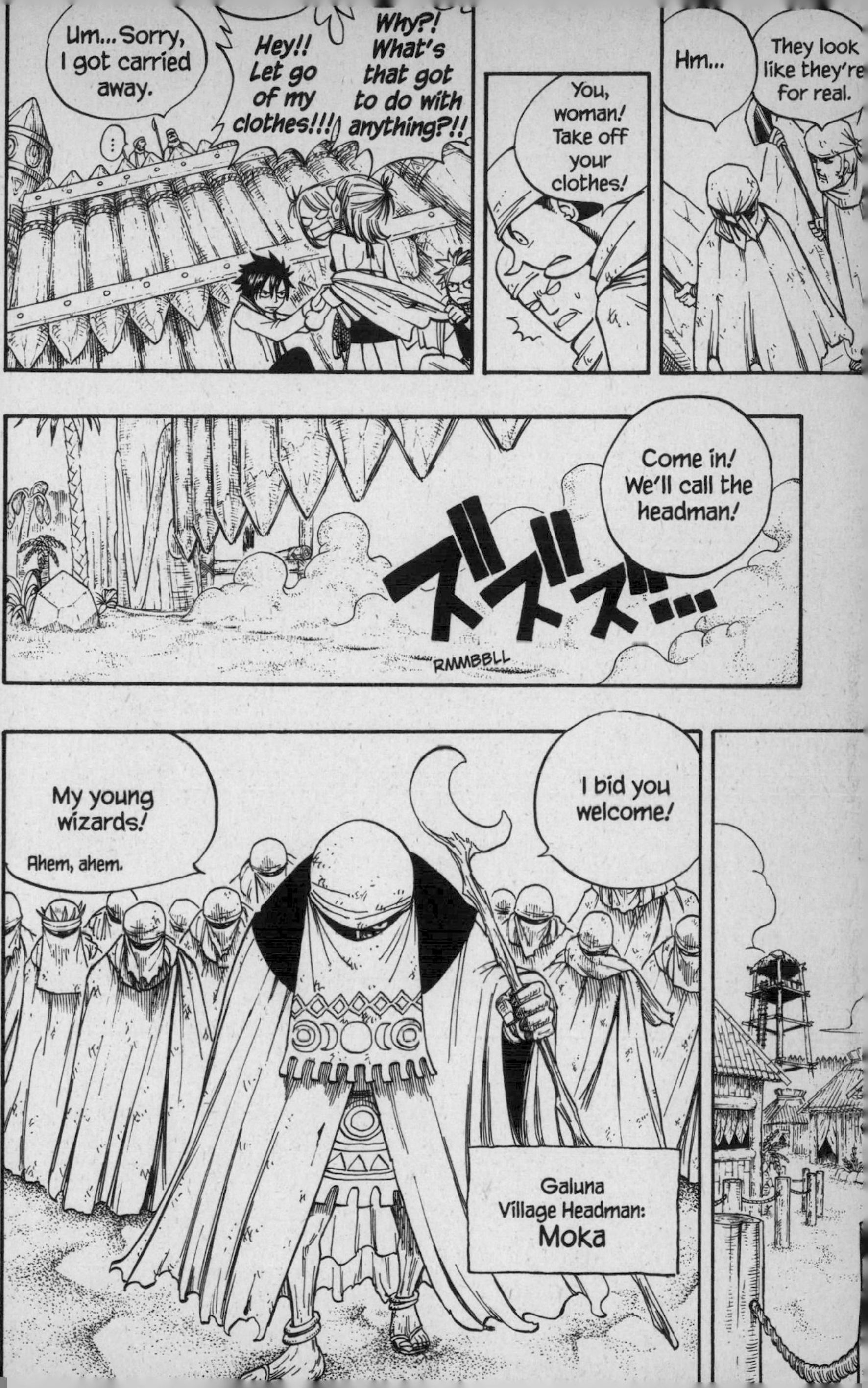
They look like they're for real.
Hm...
You, woman! Take off your clothes!
Why?! What's that got to do with anything?!!
Hey!! Let go of my clothes!!!
Um... Sorry, I got carried away.
Come in! We'll call the headman!
ズズズ...
RMMBBLL
I bid you welcome!
My young wizards!
Ahem, ahem.
Galuna Village Headman: Moka

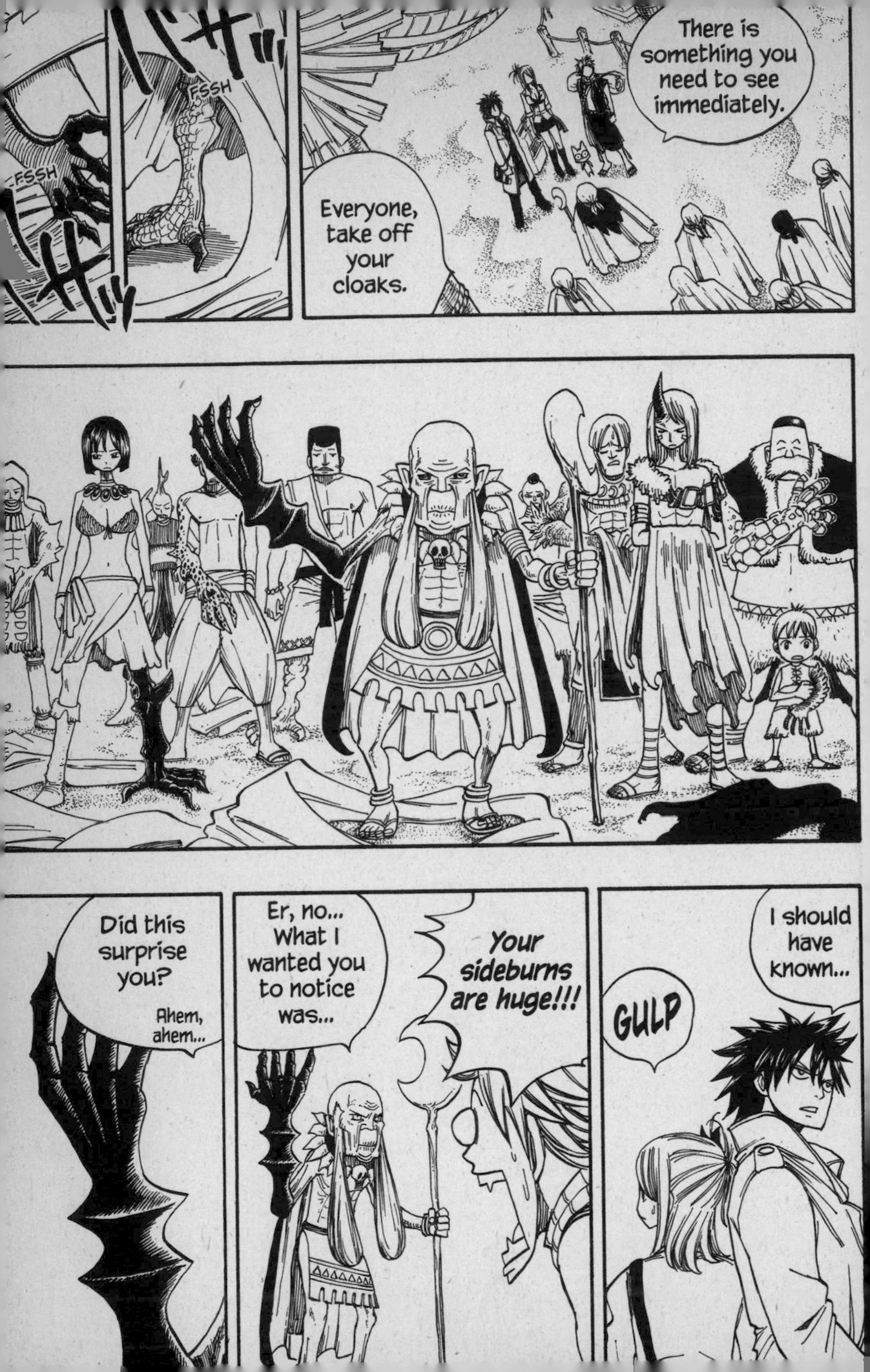
There is something you need to see immediately.
Everyone, take off your cloaks.
FSSH
FSSH
I should have known...
GULP
Your sideburns are huge!!!
Er, no... What I wanted you to notice was...
Did this surprise you?
Ahem, ahem...

...is afflicted with this very same curse!

Ahem...

...including dogs, birds, everything...

Every living being on this island...

There is no disease in the world like it.

Ahem.

We've been seen by dozens of doctors.

Couldn't it be a disease or something...?

I don't want to doubt you, but on what basis do you call this a "curse"?

...and glowing as brilliantly and beautifully as the moon itself!

Originally, this island was known for gathering in the moonlight...

The magic of the moon?

Besides... The reason we appear like this has something to do with the magic of the moon.

77

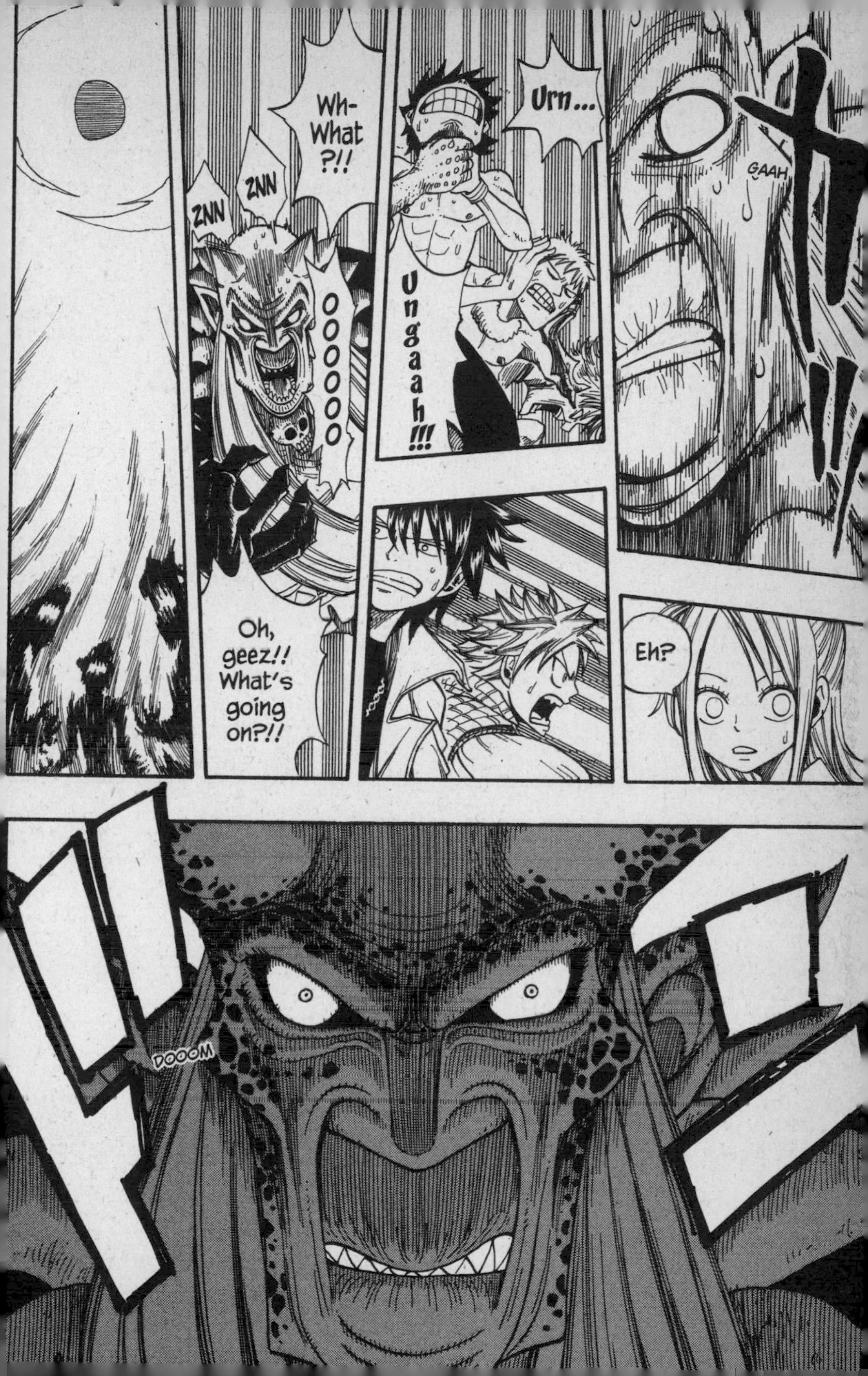
GAAH
Eh?
Urn...
Ungaaah!!!
Wh-What?!!
ZNN
ZNN
OOOOOOO
Oh, geez!! What's going on?!!
DOOOM

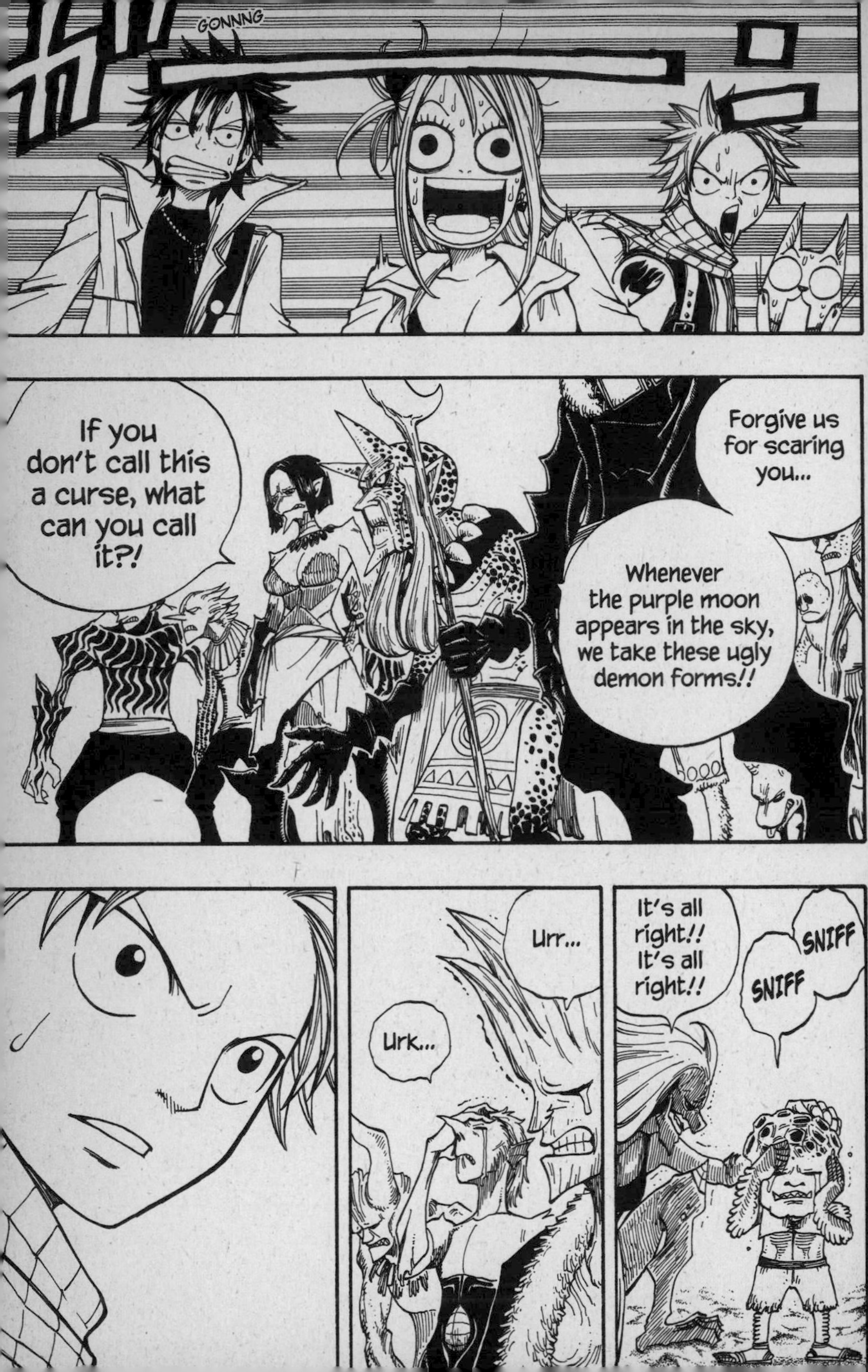
GONNNG
Forgive us for scaring you...
Whenever the purple moon appears in the sky, we take these ugly demon forms!!
If you don't call this a curse, what can you call it?!
SNIFF
It's all right!! It's all right!!
SNIFF
Urr...
Urk...

I guess he couldn't rest in peace!!

I finally understand why he disappeared.

Shh!!

But... Yesterday, we...

Him?!!

Eh?!!

．．．!!!

A ghost?!!!

We'll never let that happen!!!

There is only one way to remove the curse.

If it goes on much longer... all of us will have our souls stolen... We'll all become demons.

I thank you for coming, wizards of renown, and I beg you to please save our poor island.

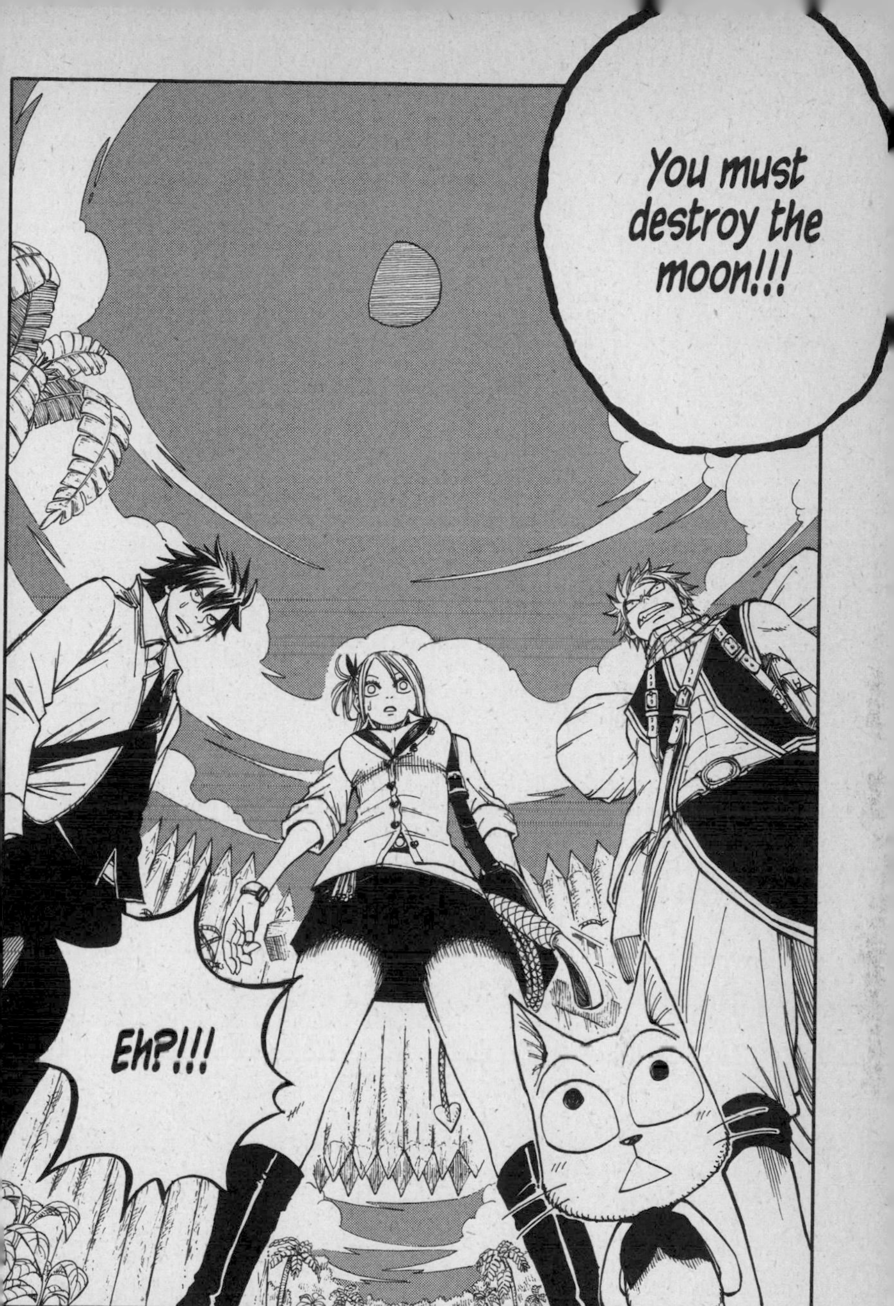
You must destroy the moon!!!
Eh?!!!

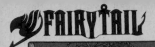

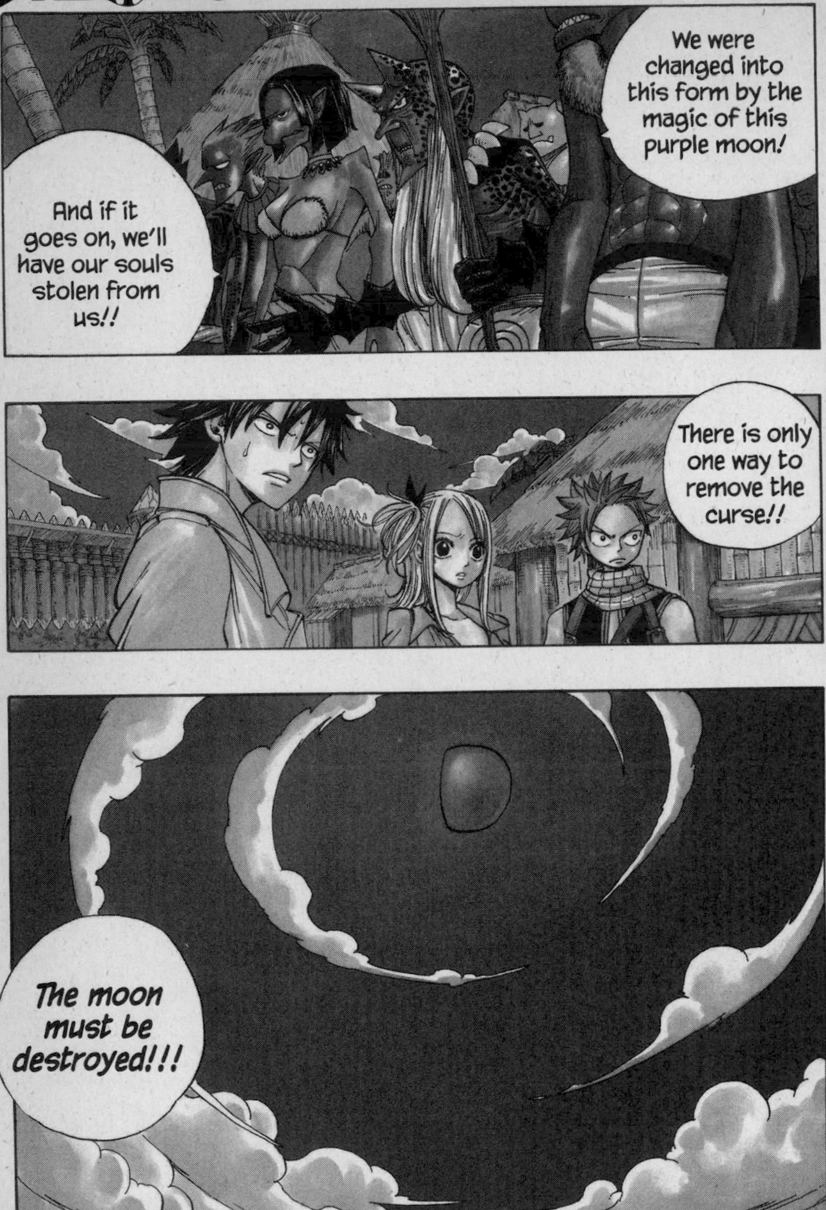
We were changed into this form by the magic of this purple moon!
And if it goes on, we'll have our souls stolen from us!!
There is only one way to remove the curse!!
The moon must be destroyed!!!

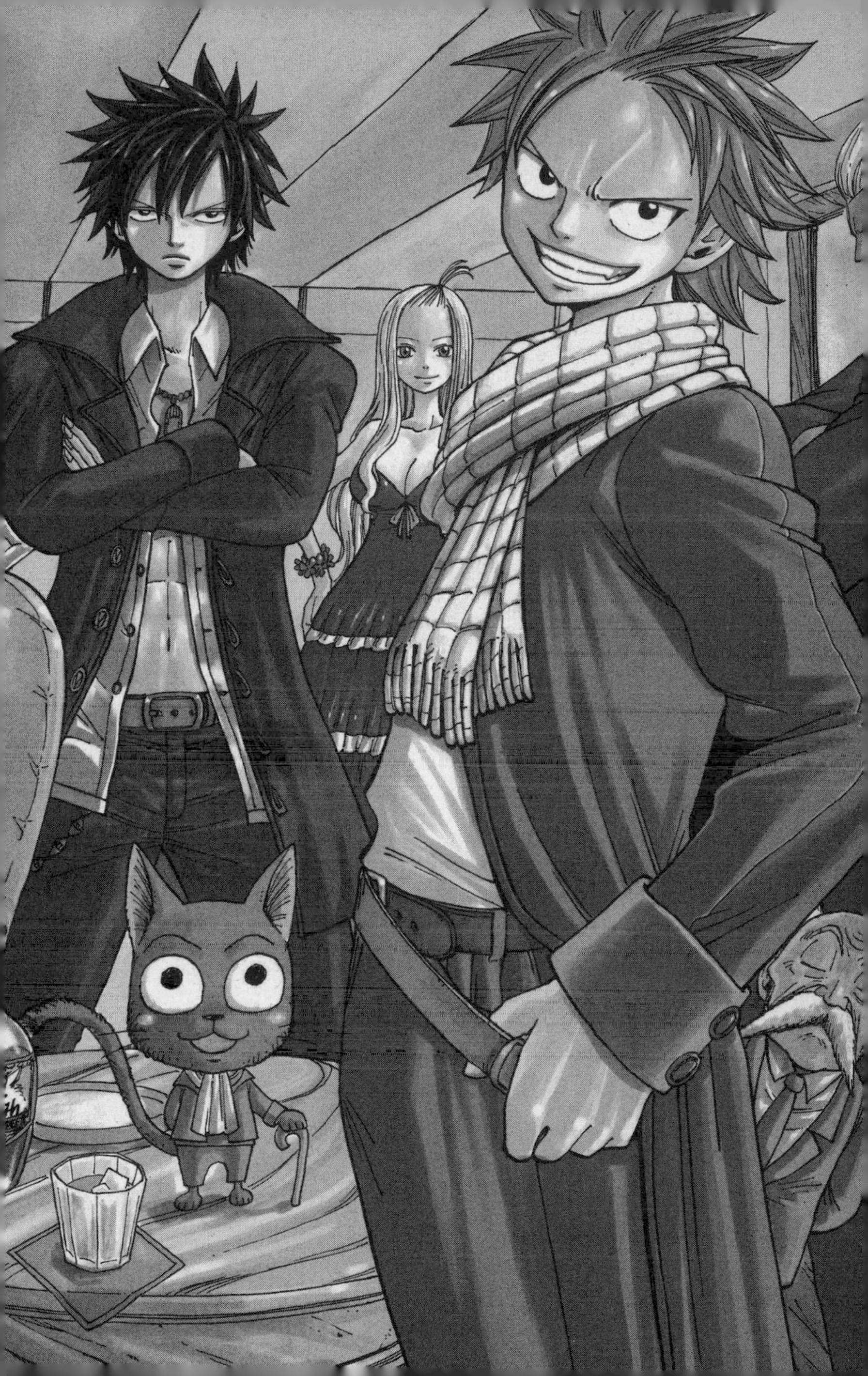

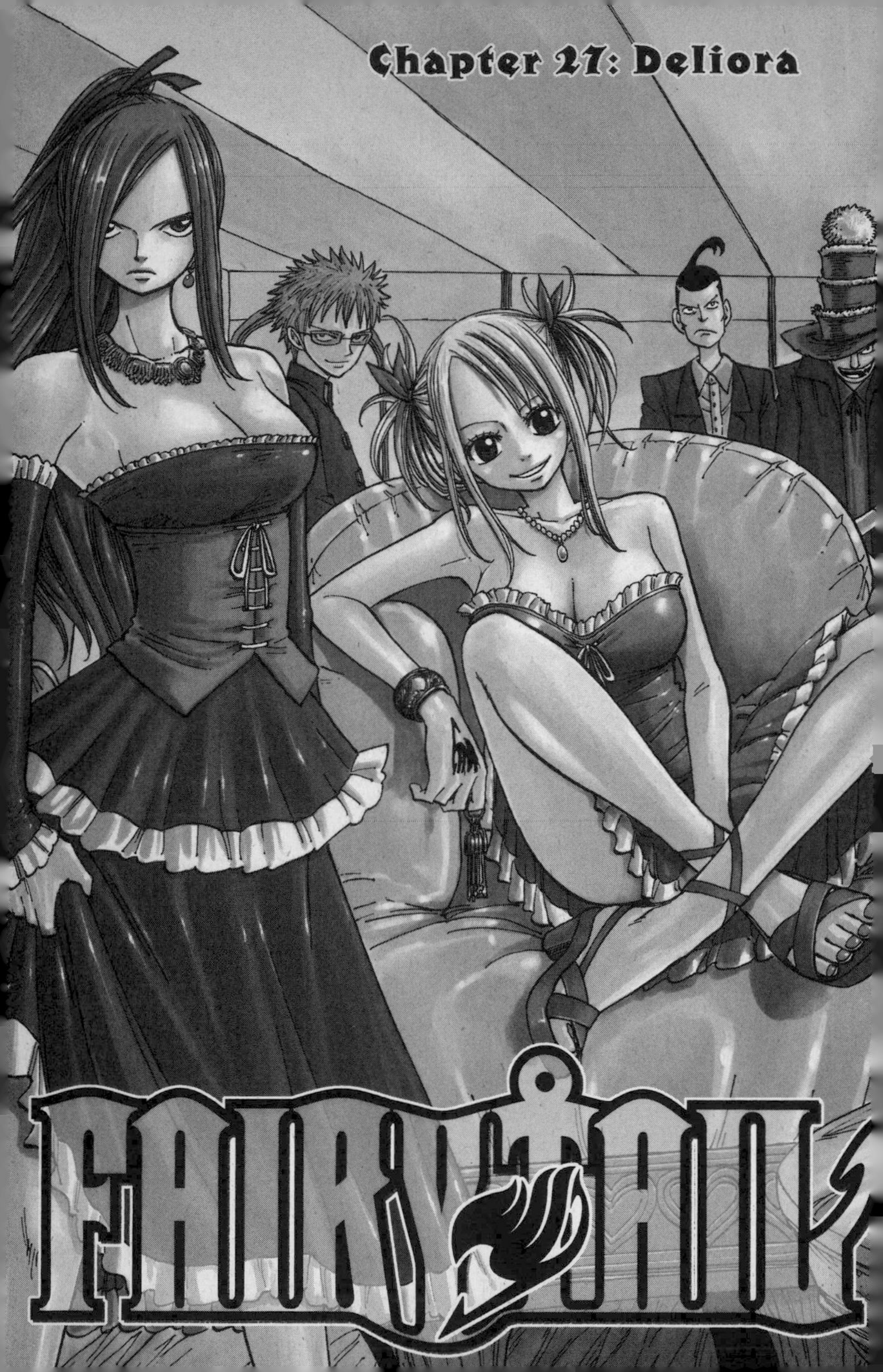
Chapter 27: Deliora
FAIRY TAIL

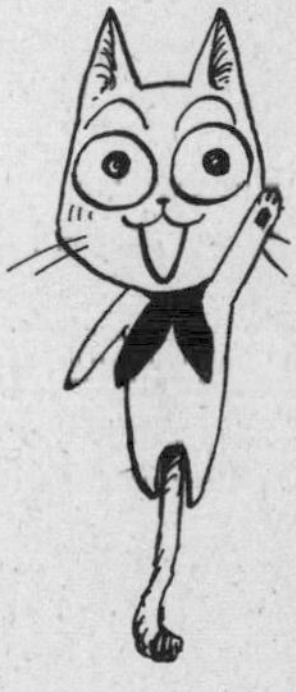

FAIRY TAIL

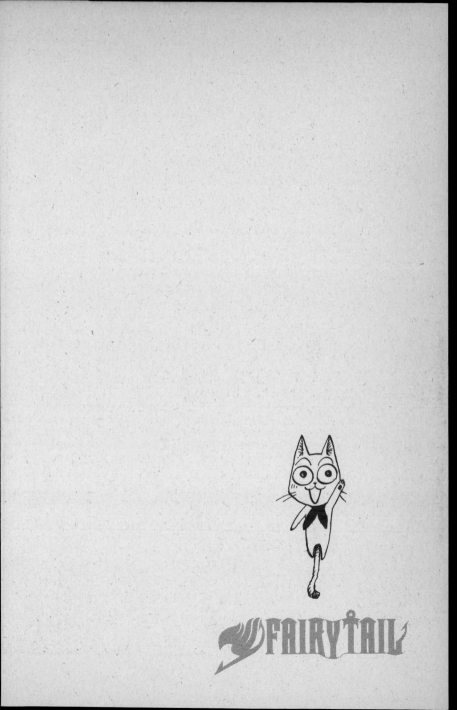

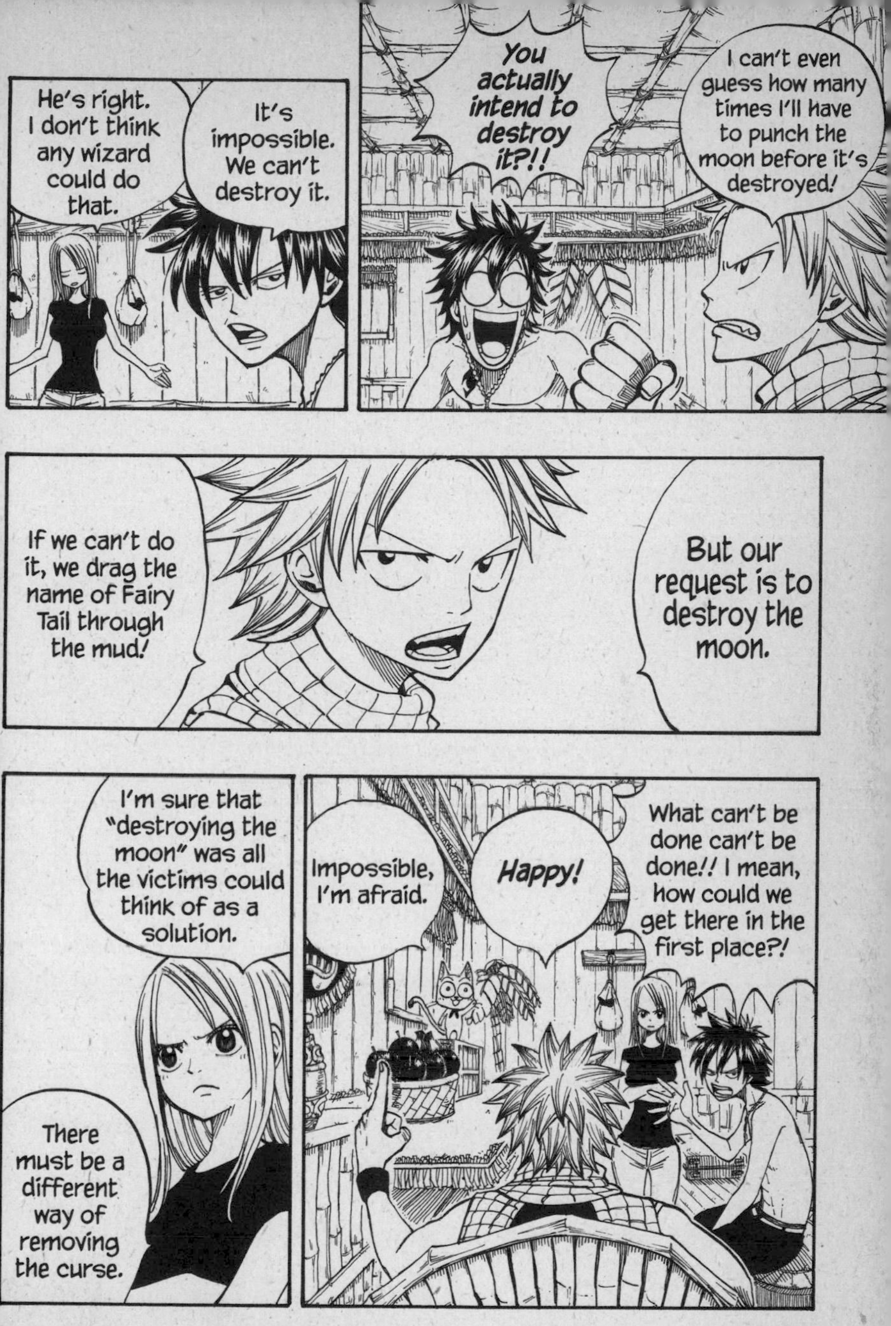
I can't even guess how many times I'll have to punch the moon before it's destroyed!
You actually intend to destroy it?!!
It's impossible. We can't destroy it.
He's right. I don't think any wizard could do that.
But our request is to destroy the moon.
If we can't do it, we drag the name of Fairy Tail through the mud!
What can't be done can't be done!! I mean, how could we get there in the first place?!
Happy!
Impossible, I'm afraid.
I'm sure that "destroying the moon" was all the victims could think of as a solution.
There must be a different way of removing the curse.

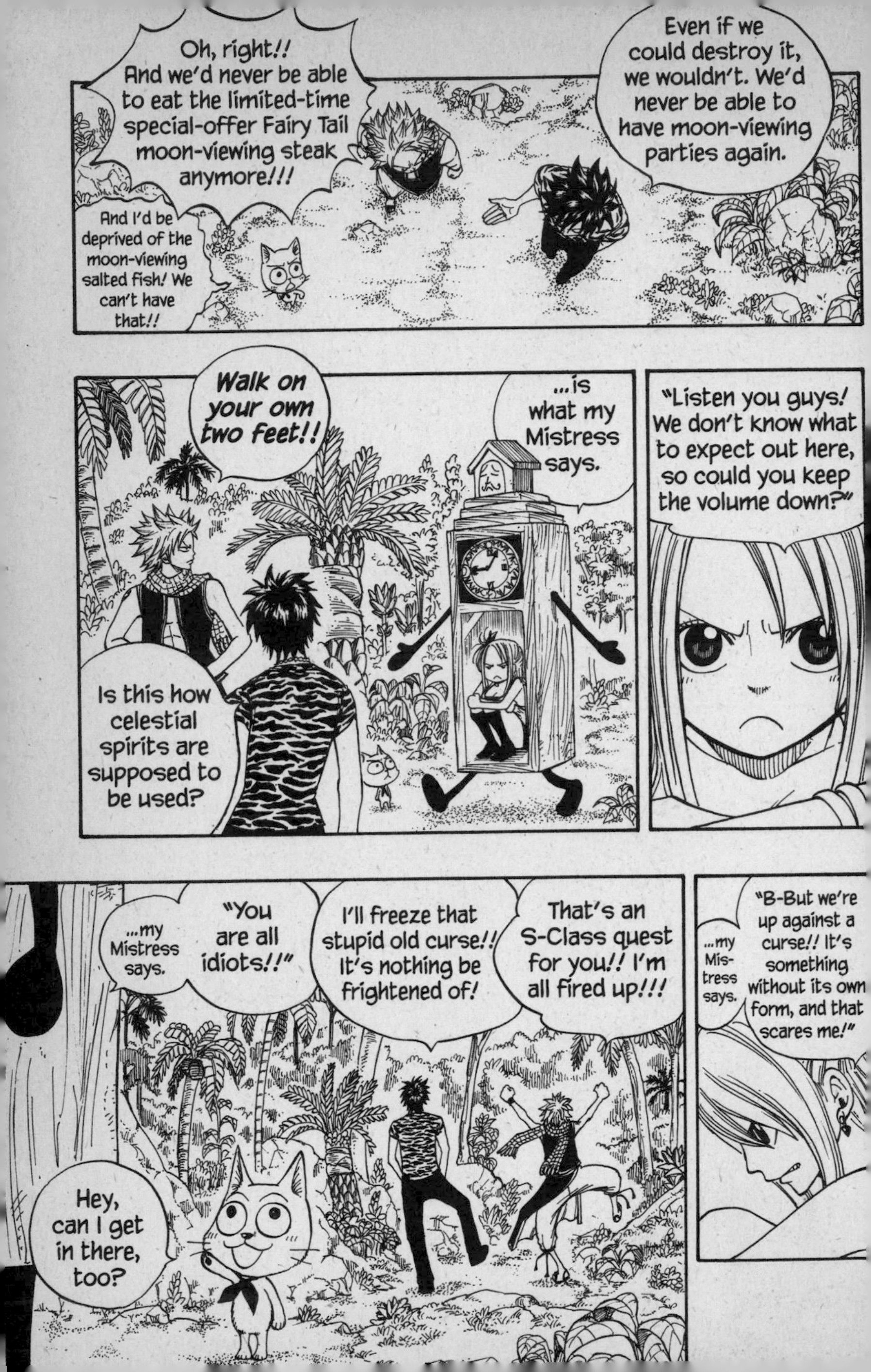
Even if we could destroy it, we wouldn't. We'd never be able to have moon-viewing parties again.
Oh, right!! And we'd never be able to eat the limited-time special-offer Fairy Tail moon-viewing steak anymore!!!
And I'd be deprived of the moon-viewing salted fish! We can't have that!!
"Listen you guys! We don't know what to expect out here, so could you keep the volume down?"
Walk on your own two feet!!
...is what my Mistress says.
Is this how celestial spirits are supposed to be used?
"B-But we're up against a curse!! It's something without its own form, and that scares me!"
...my Mis-tress says.
That's an S-Class quest for you!! I'm all fired up!!!
I'll freeze that stupid old curse!! It's nothing be frightened of!
"You are all idiots!!"
...my Mistress says.
Hey, can I get in there, too?

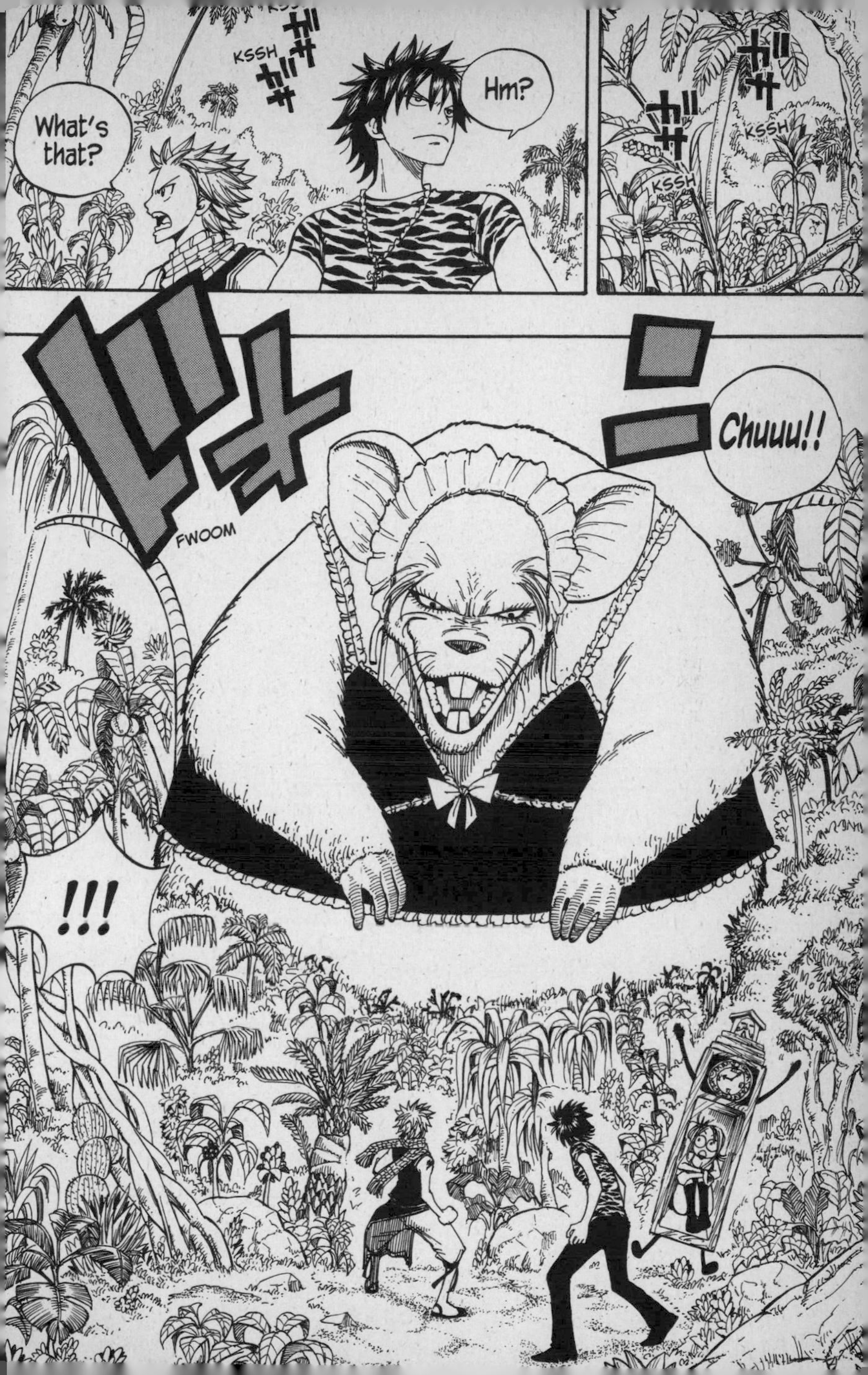
KSSH
KSSH
KSSH
Hm?
What's that?
Chuuu!!
FWOOM
!!!

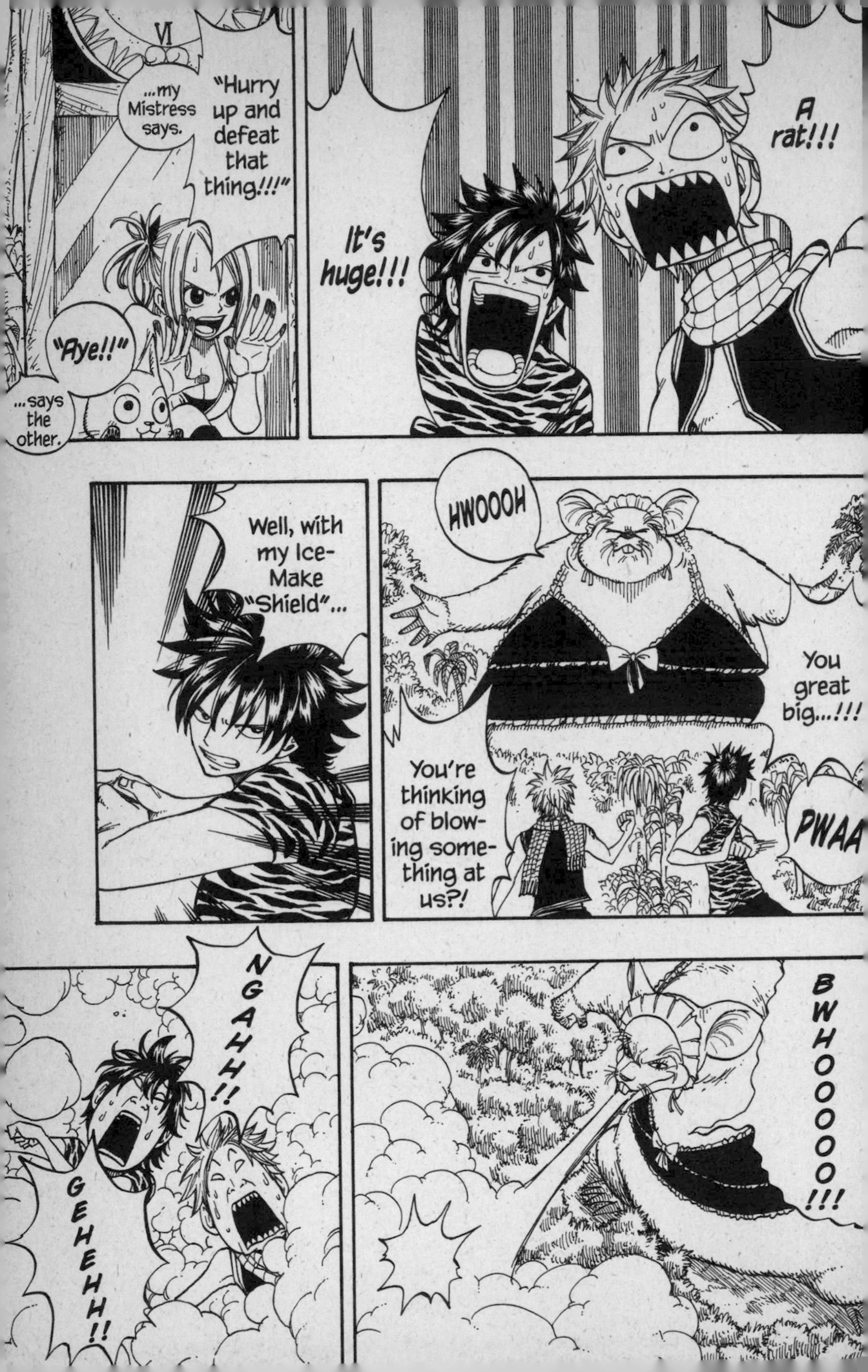
A rat!!!
It's huge!!!
"Hurry up and defeat that thing!!!"
...my Mistress says.
"Aye!!"
...says the other.
HWOOOH
You great big...!!!
You're thinking of blowing something at us?!
PWAA
Well, with my Ice-Make "Shield"...
BWHOOOOOO!!!
NGAHH!!
GEHEHH!!

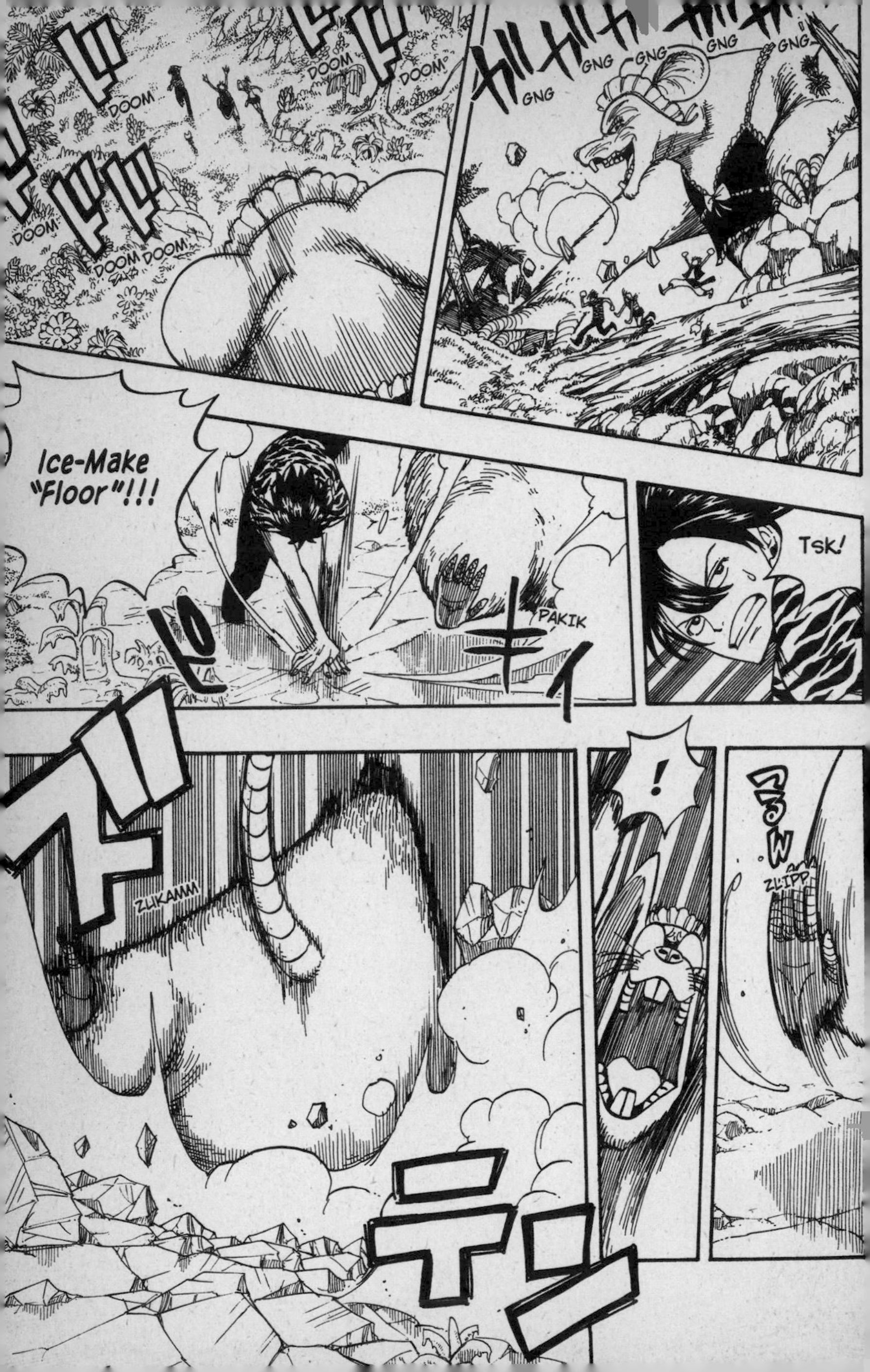
GNG GNG GNG GNG GNG
DOOM DOOM DOOM
DOOM DOOM DOOM
Ice-Make "Floor"!!!
PAKIK
TSK!
ZLIPP
!
ZLKAMM

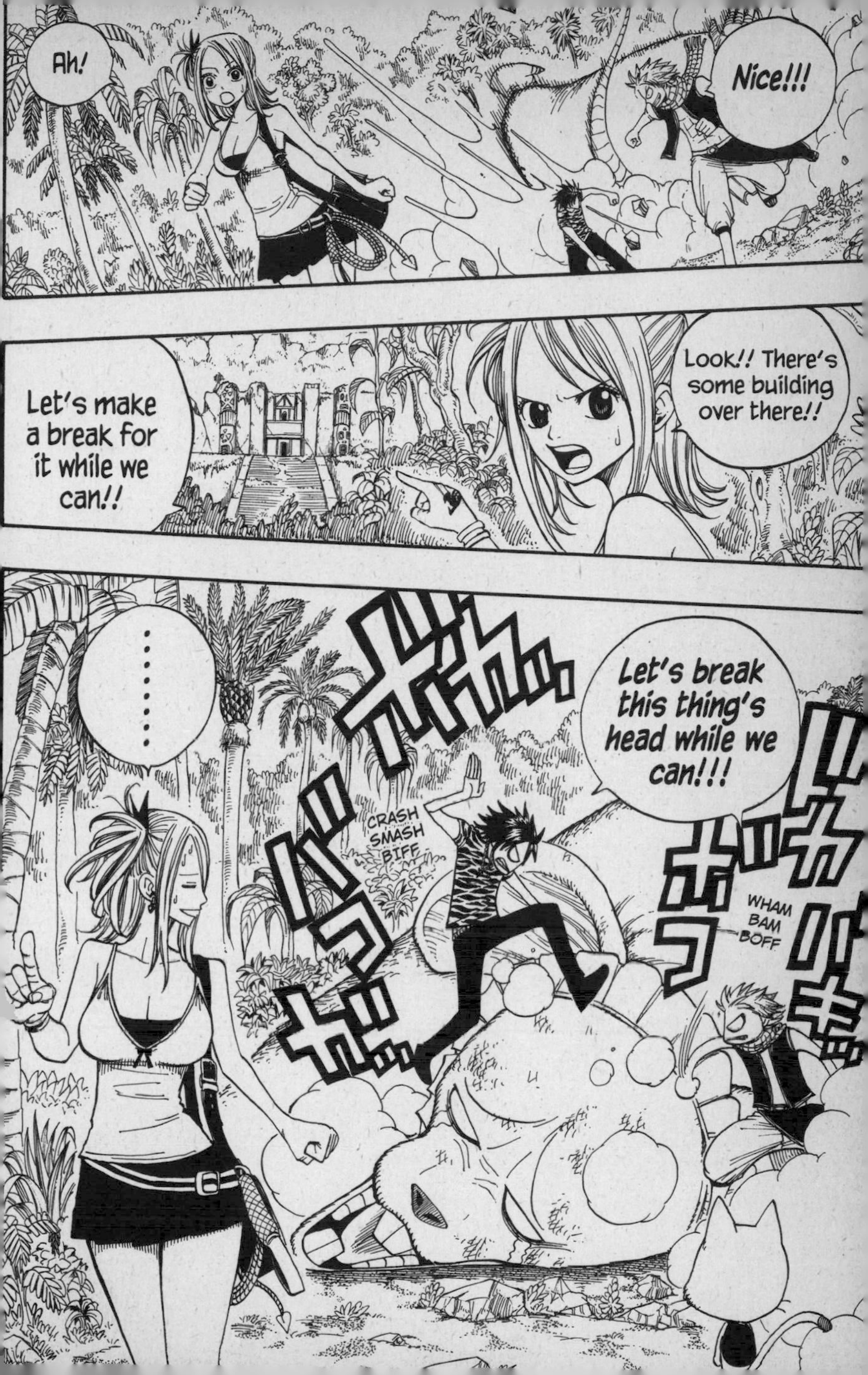
Nice!!!
Ah!
Look!! There's some building over there!!
Let's make a break for it while we can!!
Let's break this thing's head while we can!!!
WHAM BAM BOFF
CRASH SMASH BIFF
....

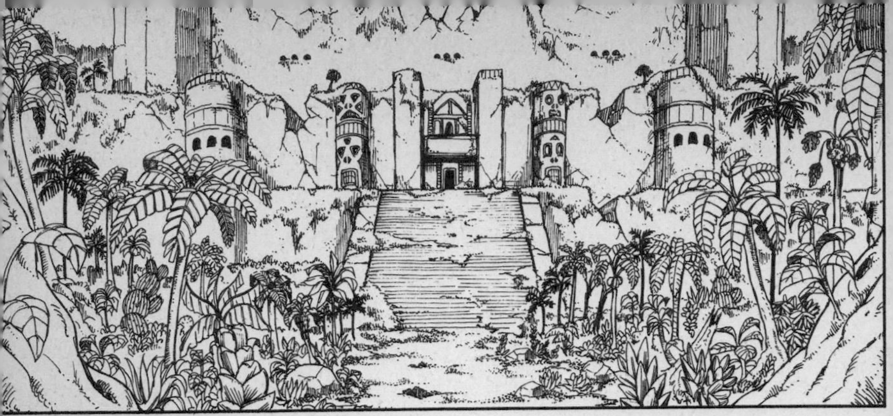

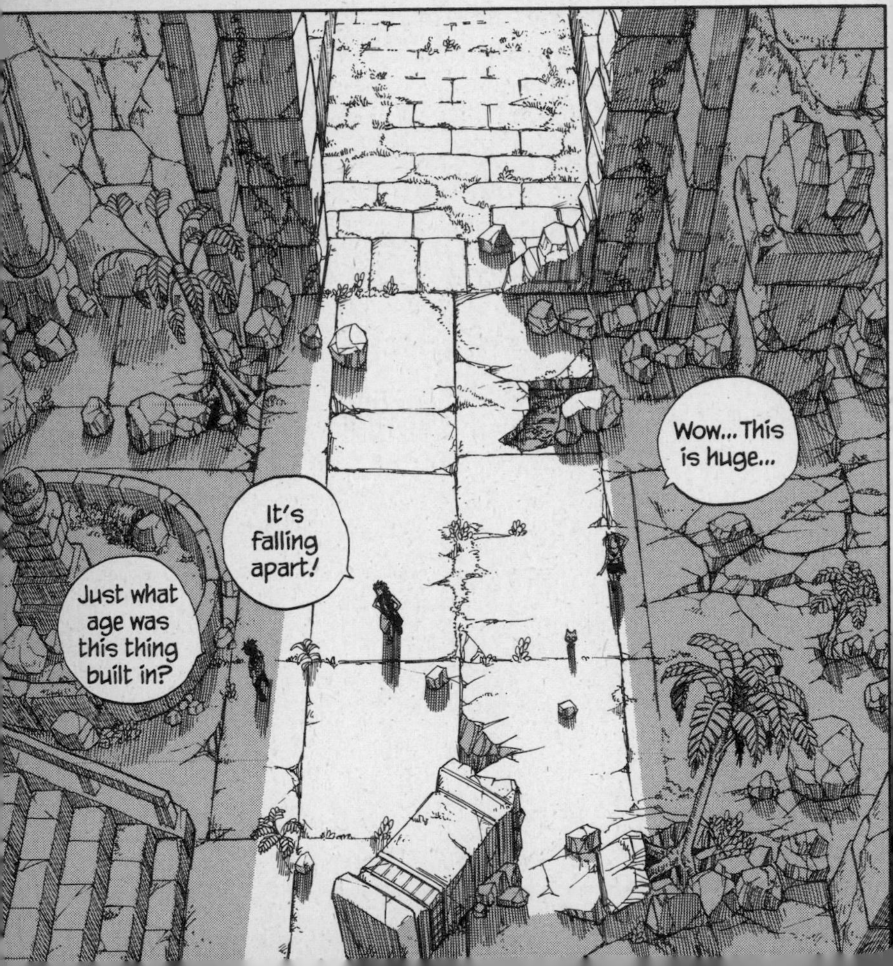
Wow... This is huge...
It's falling apart!
Just what age was this thing built in?

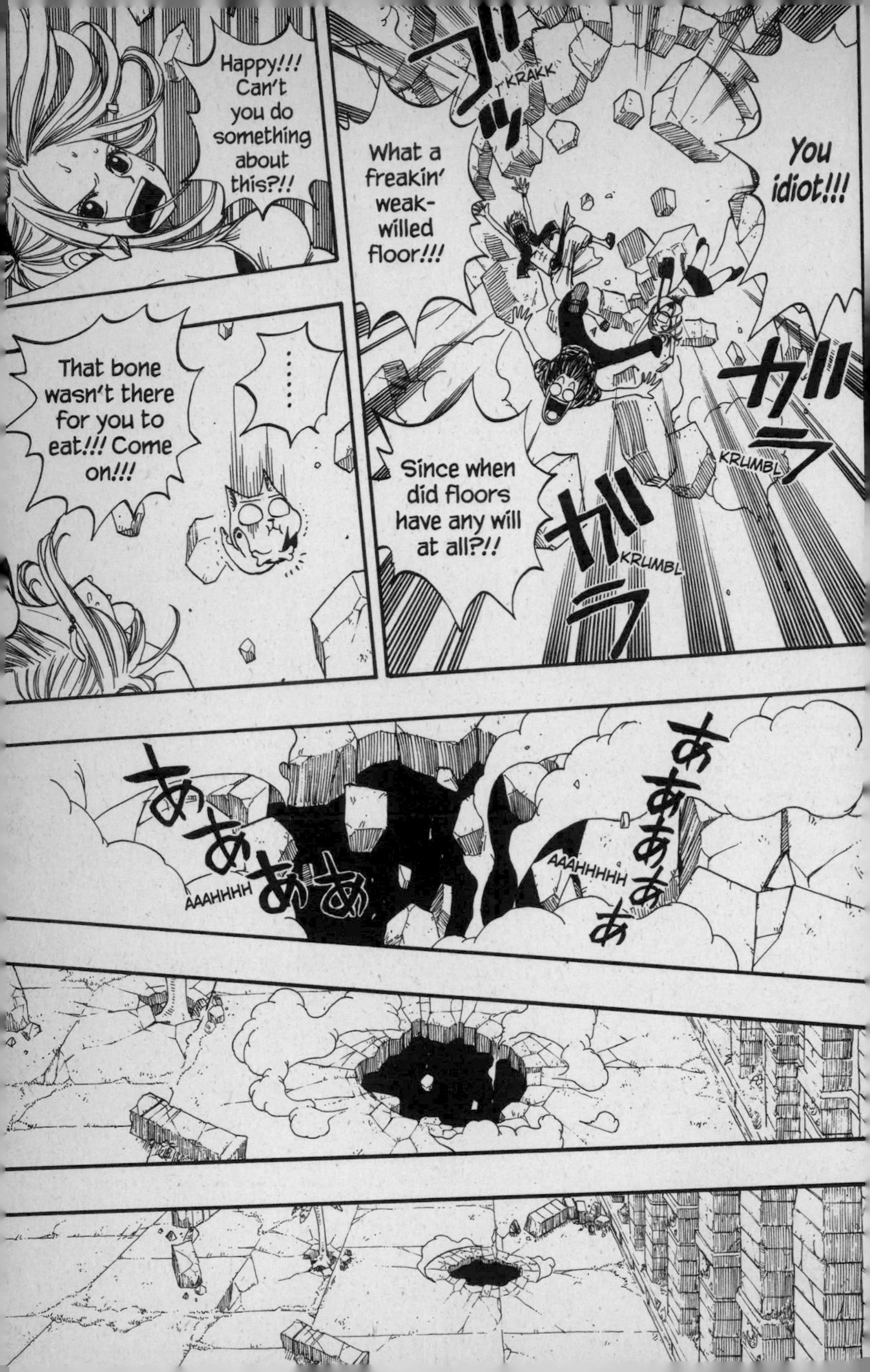

ゴッ
KRAKK
You idiot!!!
What a freakin' weak-willed floor!!!
ガラ
KRUMBL
Since when did floors have any will at all?!!
ガラ
KRUMBL
Happy!!! Can't you do something about this?!!
......
That bone wasn't there for you to eat!!! Come on!!!
あああああ
AAAHHHHH
ああああ
AAAHHHH

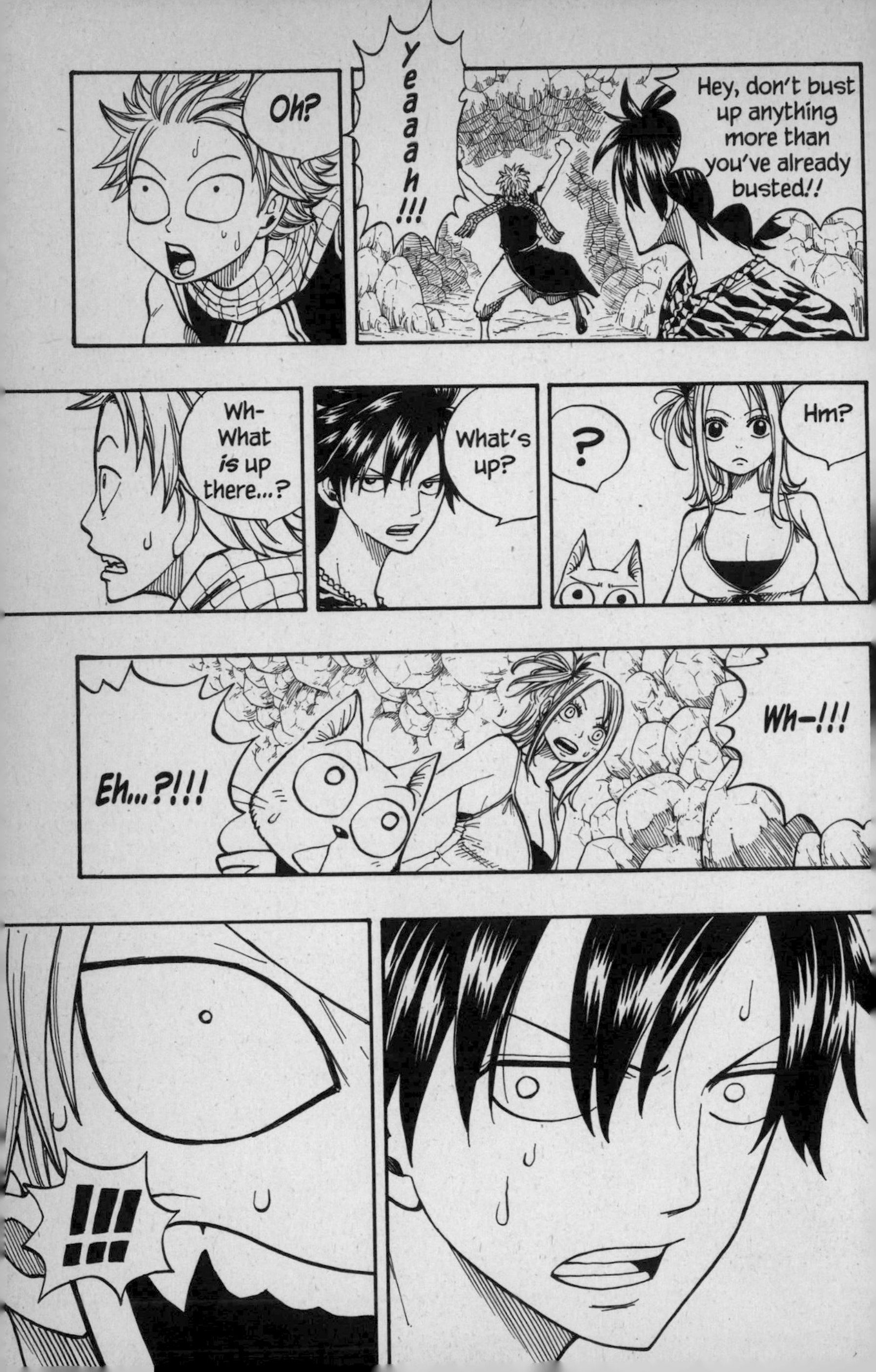
Hey, don't bust up anything more than you've already busted!!
Yeaaaah!!!
Oh?
Hm?
?
What's up?
Wh- What is up there...?
Wh-!!!
Eh...?!!!
!!!

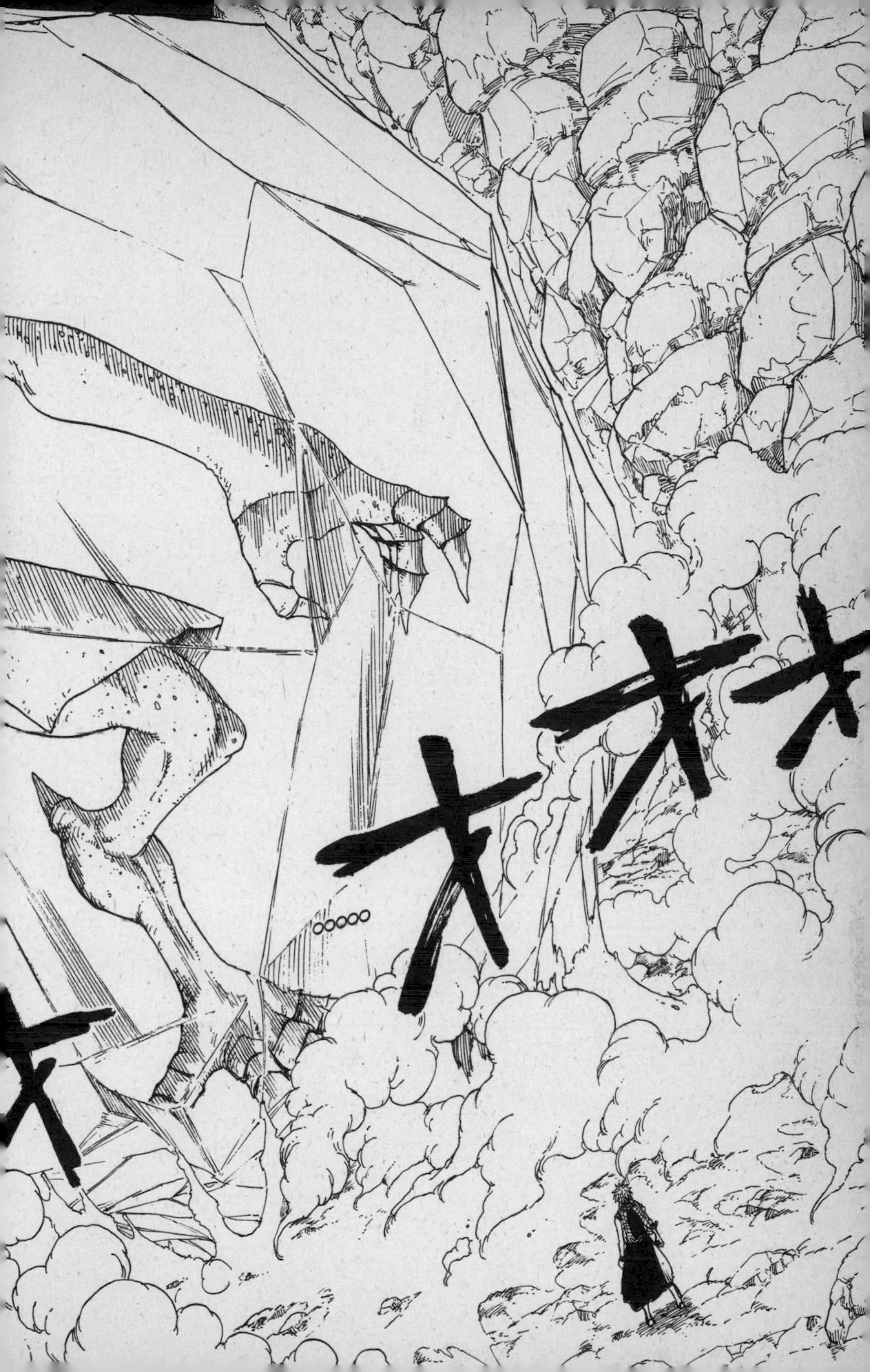

オオオ
OOOOO

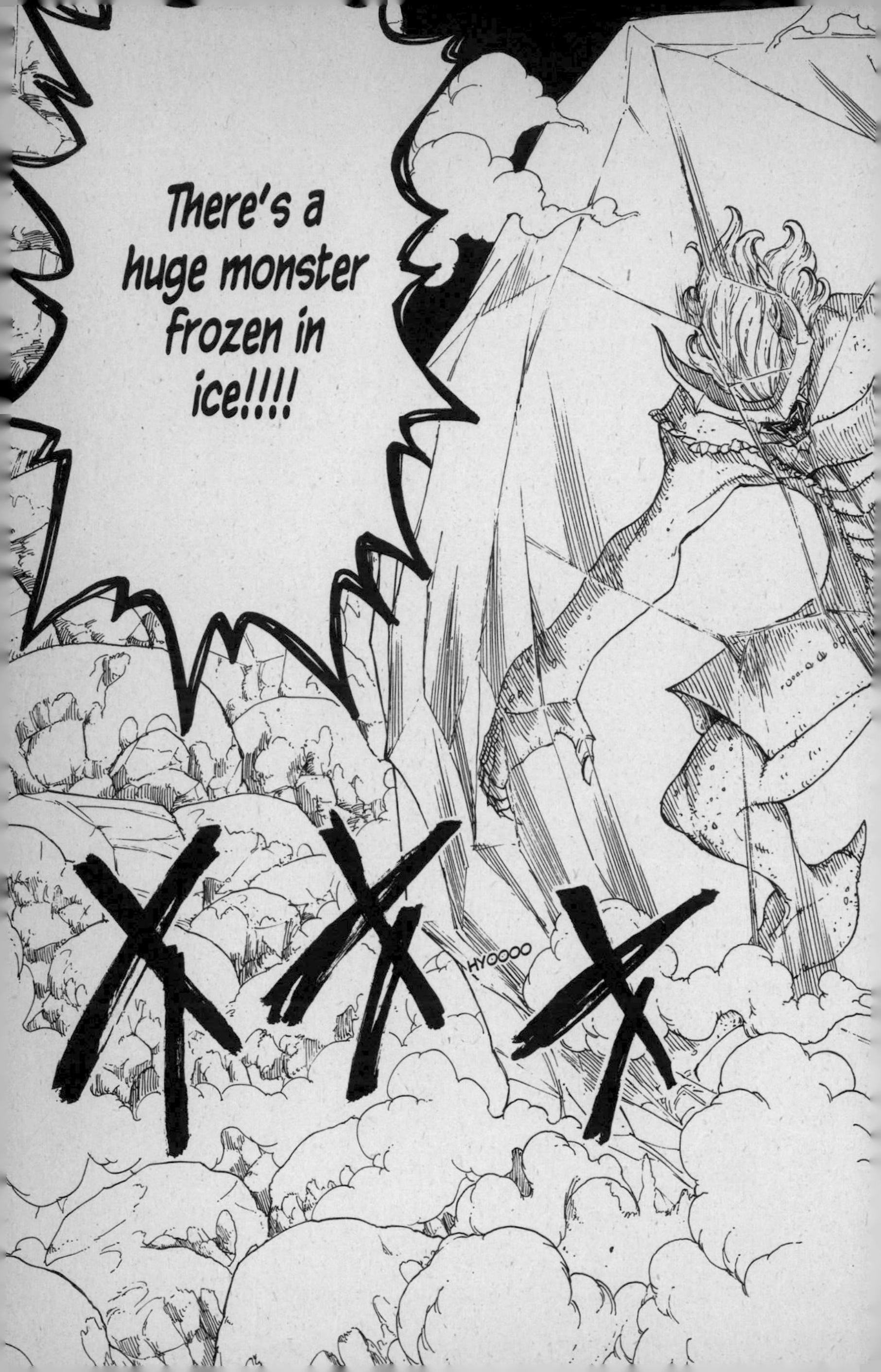
There's a huge monster frozen in ice!!!!
HYOOOO

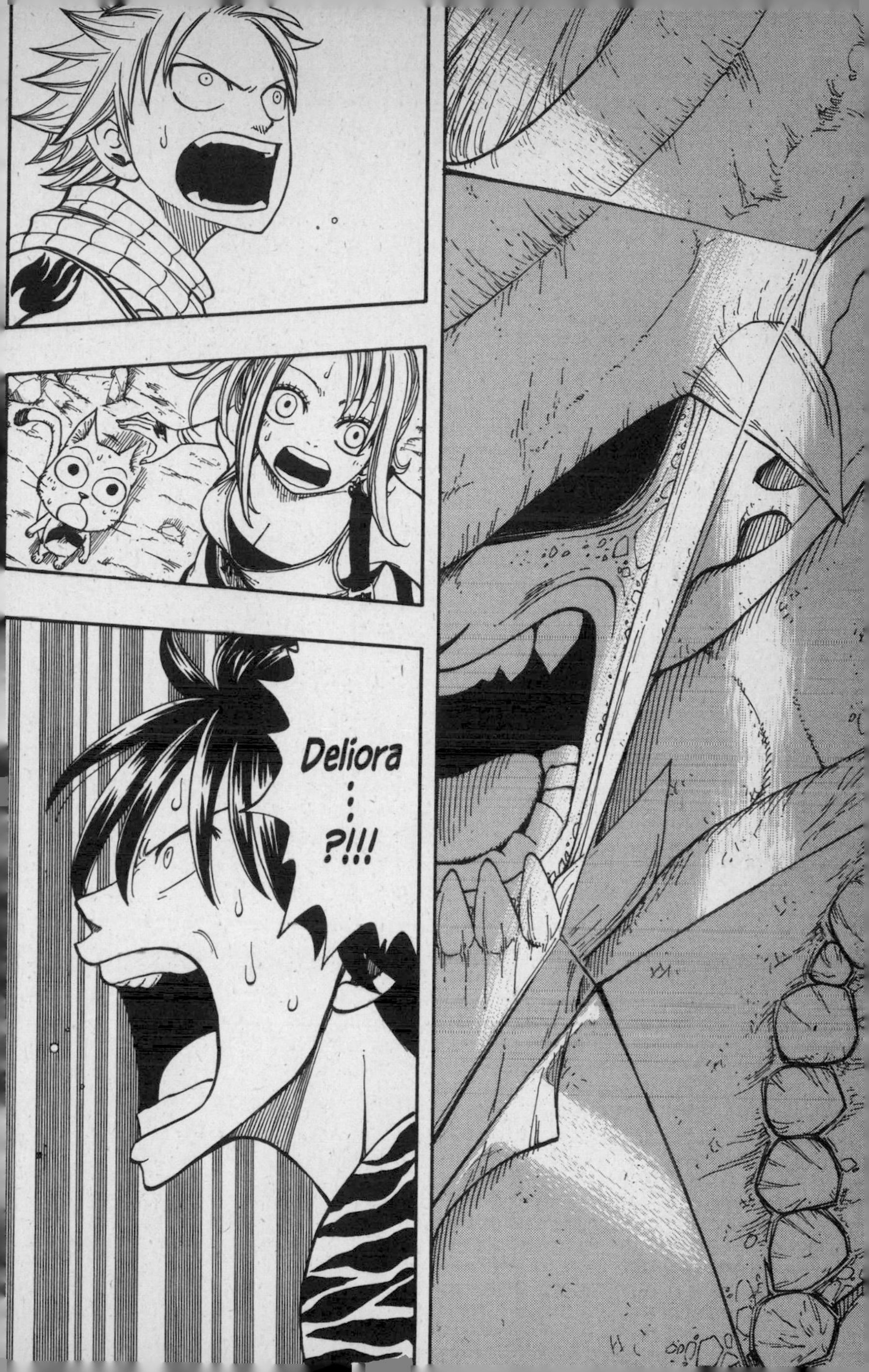
Deliora . . . ?!!!

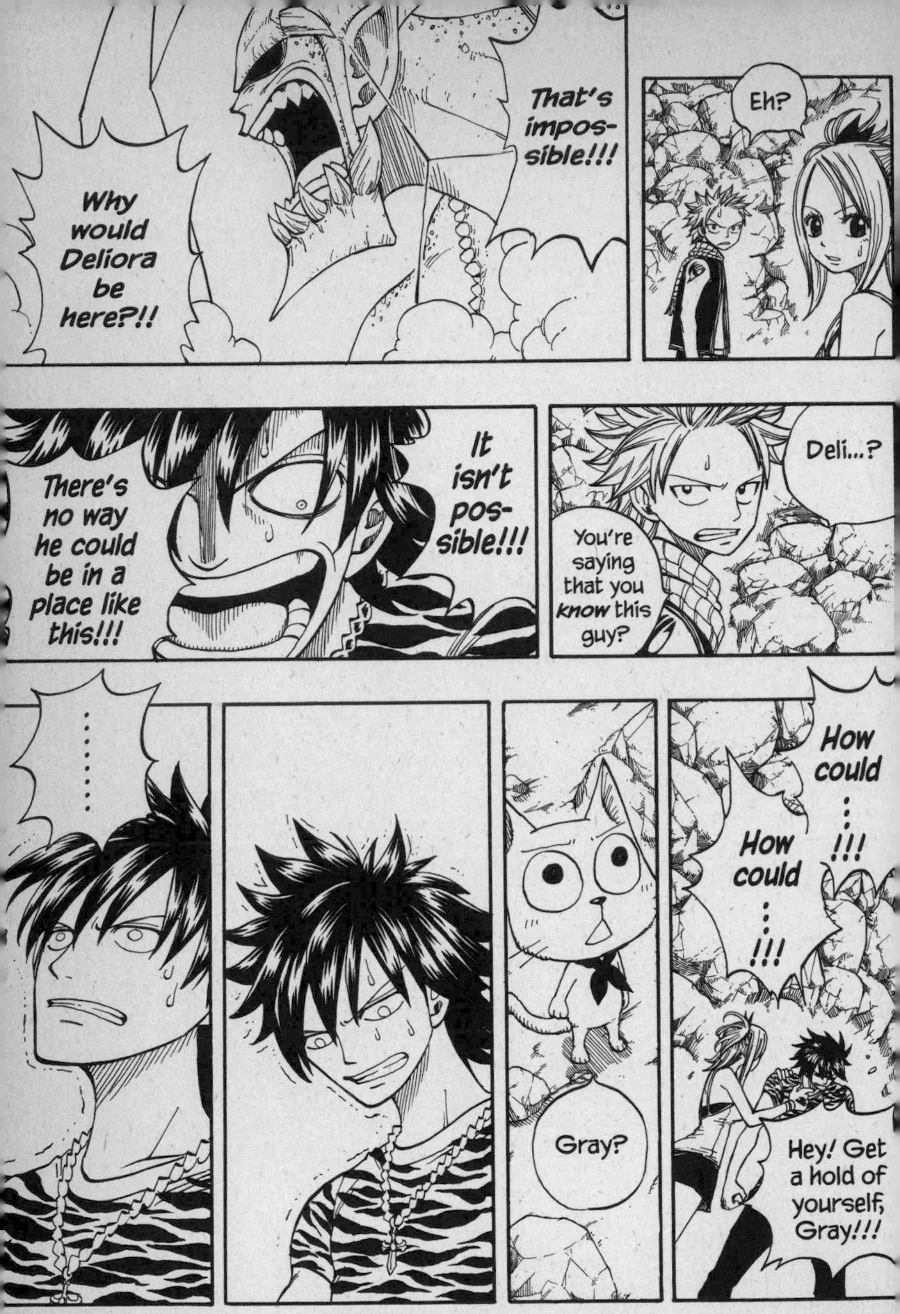
Eh?
That's impos-sible!!!
Why would Deliora be here?!!
Deli...?
You're saying that you know this guy?
It isn't pos-sible!!!
There's no way he could be in a place like this!!!
How could...!!!
How could...!!!
Hey! Get a hold of yourself, Gray!!!
Gray?
......

The Demon of Disaster ¦

Deliora ¦

Come on, Gray! What is that thing?!

The Demon of Disaster...?

What happened to it?!

It's in the same position it was in back when...

First thing to do is hide!

What for?

Never mind! Just do it!!

Shh!

Some-body's coming!!

!

†"" KAK
†"" †" KAK KAK

†" "" KAK
†"" KAK
"" KAK

106

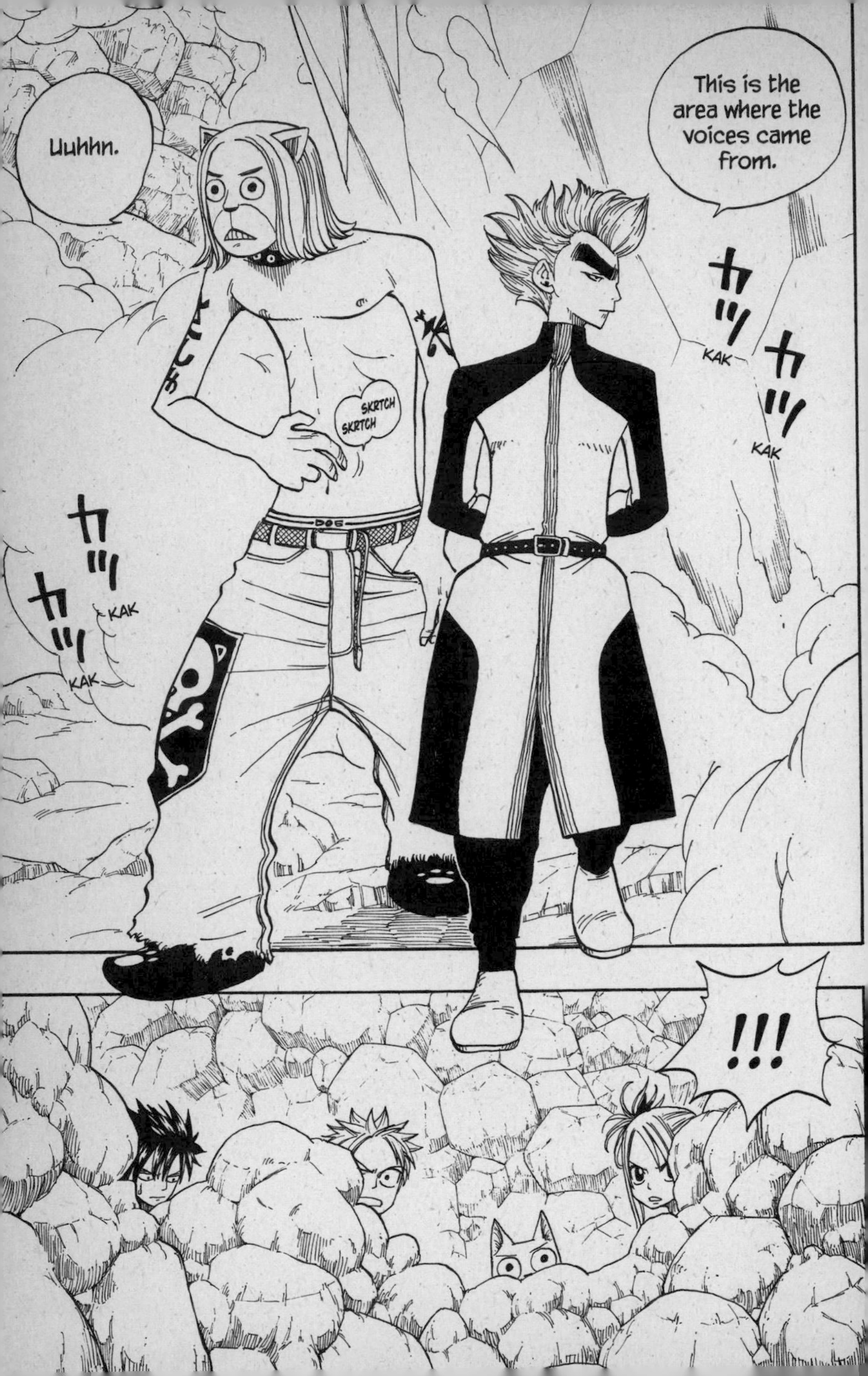
This is the area where the voices came from.
カッ
KAK
カッ
KAK
Uuhhn.
SKRTCH SKRTCH
カッ
KAK
カッ
KAK
!!!

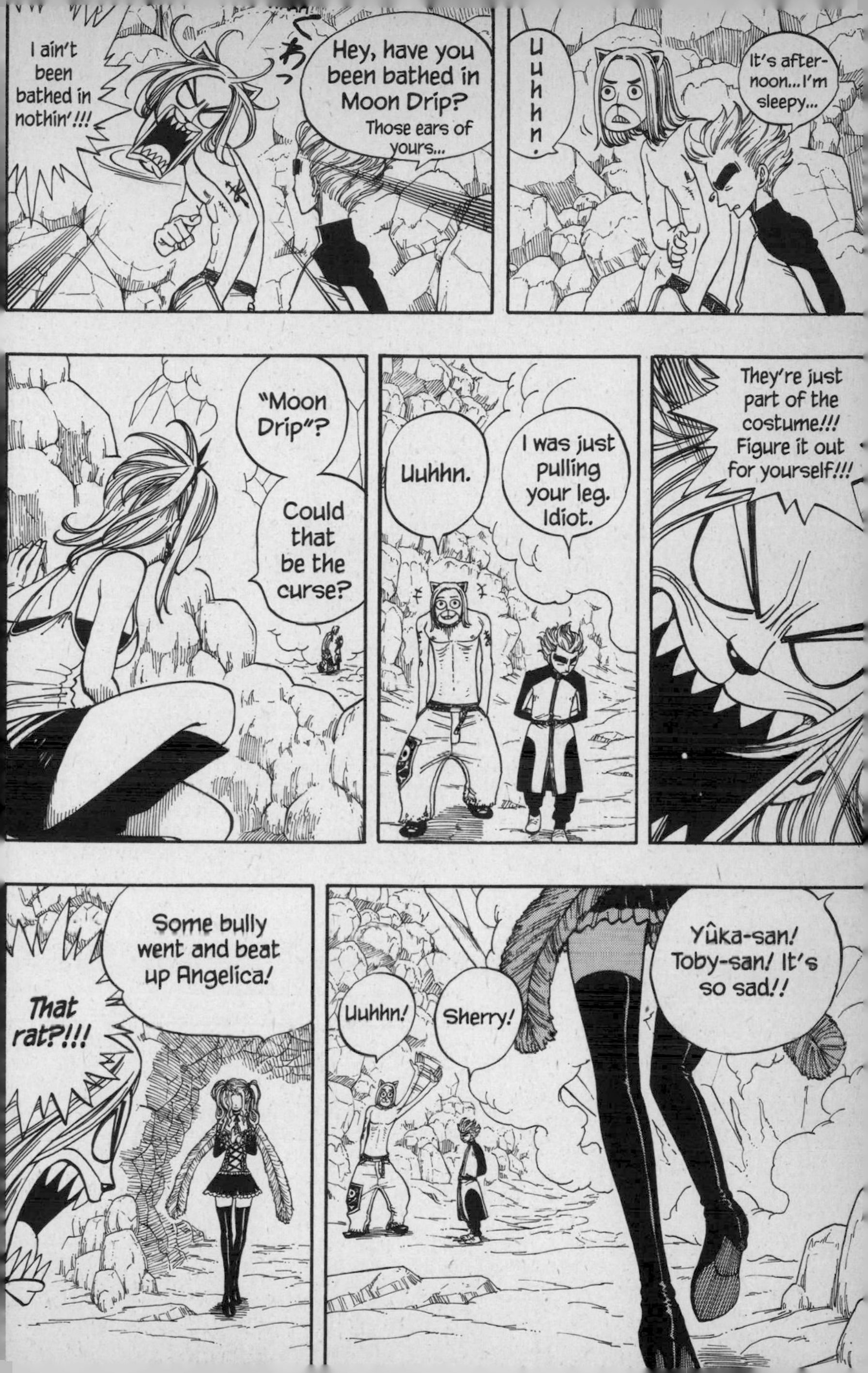
It's after-noon...I'm sleepy...
Uuhhn.
Hey, have you been bathed in Moon Drip?
Those ears of yours...
I ain't been bathed in nothin'!!!
They're just part of the costume!!! Figure it out for yourself!!!
I was just pulling your leg. Idiot.
Uuhhn.
"Moon Drip"?
Could that be the curse?
Yûka-san! Toby-san! It's so sad!!
Sherry!
Uuhhn!
Some bully went and beat up Angelica!
That rat?!!!

112

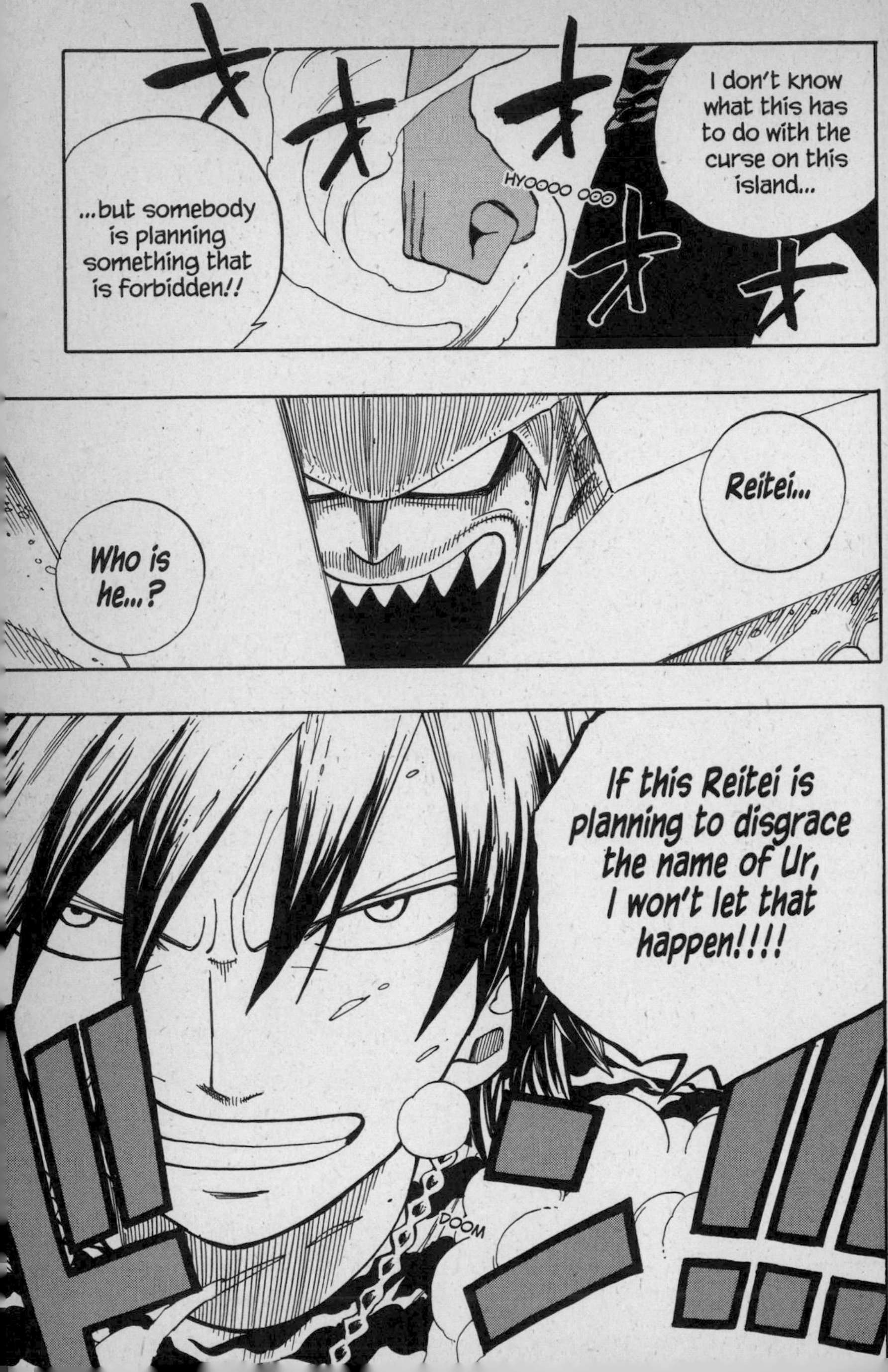
I don't know what this has to do with the curse on this island...
HYOOOO OOO
...but somebody is planning something that is forbidden!!
Reitei...
Who is he...?
If this Reitei is planning to disgrace the name of Ur, I won't let that happen!!!!
DOOM

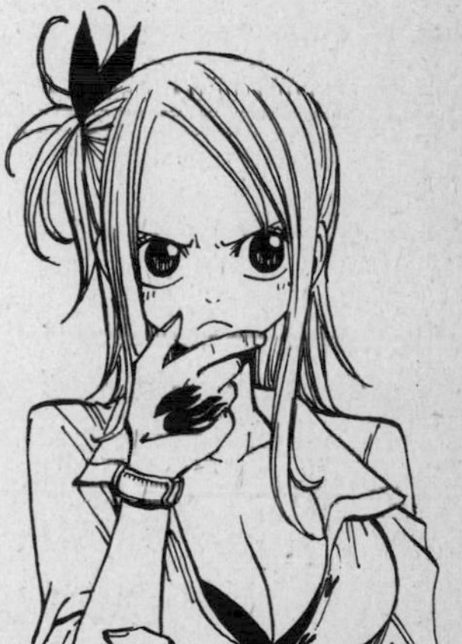

FAIRY TAIL

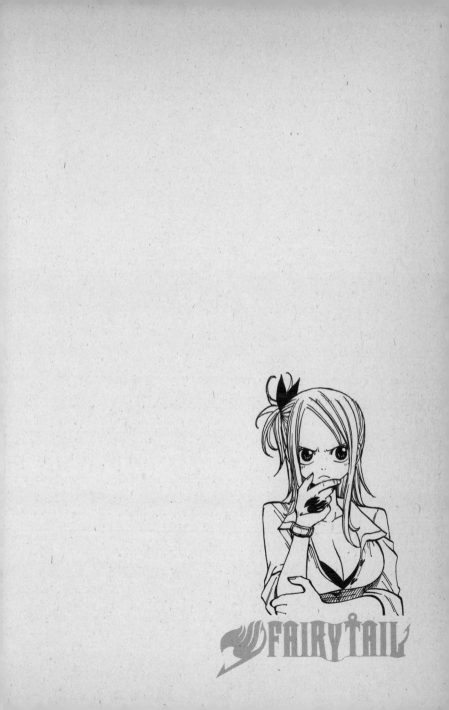

FAIRY TAIL

FAIRY TAIL

Name: Mirajane   **Age:** 19 Yrs.

Magic: Transformation

Likes: Cooking   **Dislikes:** Cockroaches

Remarks

An employee at Fairy Tail. Originally she
was a wizard doing jobs for the guild, but
due to the events of a certain mission,
she retired from active service. Her
ability to play the "pretty dumb girl,"
and her sweet smile have given her the
moniker of poster girl for Fairy Tail.
Although she doesn't encourage talent
scouts, she has done pin-up spreads
for magazines. And because of it, she's
become a minor celebrity.

Chapter 28:
Moon Drip

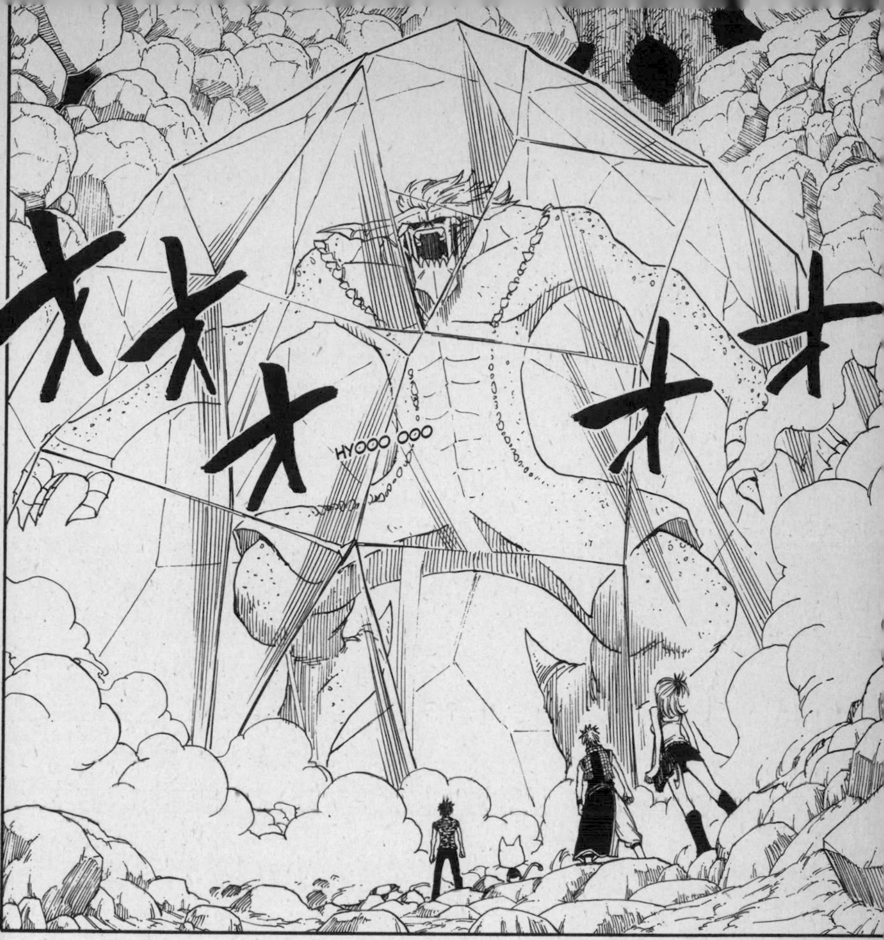
HYOOO OOO

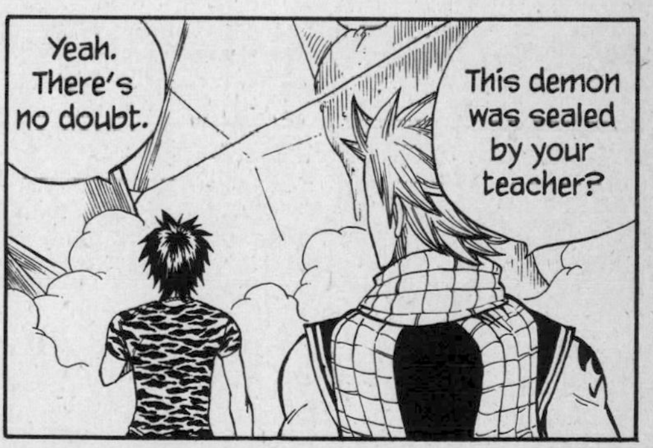
This demon was sealed by your teacher?
Yeah. There's no doubt.

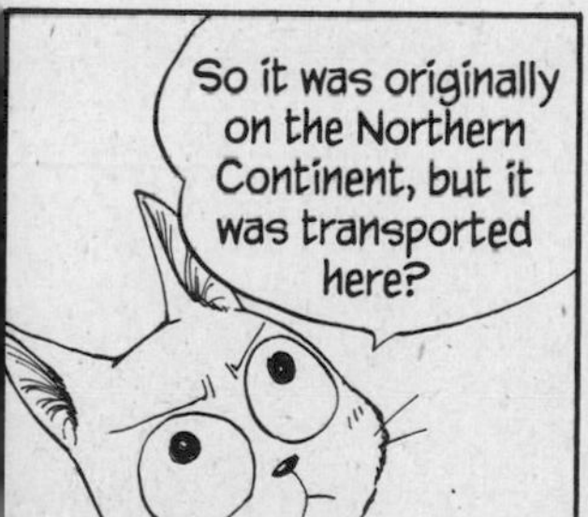
So it was originally on the Northern Continent, but it was transported here?

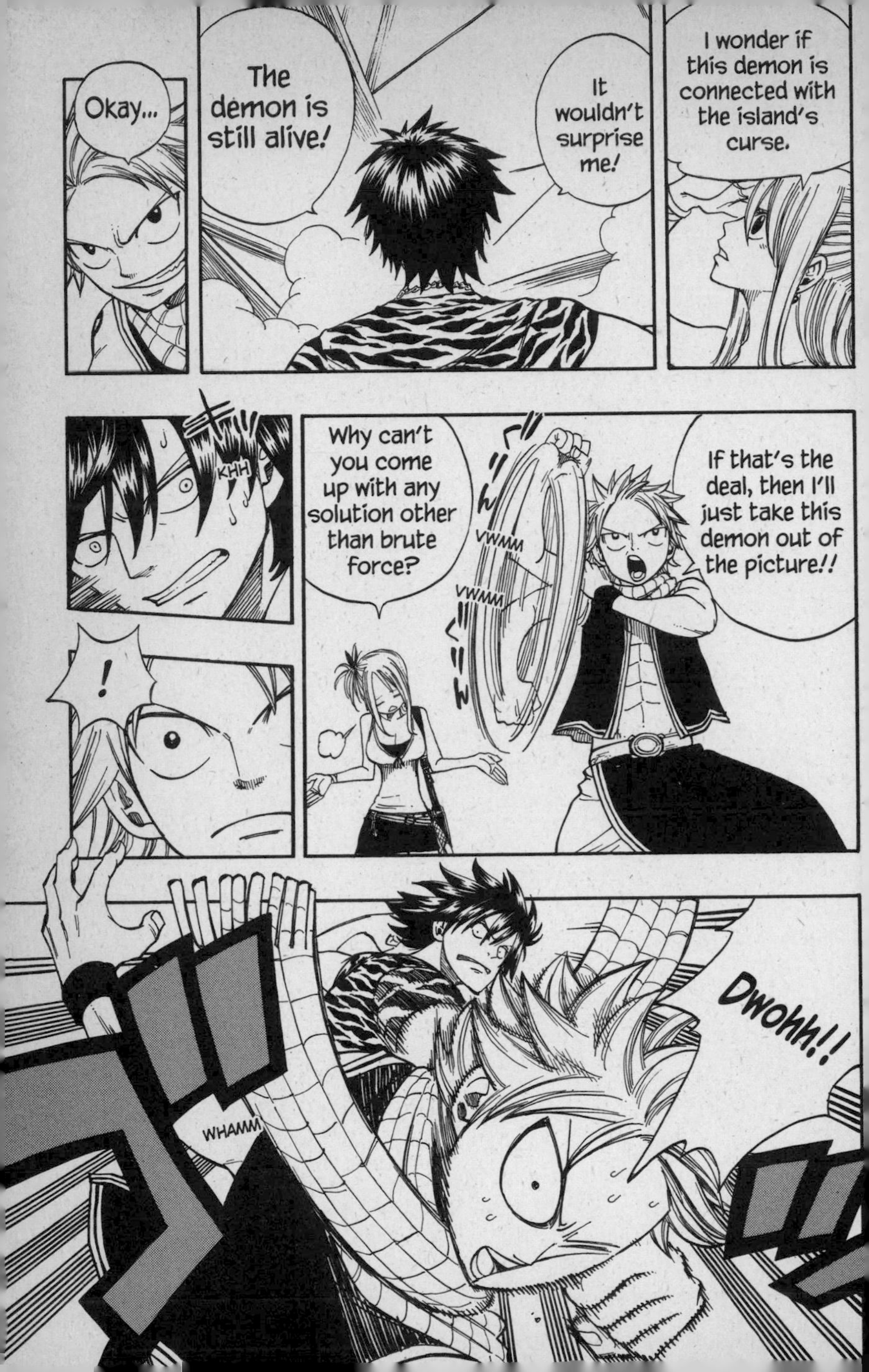
I wonder if this demon is connected with the island's curse.
It wouldn't surprise me!
The demon is still alive!
Okay...
If that's the deal, then I'll just take this demon out of the picture!!
VWMM
VWMM
Why can't you come up with any solution other than brute force?
KHH
!
Dwohh!!
WHAMM

Who would bring Deliora here? And for what reason...?

Dammit...!!! I don't like this!

Tsk!!

This is simple!!

All we have to do is follow those guys!!

?!

We should wait here!

That's true.

Wait here until the moon comes out.

No!

120

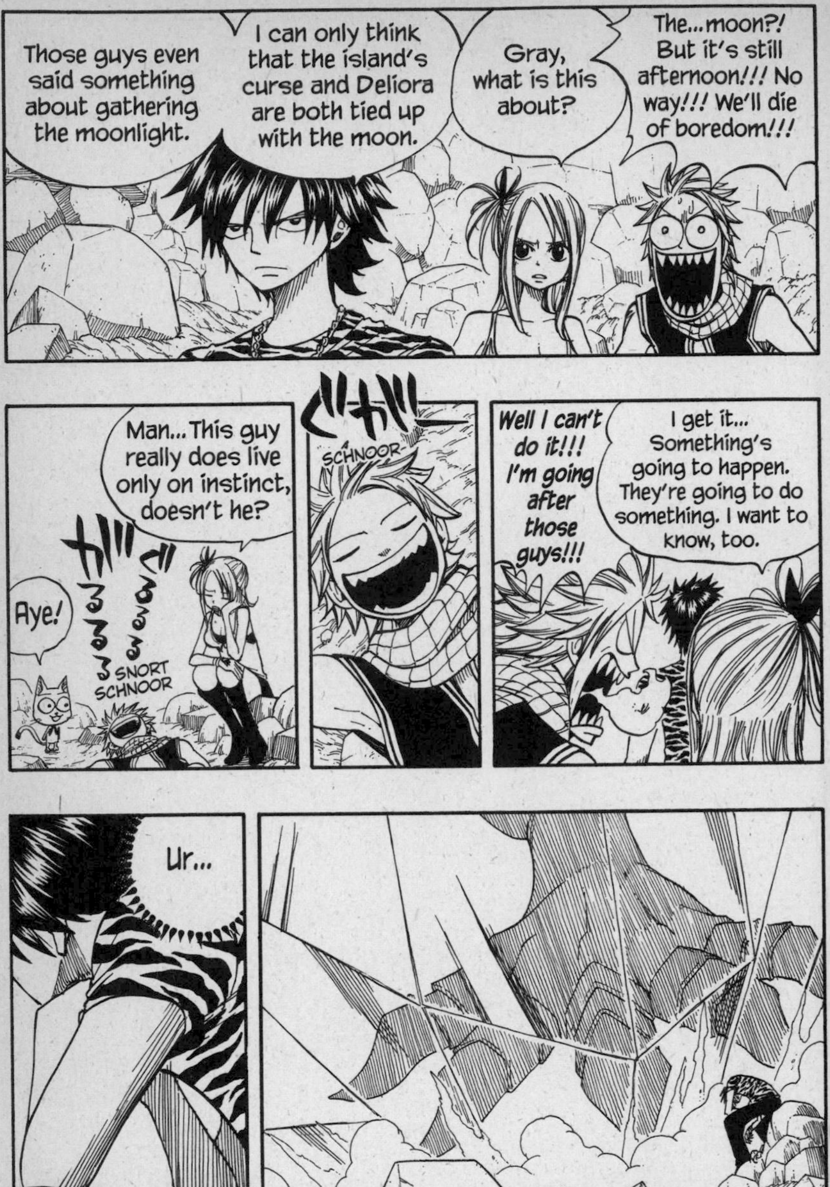
The...moon?! But it's still afternoon!!! No way!!! We'll die of boredom!!!
Gray, what is this about?
I can only think that the island's curse and Deliora are both tied up with the moon.
Those guys even said something about gathering the moonlight.
I get it... Something's going to happen. They're going to do something. I want to know, too.
Well I can't do it!!! I'm going after those guys!!!
SCHNOOR
Man... This guy really does live only on instinct, doesn't he?
Aye!
SNORT SCHNOOR
Ur...

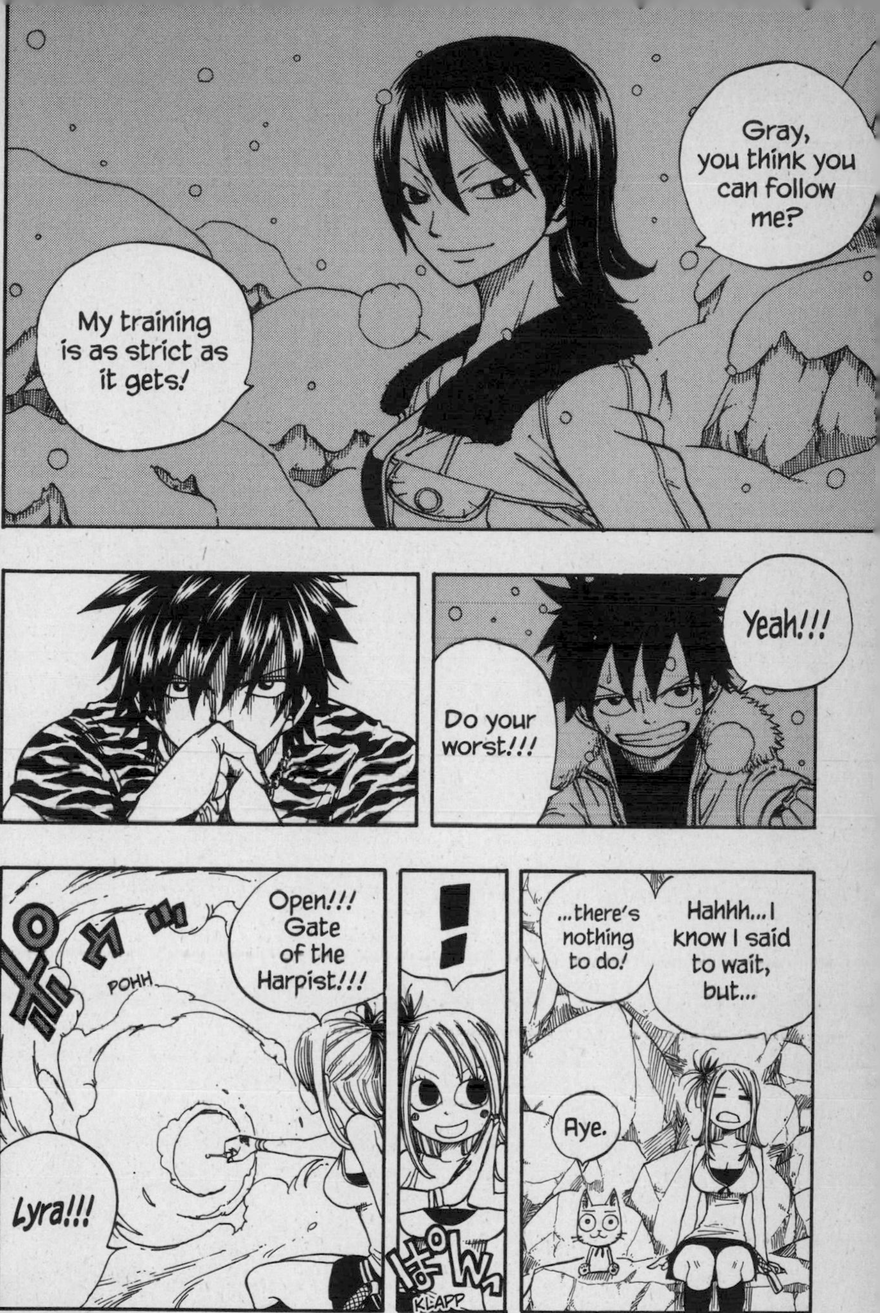
Gray, you think you can follow me?
My training is as strict as it gets!
Yeah!!!
Do your worst!!!
Hahhh... I know I said to wait, but...
...there's nothing to do!
Aye.
!
KLAPP
Open!!! Gate of the Harpist!!!
POHH
Lyra!!!

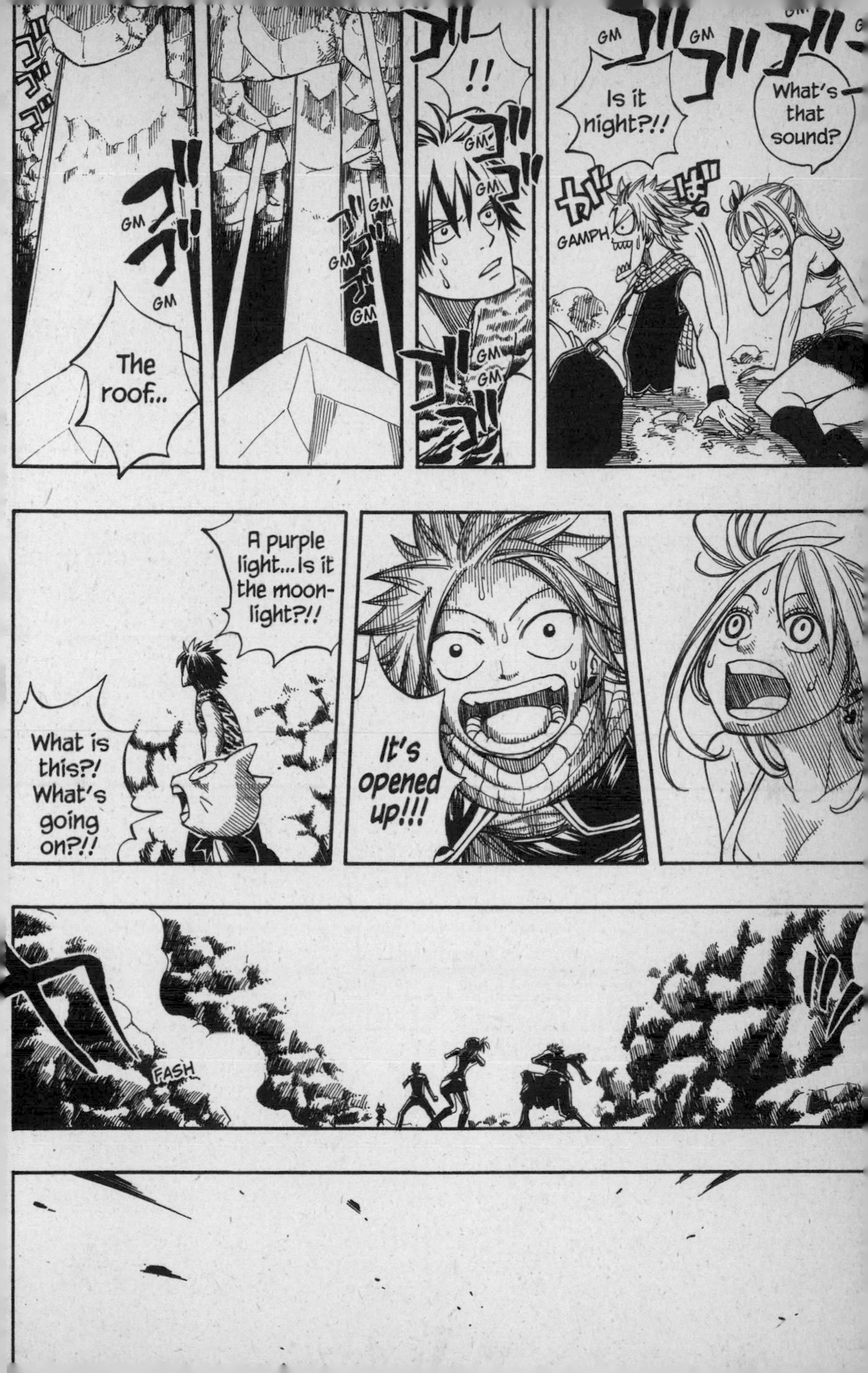
What's that sound?
GM
GM
Is it night?!!
GAMPH
!!
GM
GM
GM
GM
GM
GM
GM
GM
The roof...
GM
GM
It's opened up!!!
A purple light...Is it the moon-light?!!
What is this?! What's going on?!!
FASH

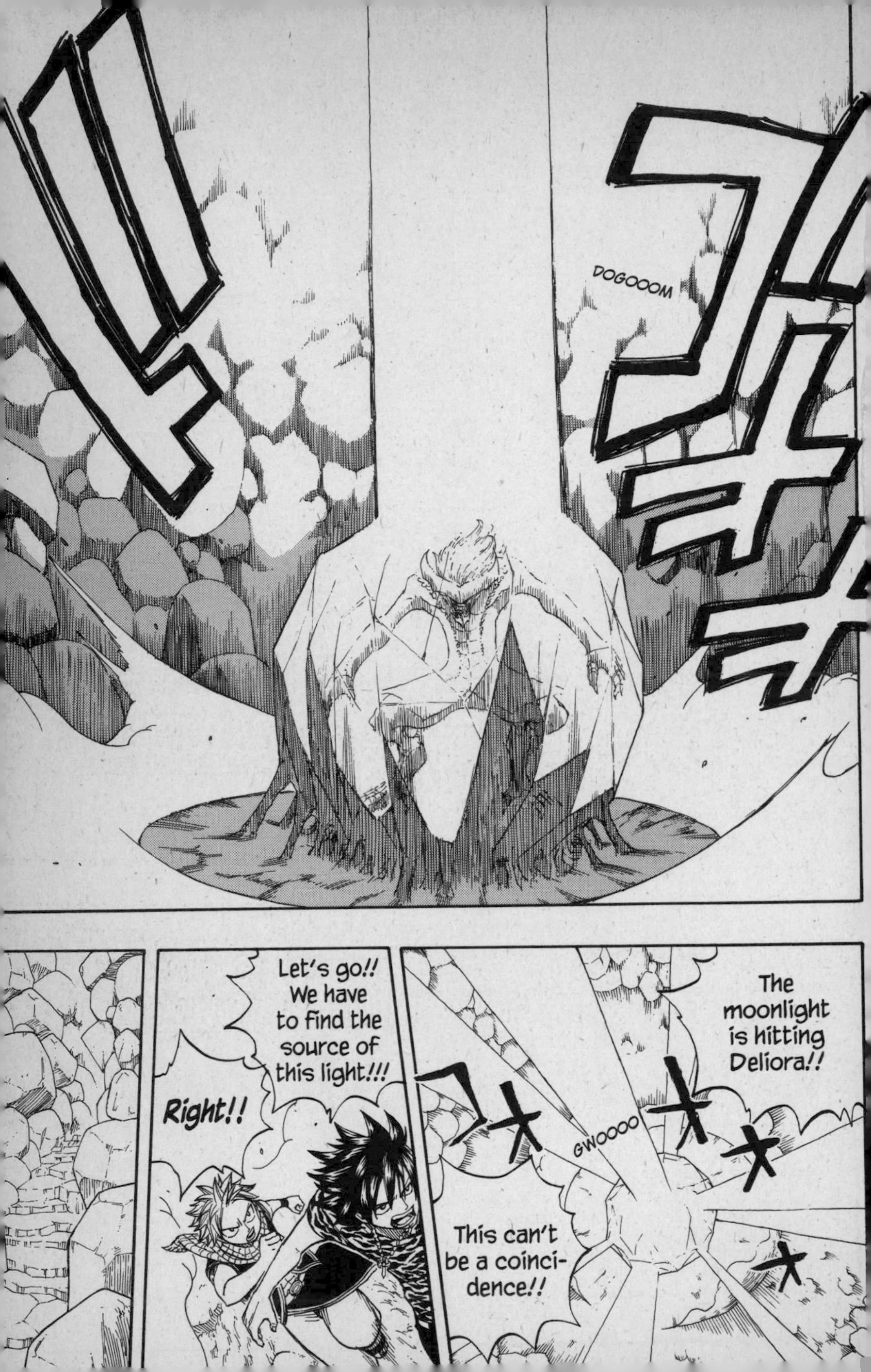
DOGOOOM
The moonlight is hitting Deliora!!
GWOOOO
This can't be a coincidence!!
Let's go!! We have to find the source of this light!!!
Right!!

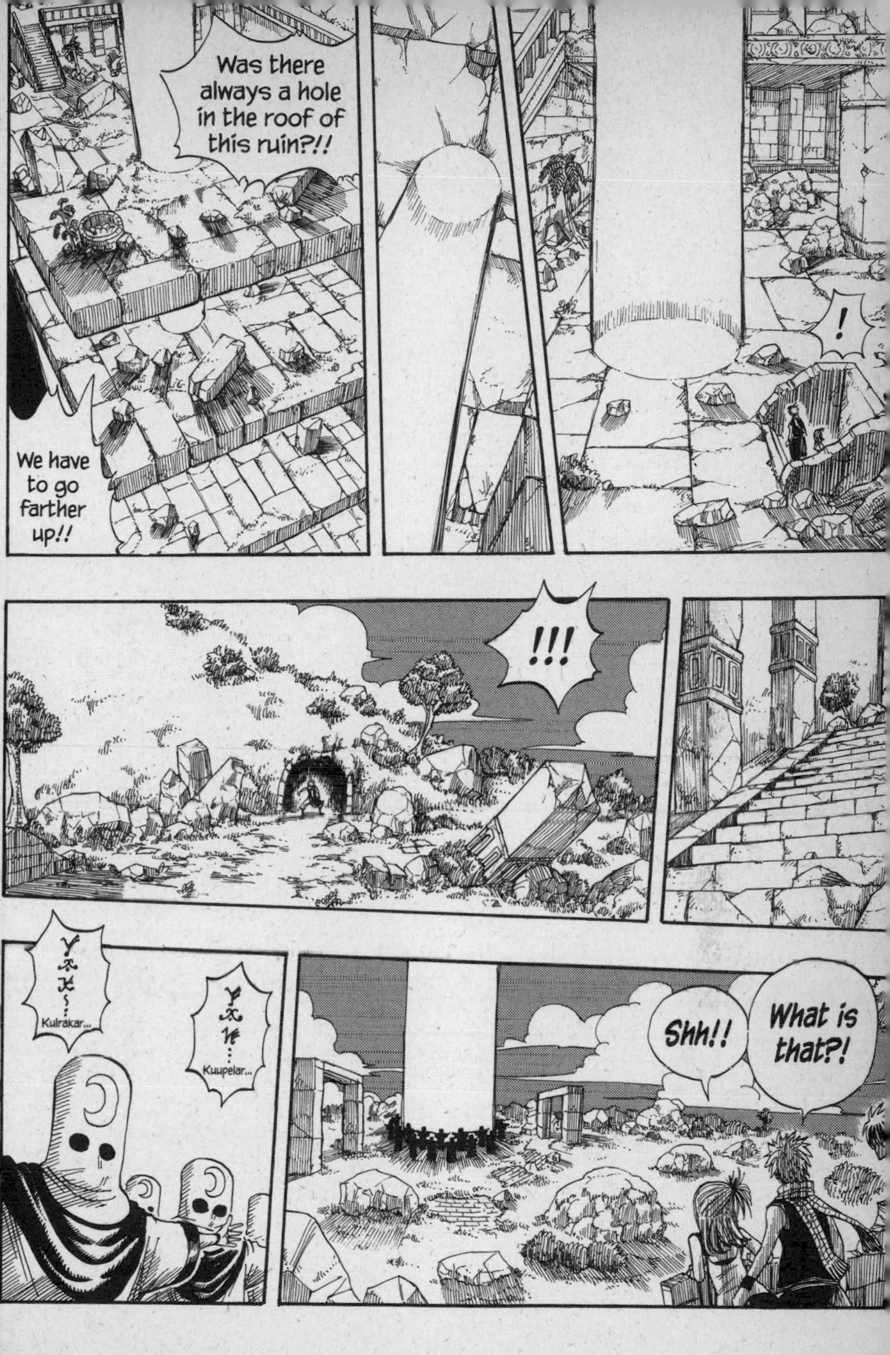
!
Was there always a hole in the roof of this ruin?!!
We have to go farther up!!
!!!
What is that?!
Shh!!
Kuupelar...
Kulrakar...

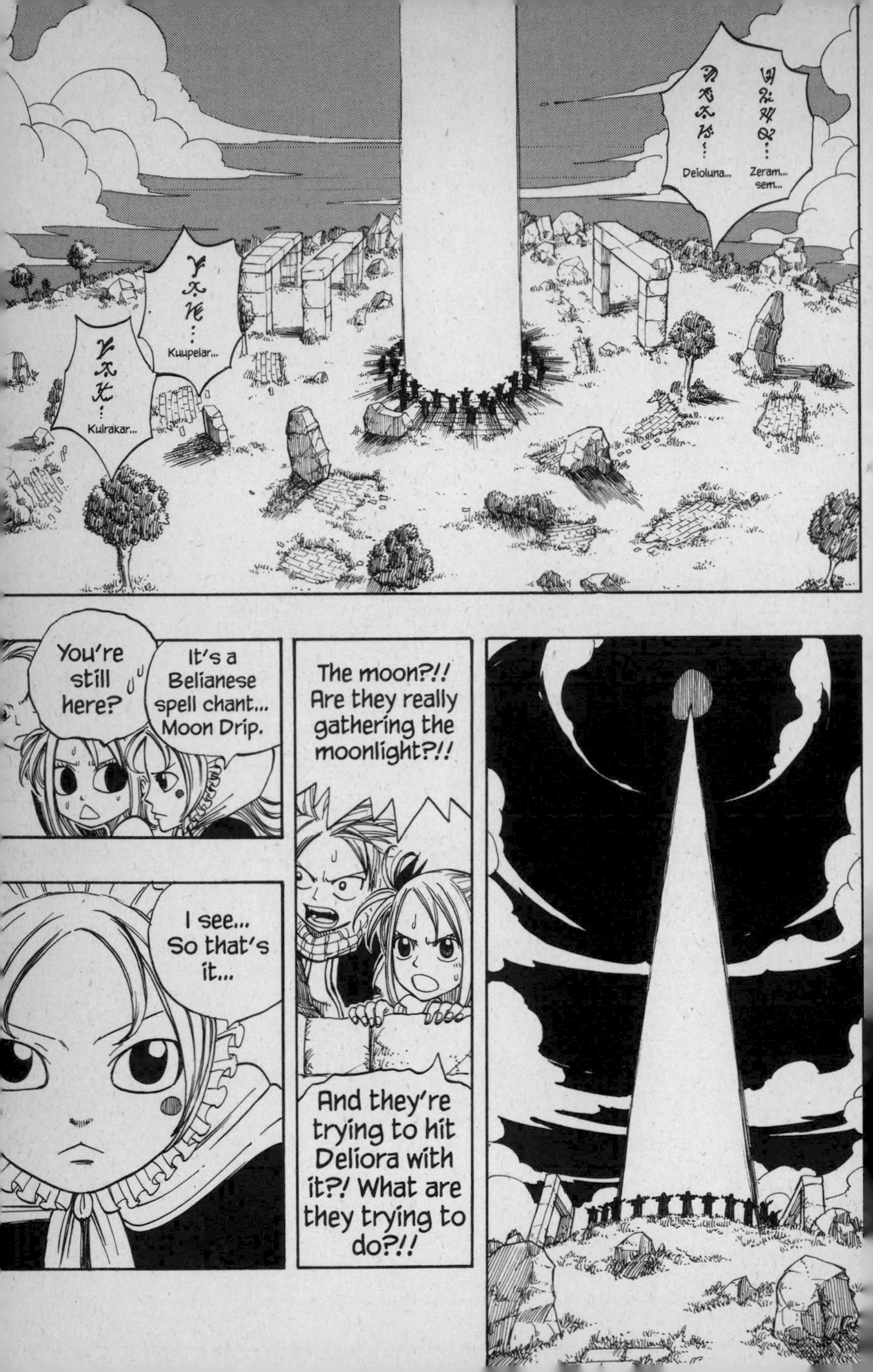
Zeram... sem...
Deioluna...
Kuupelar...
Kulrakar...
The moon?!! Are they really gathering the moonlight?!!
And they're trying to hit Deliora with it?! What are they trying to do?!!
It's a Belianese spell chant... Moon Drip.
You're still here?
I see... So that's it...

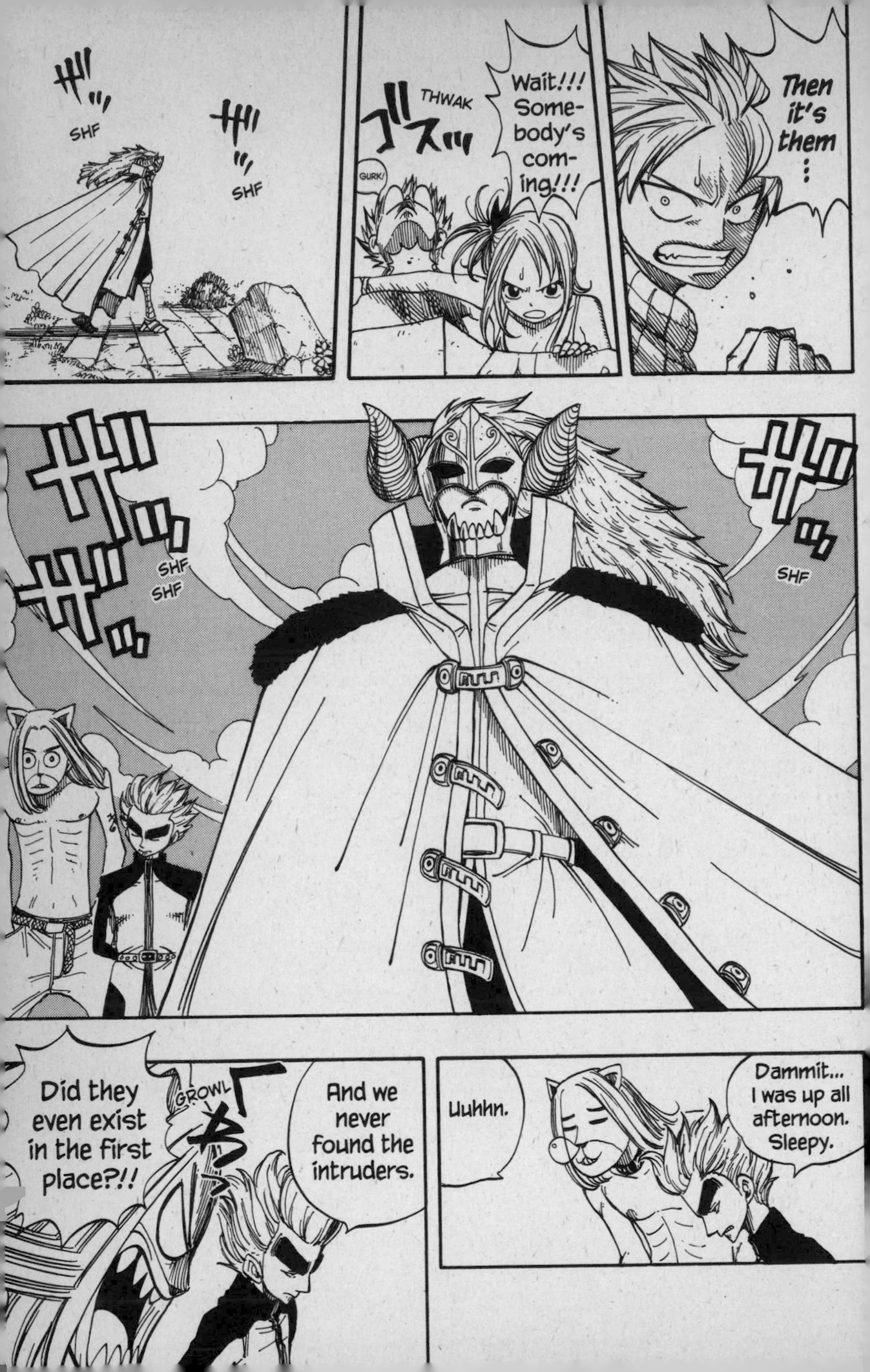
Then it's them...
Wait!!! Somebody's coming!!!
THWAK
GURK!
SHF
SHF
SHF
SHF
SHF
Dammit... I was up all afternoon. Sleepy.
Uuhhn.
And we never found the intruders.
GROWL
Did they even exist in the first place?!!

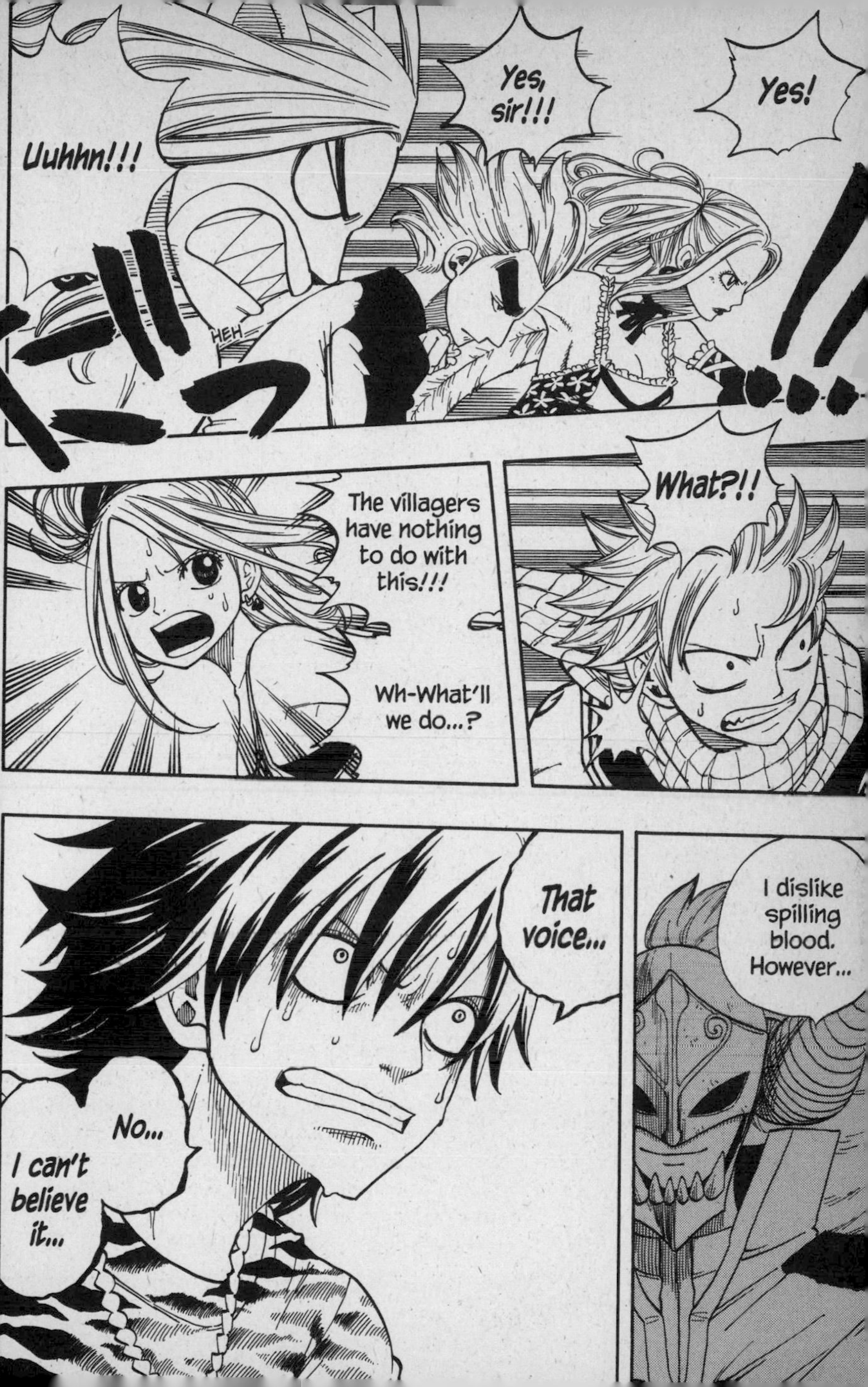
Yes!
Yes, sir!!!
Uuhhn!!!
HEH
What?!!
The villagers have nothing to do with this!!!
Wh-What'll we do...?
I dislike spilling blood. However...
That voice...
No... I can't believe it...

FAIRY TAIL

Chapter 29: Gray and Lyon

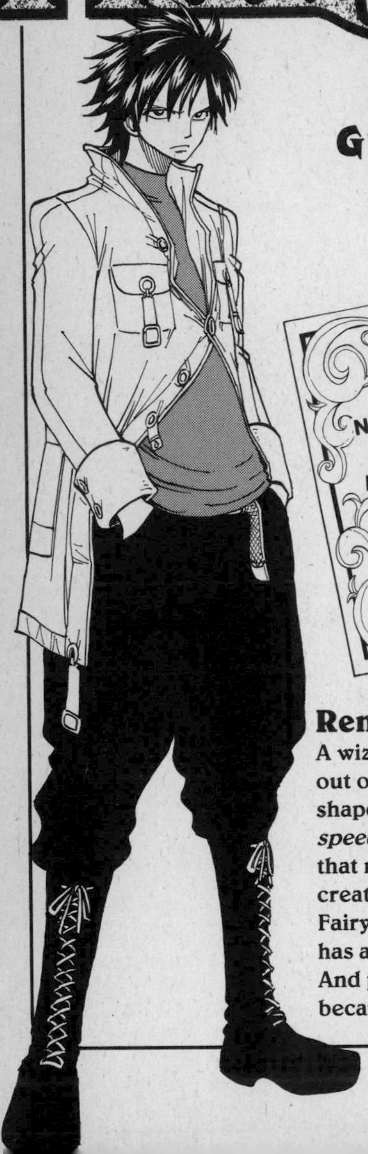

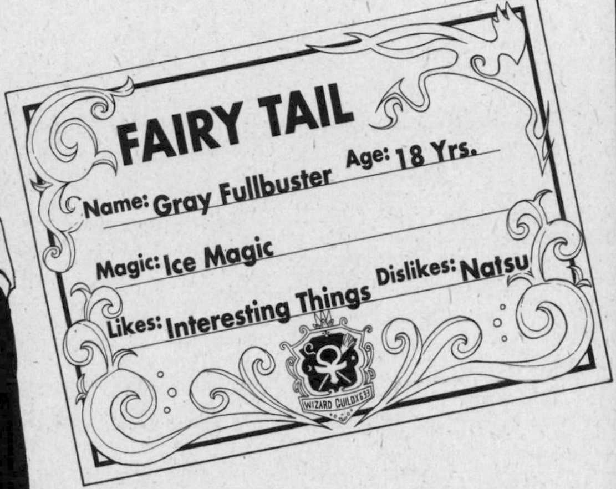
FAIRY TAIL
Name: Gray Fullbuster
Age: 18 Yrs.
Magic: Ice Magic
Likes: Interesting Things
Dislikes: Natsu
WIZARD GUILDX637

Remarks

A wizard whose magical power is making objects out of ice. He can form ice into many different shapes and use them as weapons. But it's the *speed* at which those objects can be made that makes ice magic stand out from the other creation magics. He's near the top of the list of Fairy Tail's most talented wizards, but he also has an odd habit of stripping off his clothes. And perhaps his rivalry with Natsu exists simply because fire and ice don't mix!

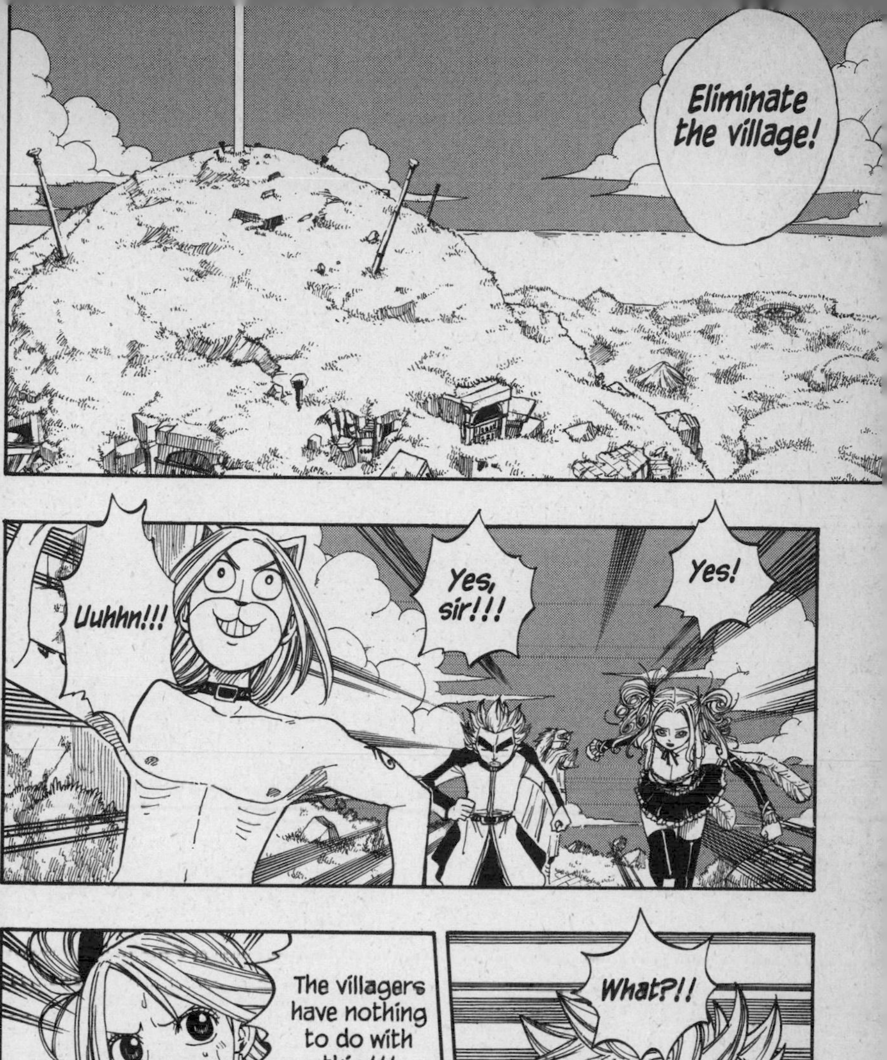
Eliminate the village!
Yes!
Yes, sir!!!
Uuhhn!!!
What?!!
The villagers have nothing to do with this!!!
Wh-What'll we do...?
Only one thing to do!!!

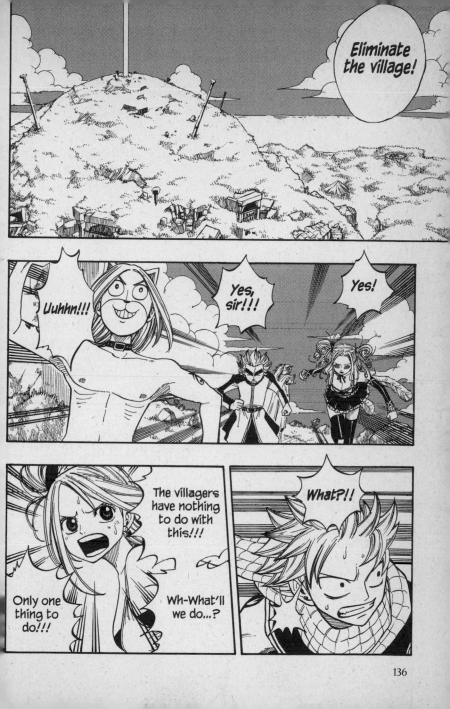

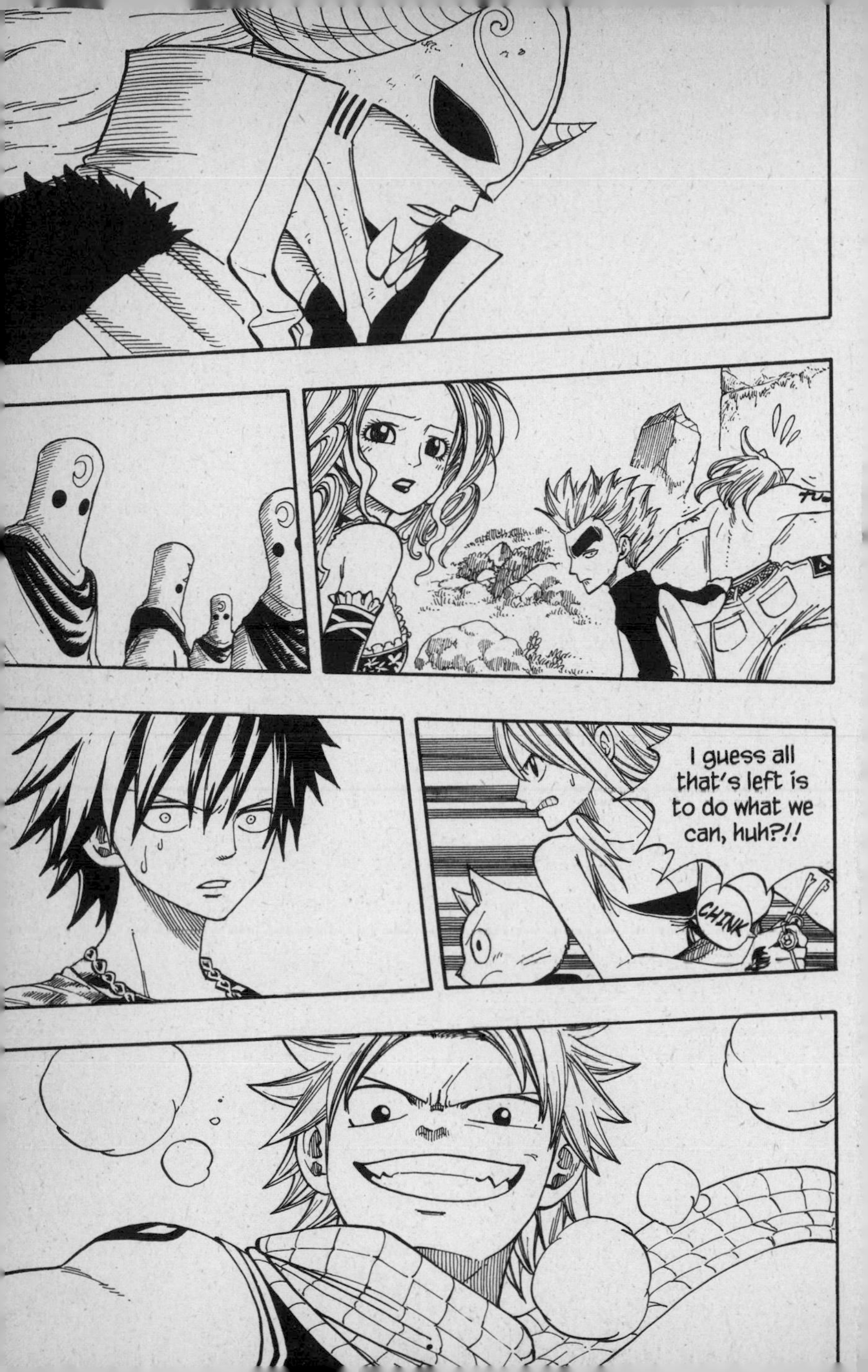
I guess all that's left is to do what we can, huh?!!
CHINK

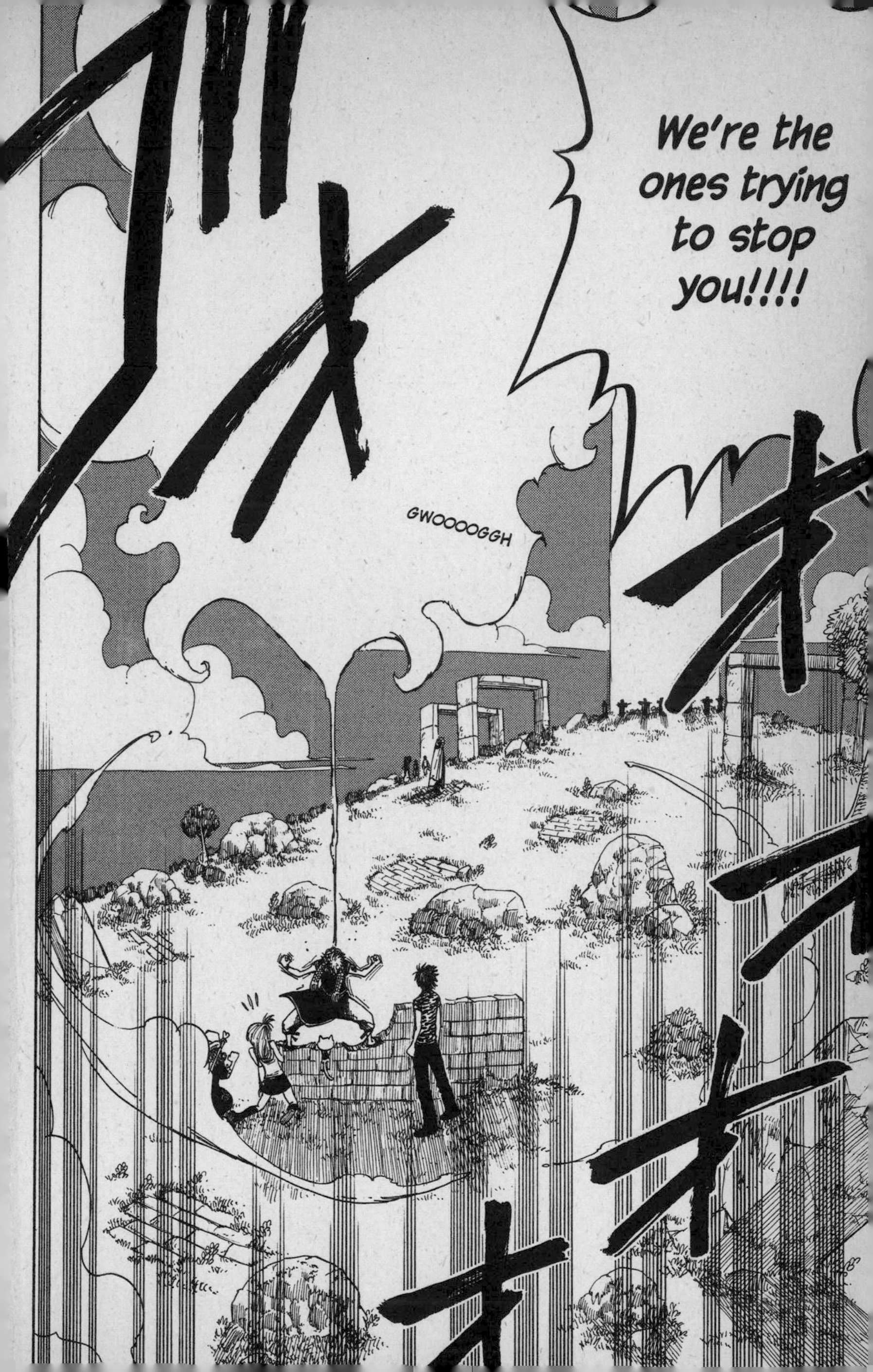
We're the ones trying to stop you!!!!
GWOOOOGGH

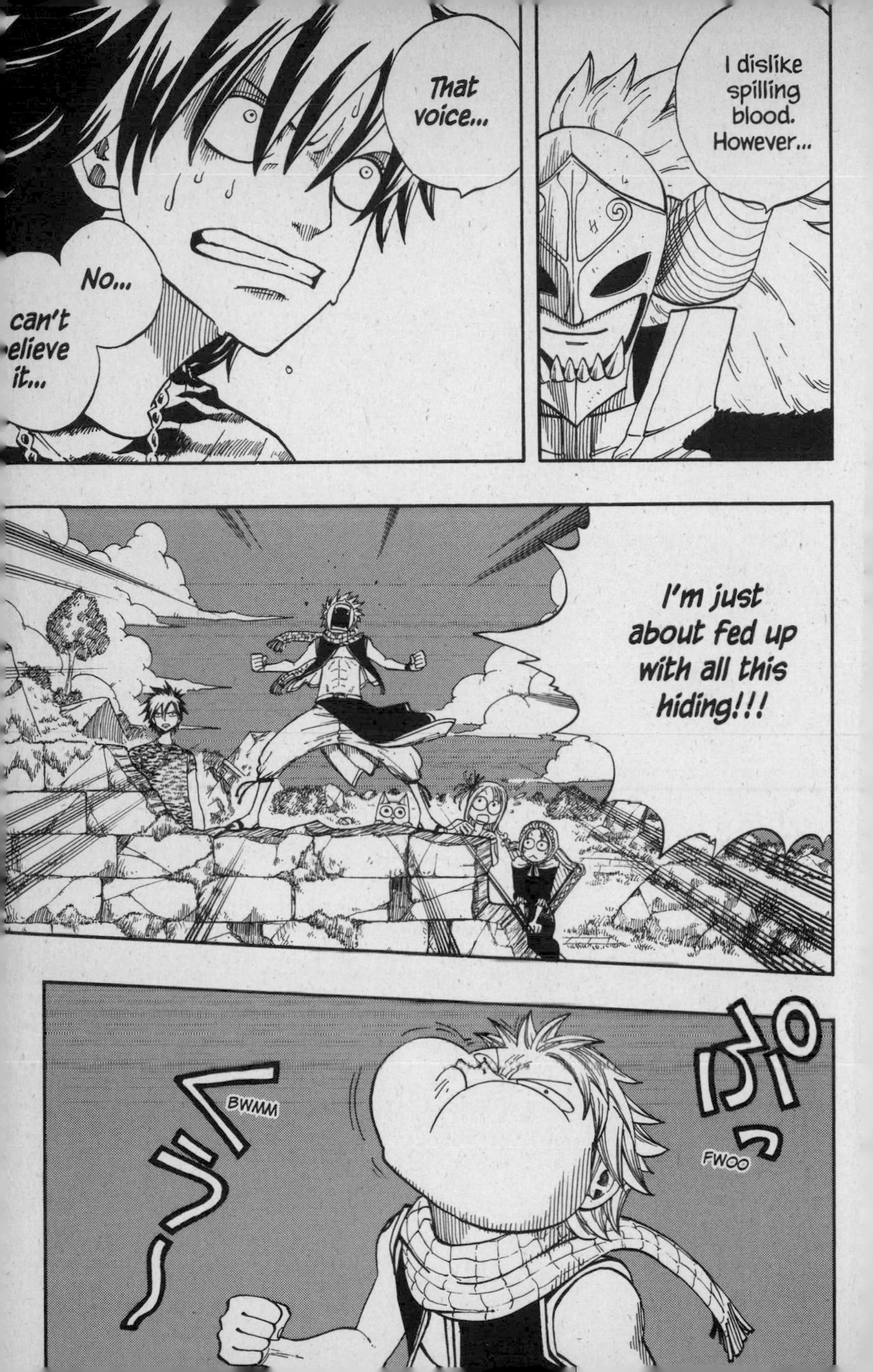
I dislike spilling blood. However...
That voice...
No...
can't elieve it...
I'm just about fed up with all this hiding!!!
FWOO
BWMM

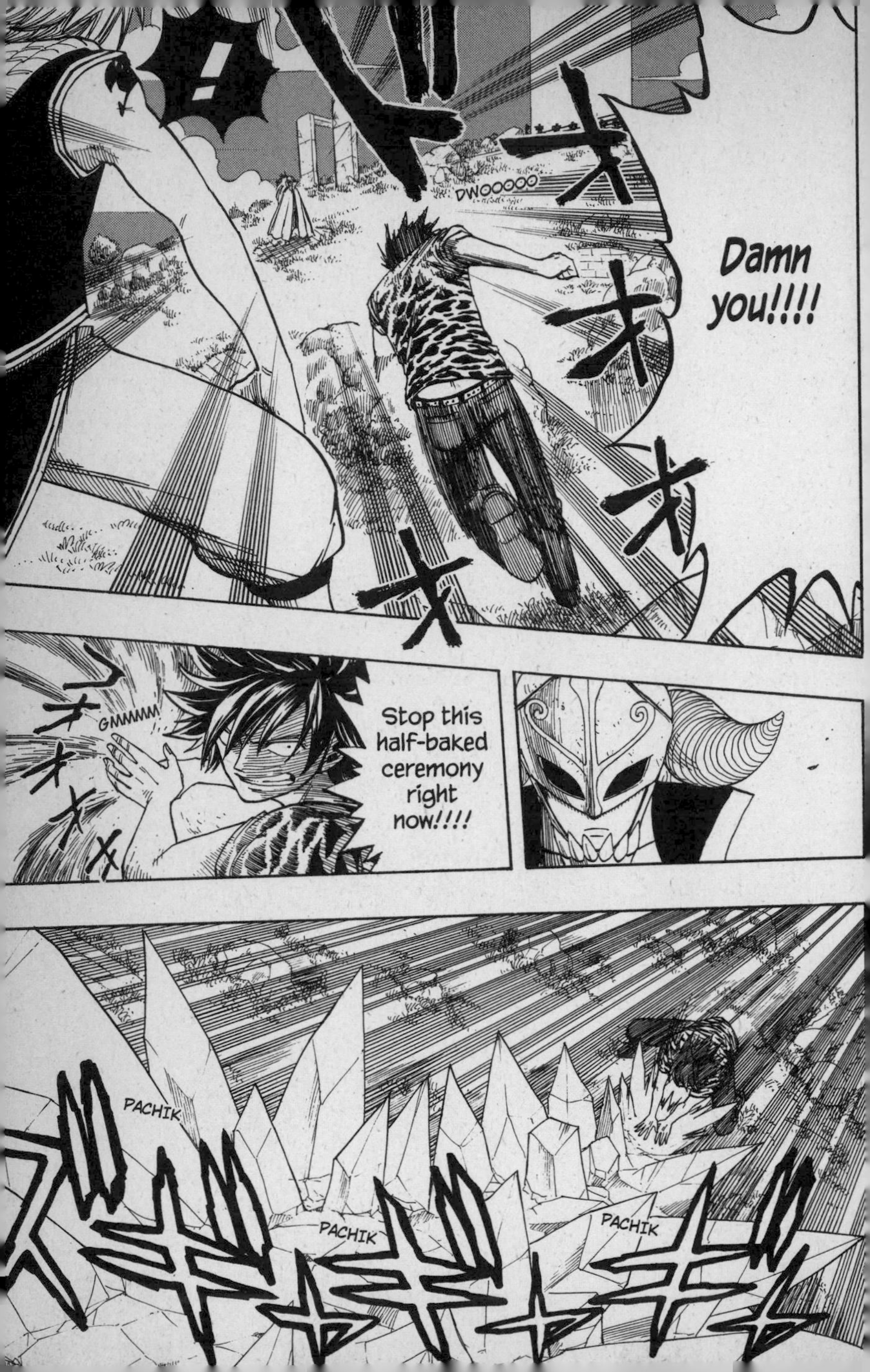
!
Damn you!!!!
DWOOOOO
Stop this half-baked ceremony right now!!!!
GMMMM
PACHIK
PACHIK
PACHIK

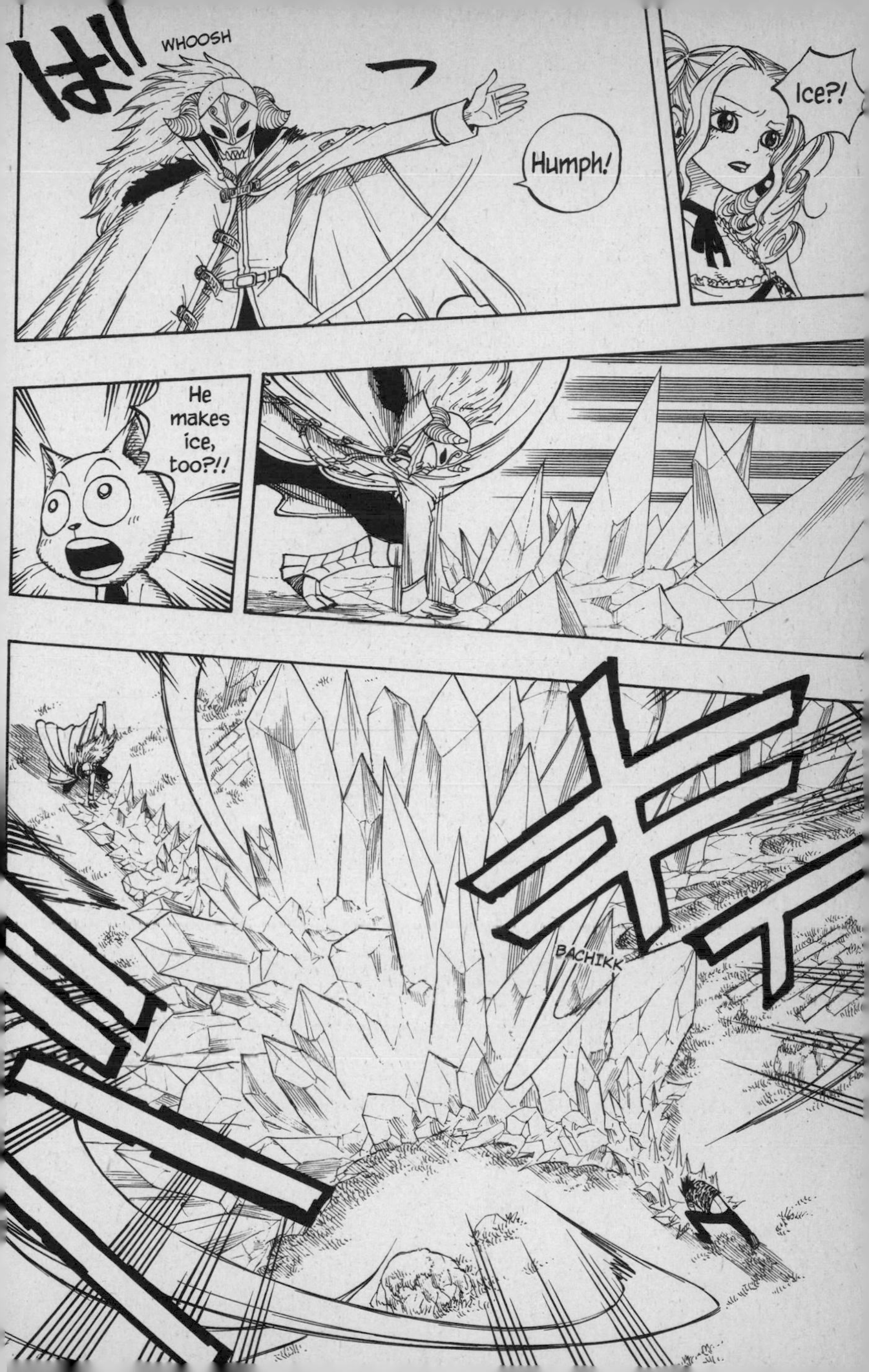
Ice?!
は!!
WHOOSH
Humph!
He makes ice, too?!!
BACHIKK

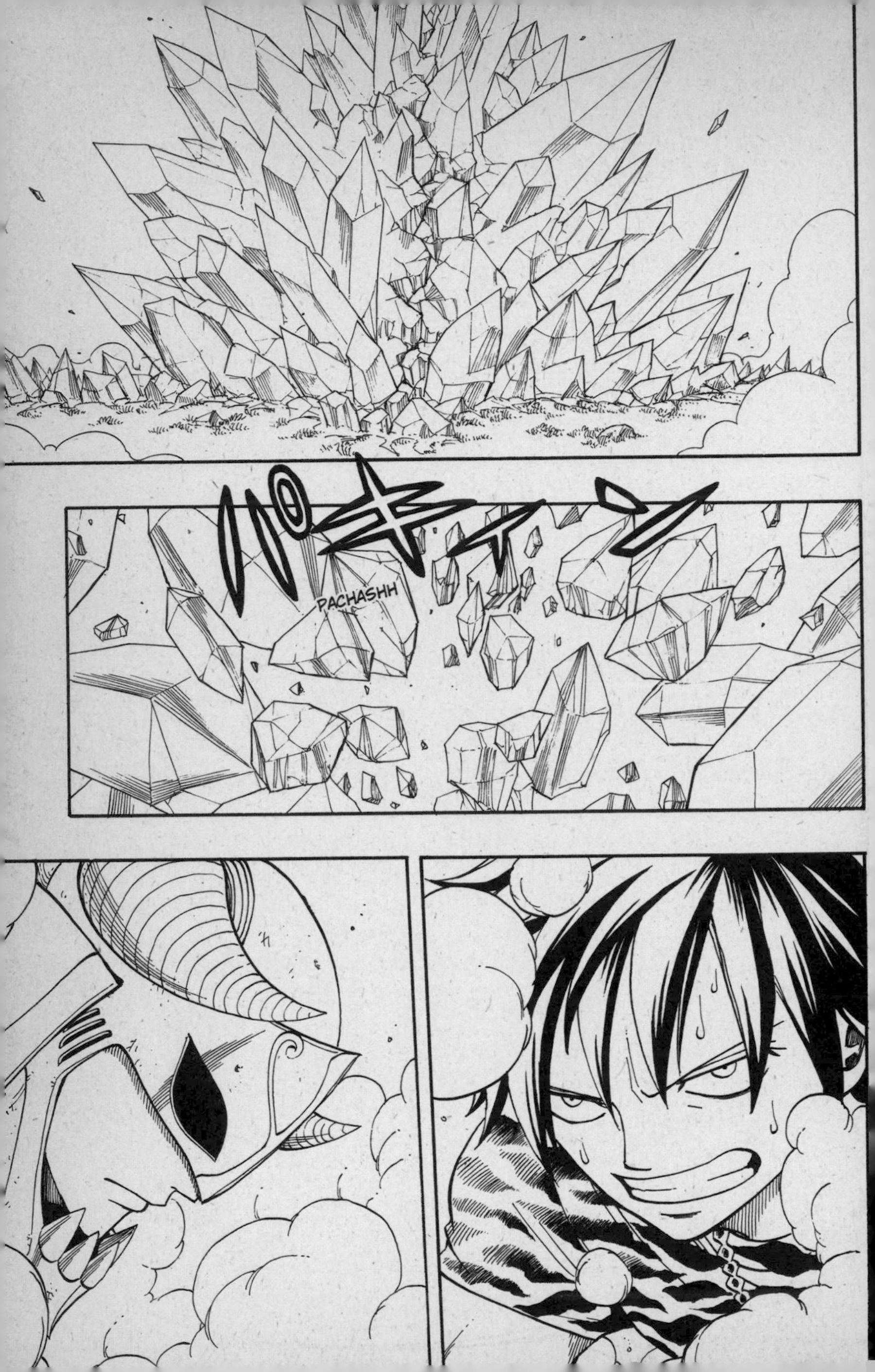

PACHASHH

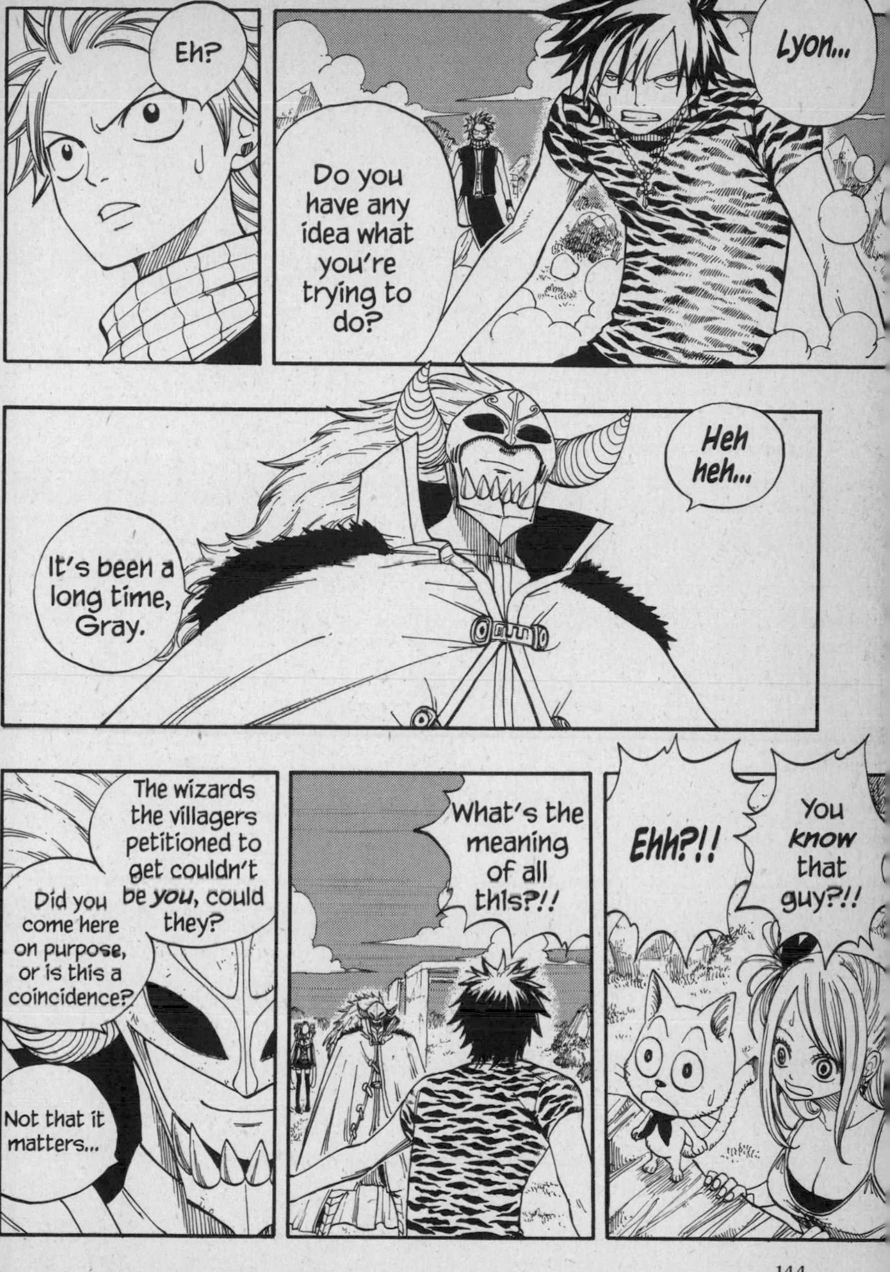
Lyon...
Do you have any idea what you're trying to do?
Eh?
Heh heh...
It's been a long time, Gray.
You *know* that guy?!!
Ehh?!!
What's the meaning of all this?!!
The wizards the villagers petitioned to get couldn't be *you*, could they?
Did you come here on purpose, or is this a coincidence?
Not that it matters...

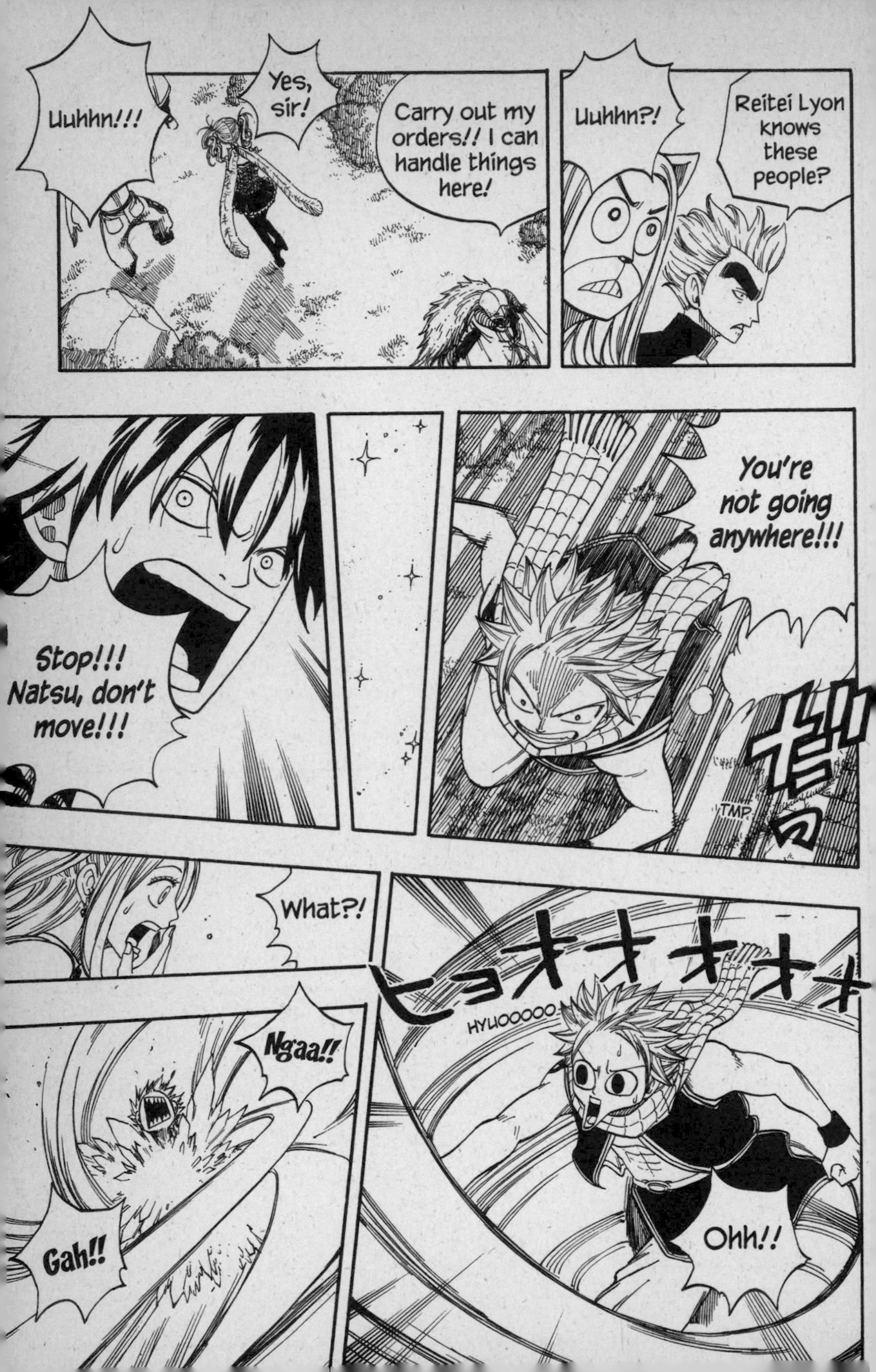
Reitei Lyon knows these people?
Uuhhn?!
Carry out my orders!! I can handle things here!
Yes, sir!
Uuhhn!!!
You're not going anywhere!!!
TMP
Stop!!! Natsu, don't move!!!
HYUOOOOO
Ohh!!
What?!
Ngaa!!
Gah!!

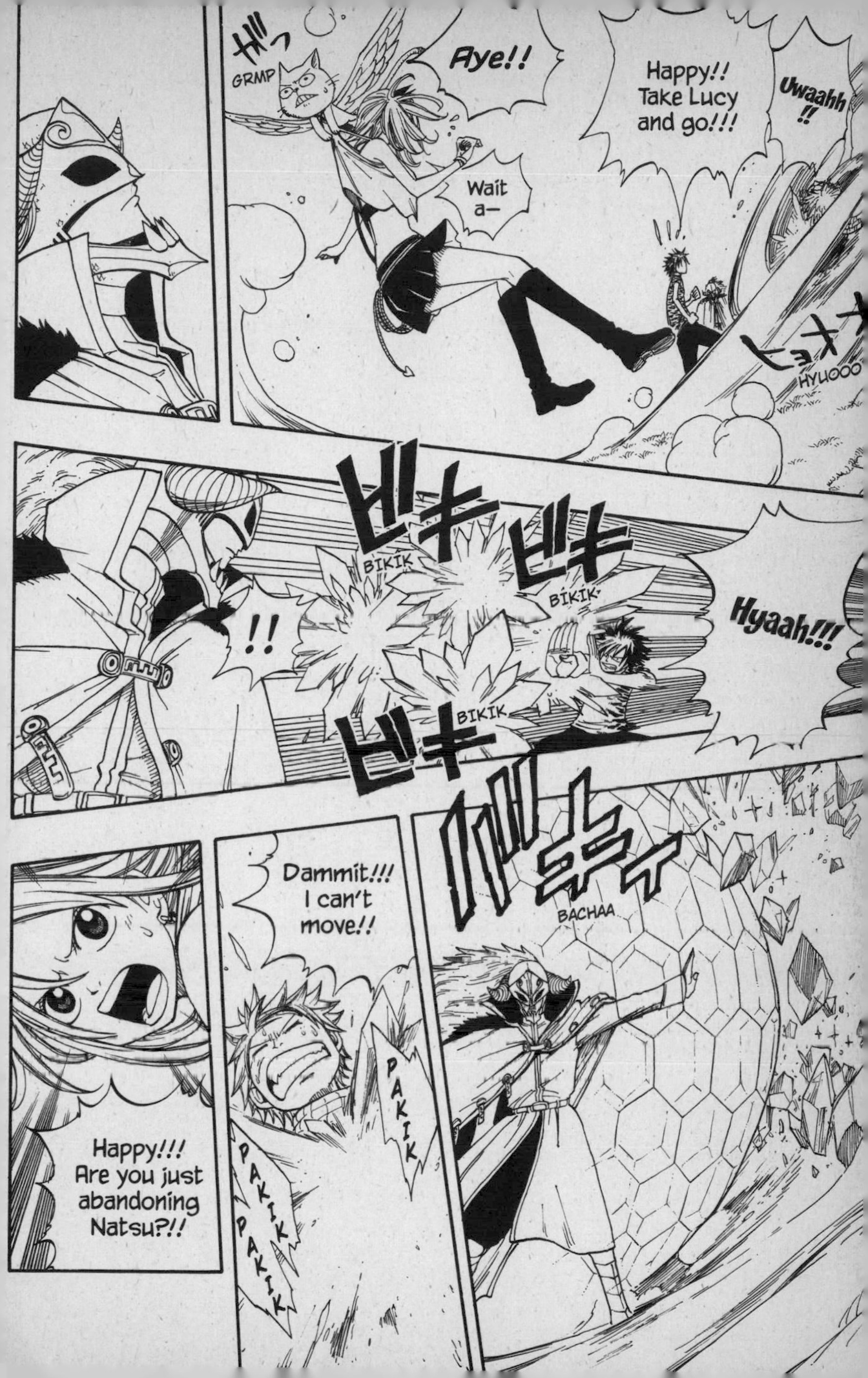
Uwaahh!!
Happy!! Take Lucy and go!!!
Aye!!
GRMP
Wait a—
HYUOOO
Hyaah!!!
BIKIK
BIKIK
BIKIK
!!
BACHAA
Dammit!!! I can't move!!
PAKIK
PAKIK
PAKIK
Happy!!! Are you just abandoning Natsu?!!

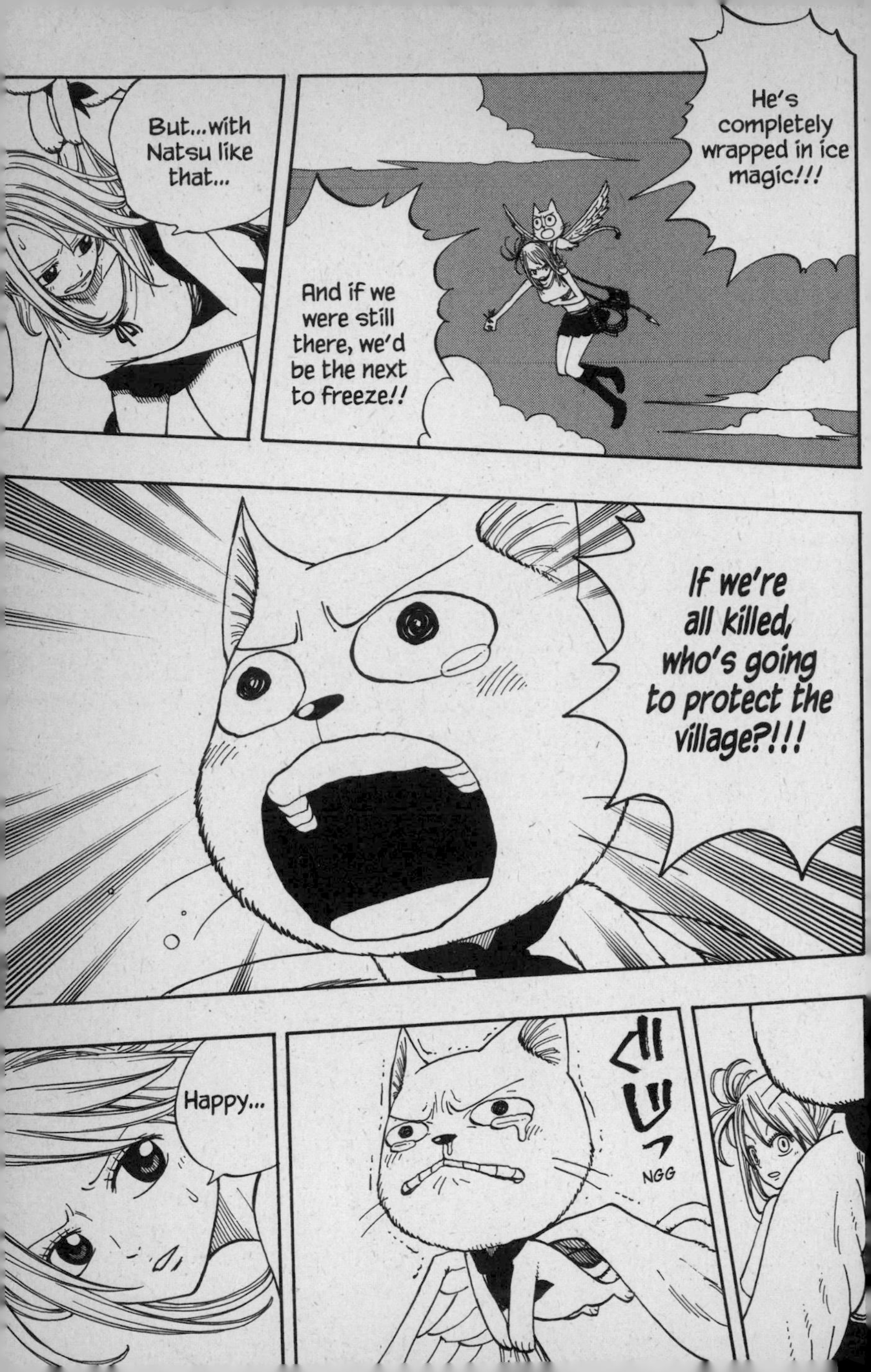
He's completely wrapped in ice magic!!!
And if we were still there, we'd be the next to freeze!!
But...with Natsu like that...
If we're all killed, who's going to protect the village?!!!
NGG
Happy...

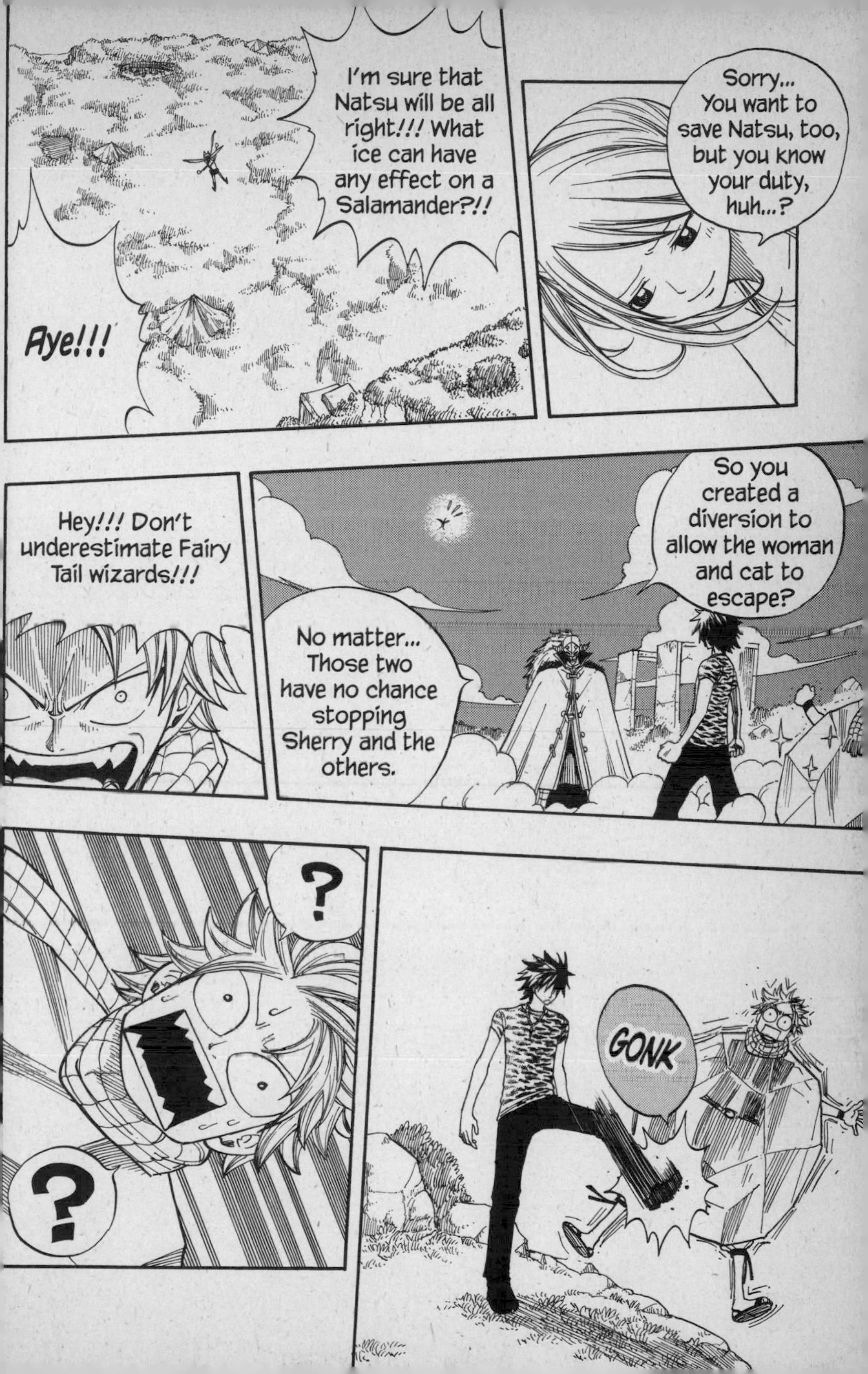
Sorry... You want to save Natsu, too, but you know your duty, huh...?
I'm sure that Natsu will be all right!!! What ice can have any effect on a Salamander?!!
Aye!!!
So you created a diversion to allow the woman and cat to escape?
No matter... Those two have no chance stopping Sherry and the others.
Hey!!! Don't underestimate Fairy Tail wizards!!!
GONK
?
?

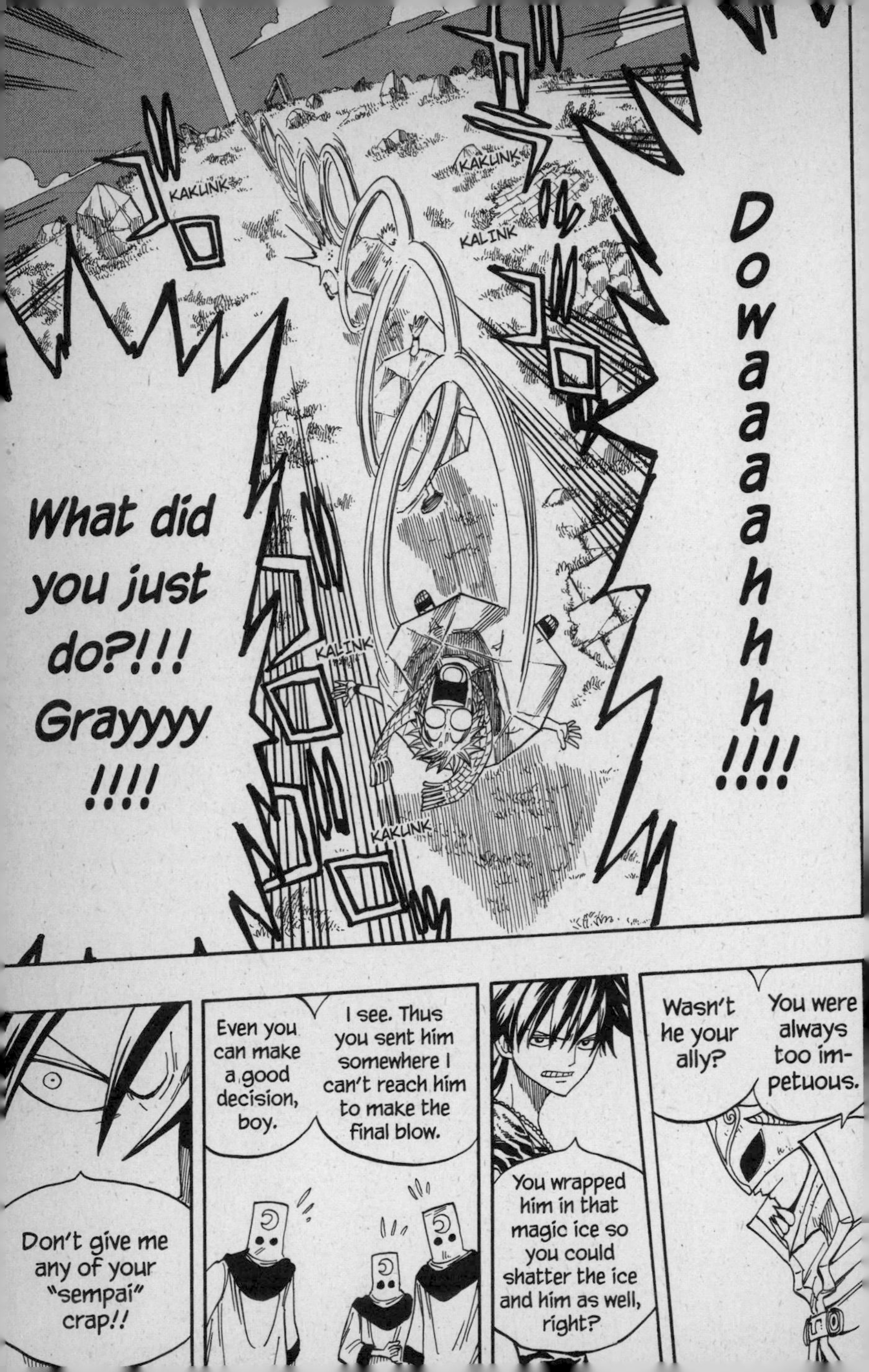

Dowaaaahhh!!!!
KAKUNK
KAKUNK
KALINK
KALINK
KAKUNK
What did you just do?!!! Grayyyy!!!!
You were always too impetuous.
Wasn't he your ally?
You wrapped him in that magic ice so you could shatter the ice and him as well, right?
I see. Thus you sent him somewhere I can't reach him to make the final blow.
Even you can make a good decision, boy.
Don't give me any of your "sempai" crap!!

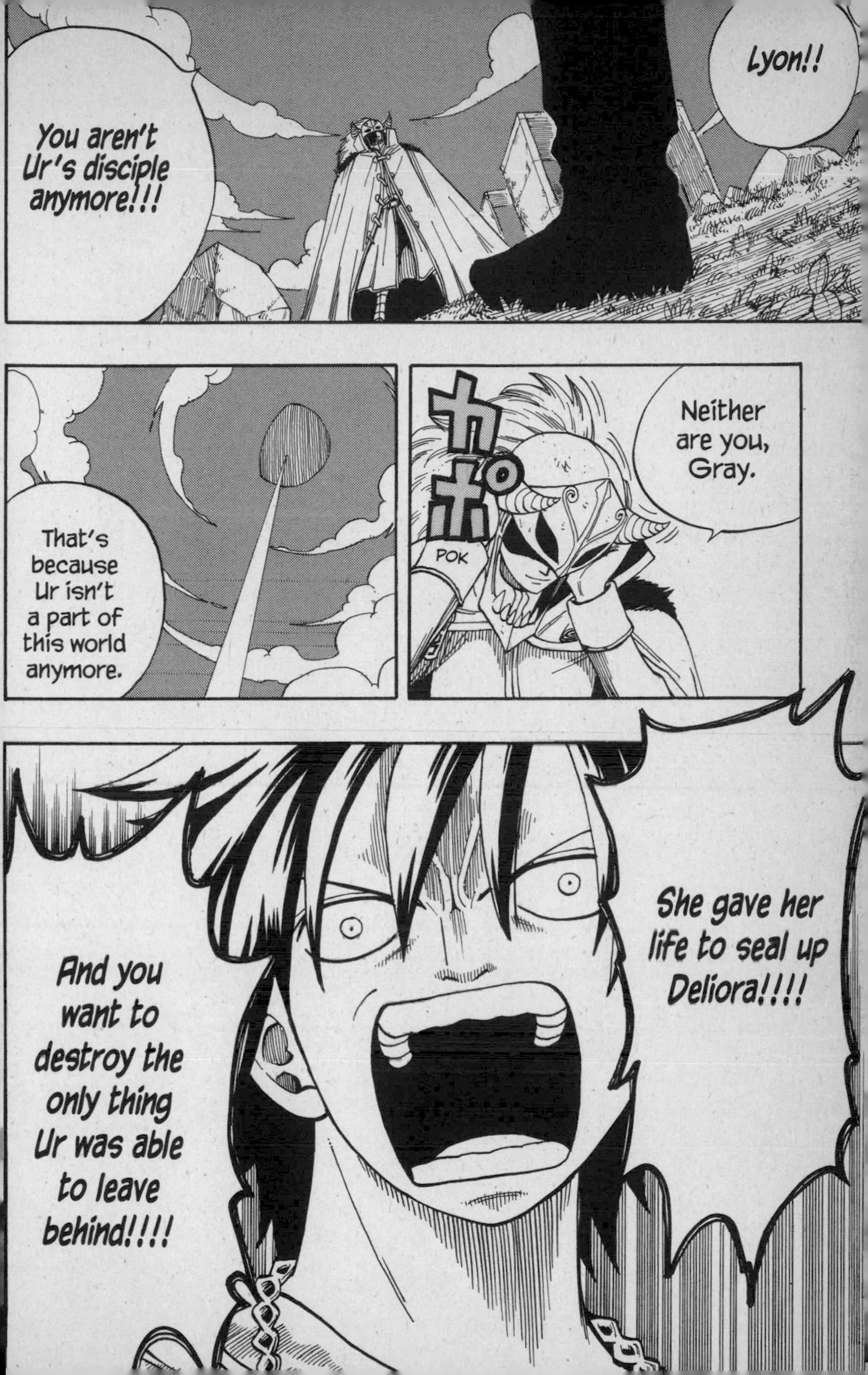
Lyon!!
You aren't Ur's disciple anymore!!!
Neither are you, Gray.
カポ
POK
That's because Ur isn't a part of this world anymore.
She gave her life to seal up Deliora!!!!
And you want to destroy the only thing Ur was able to leave behind!!!!

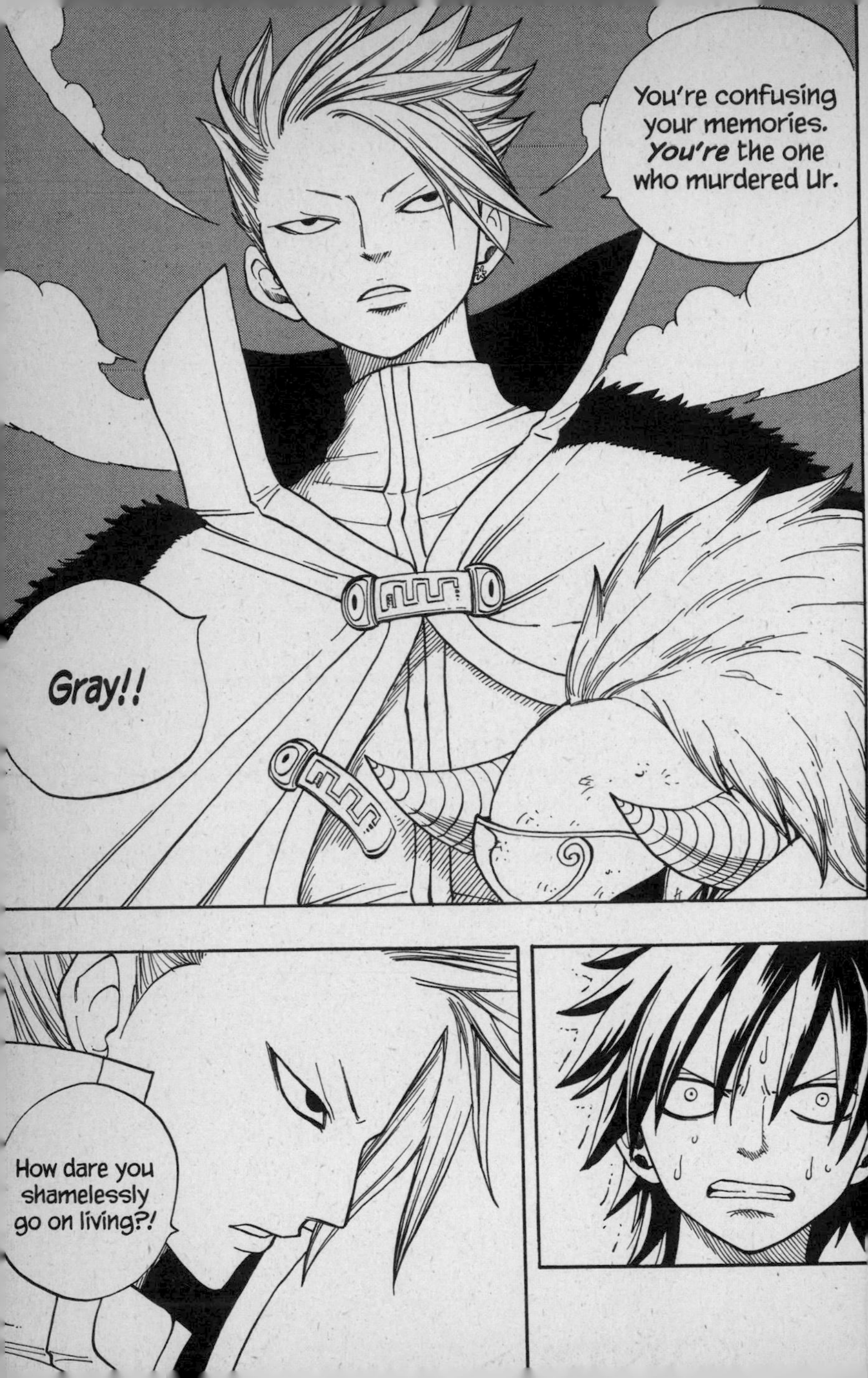
You're confusing your memories. *You're* the one who murdered Ur.
Gray!!
How dare you shamelessly go on living?!

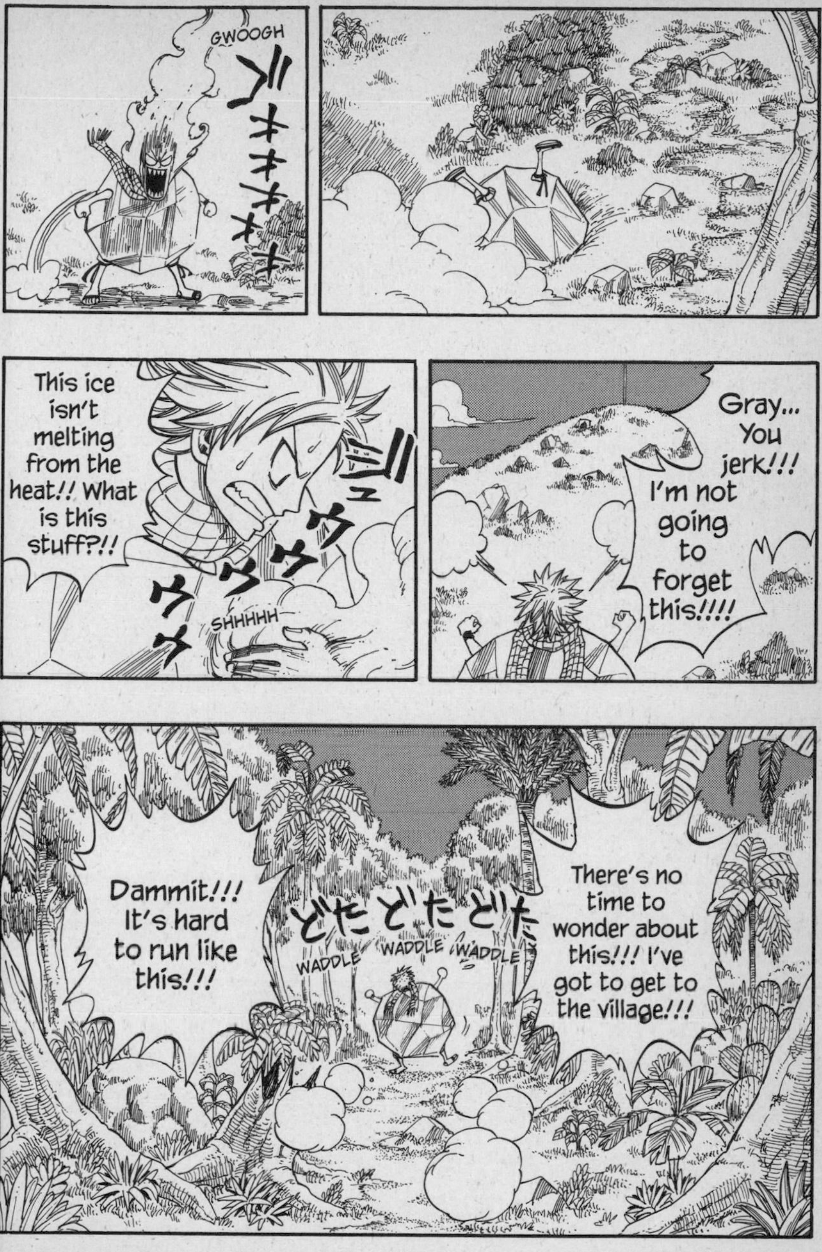

GWOOGH
ゴオオオオオ
Gray... You jerk!!! I'm not going to forget this!!!!
This ice isn't melting from the heat!! What is this stuff?!!
ジュウウウウ
SHHHHH
There's no time to wonder about this!!! I've got to get to the village!!!
どたどたどた
WADDLE WADDLE WADDLE
Dammit!!! It's hard to run like this!!!

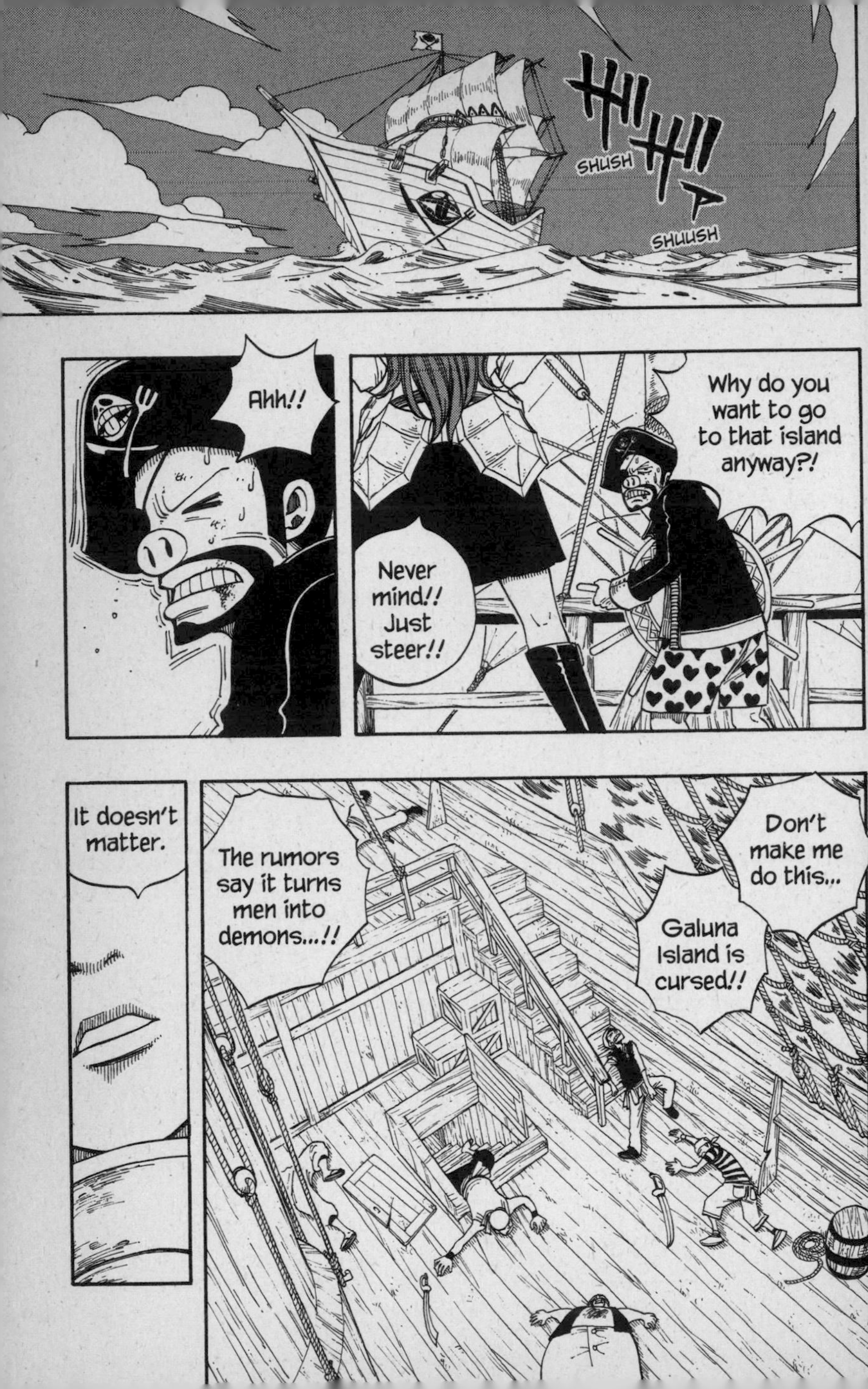
SHUSH
SHUUSH
Why do you want to go to that island anyway?!
Never mind!! Just steer!!
Ahh!!
Don't make me do this...
Galuna Island is cursed!!
The rumors say it turns men into demons...!!
It doesn't matter.

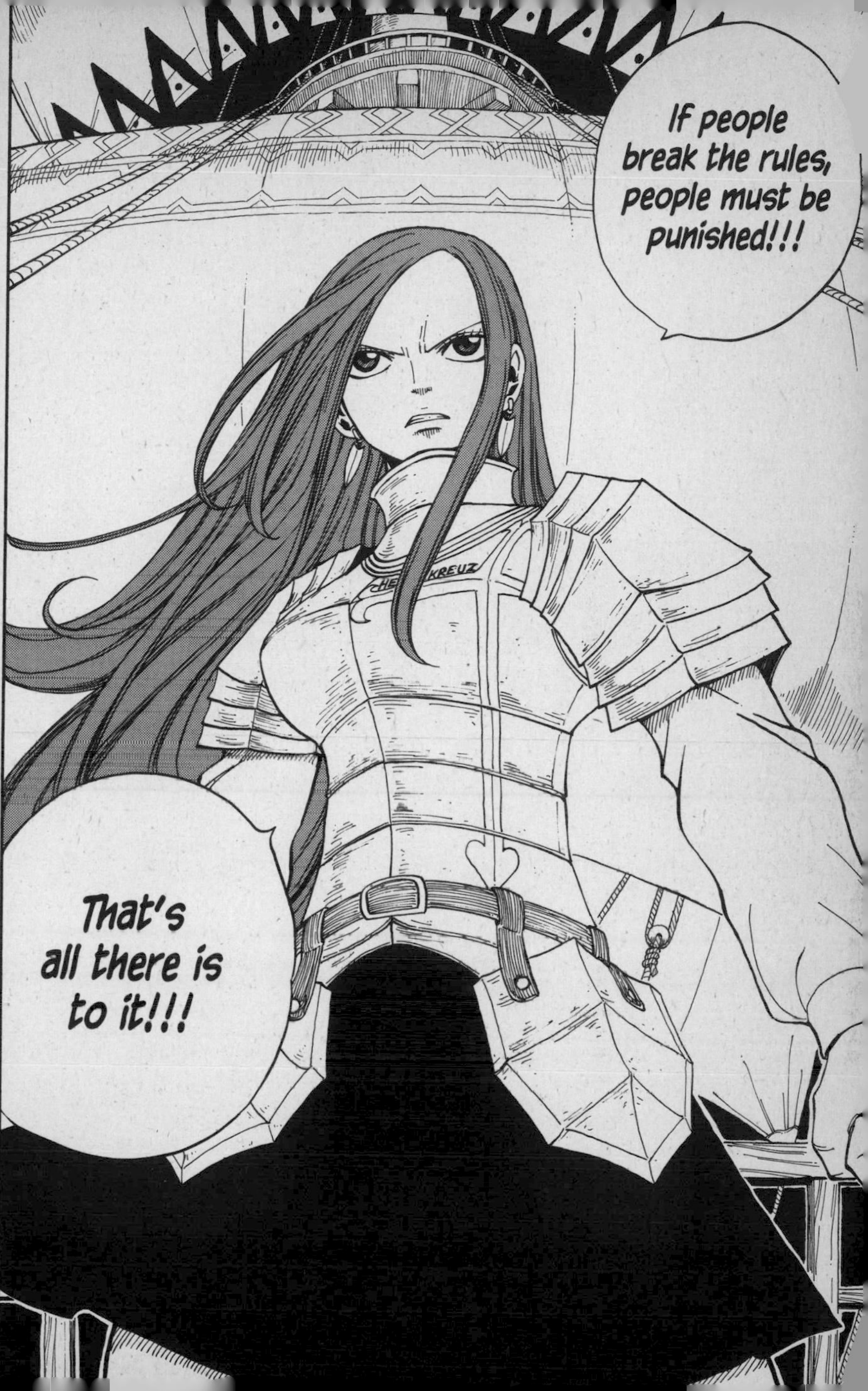
If people break the rules, people must be punished!!!
That's all there is to it!!!

FAIRY TAIL

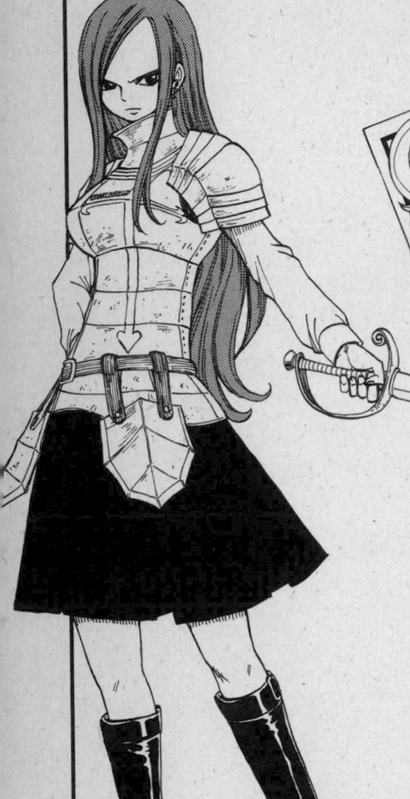

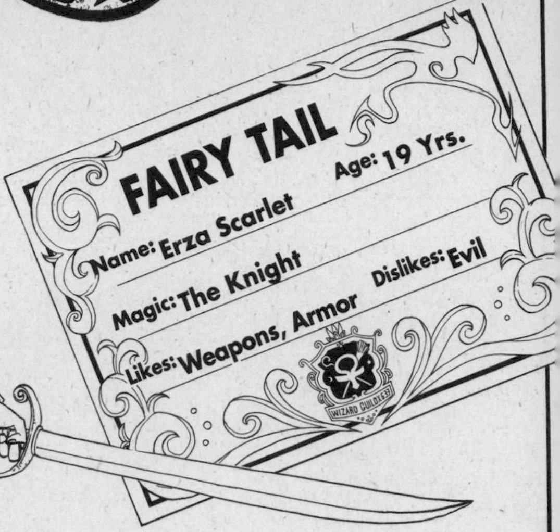
FAIRY TAIL
Age: 19 Yrs.
Name: Erza Scarlet
Magic: The Knight
Dislikes: Evil
Likes: Weapons, Armor
WIZARD GUILD

Remarks

The best female wizard in Fairy Tail, and that's how she picked up her nickname as the Fairy Queen, Titania Erza. Her magic is the ability to switch weapons and armor instantly to allow her to fight effectively in hand-to-hand combat. She is twice as strict as anybody else, and within the guild, she's referred to as the head of the disciplinary committee. By the way, the brand of armor that she normally wears is a part of a fashion line that is popular with young girls, Heart Kreuz. They'd never made armor before but were so intimidated by Erza's request for them to make hers that they grudgingly complied. She presently has more armor on order, and word has it that Heart Kreuz is tearing their hair out over her demands.

Chapter 30: The Dream Continues

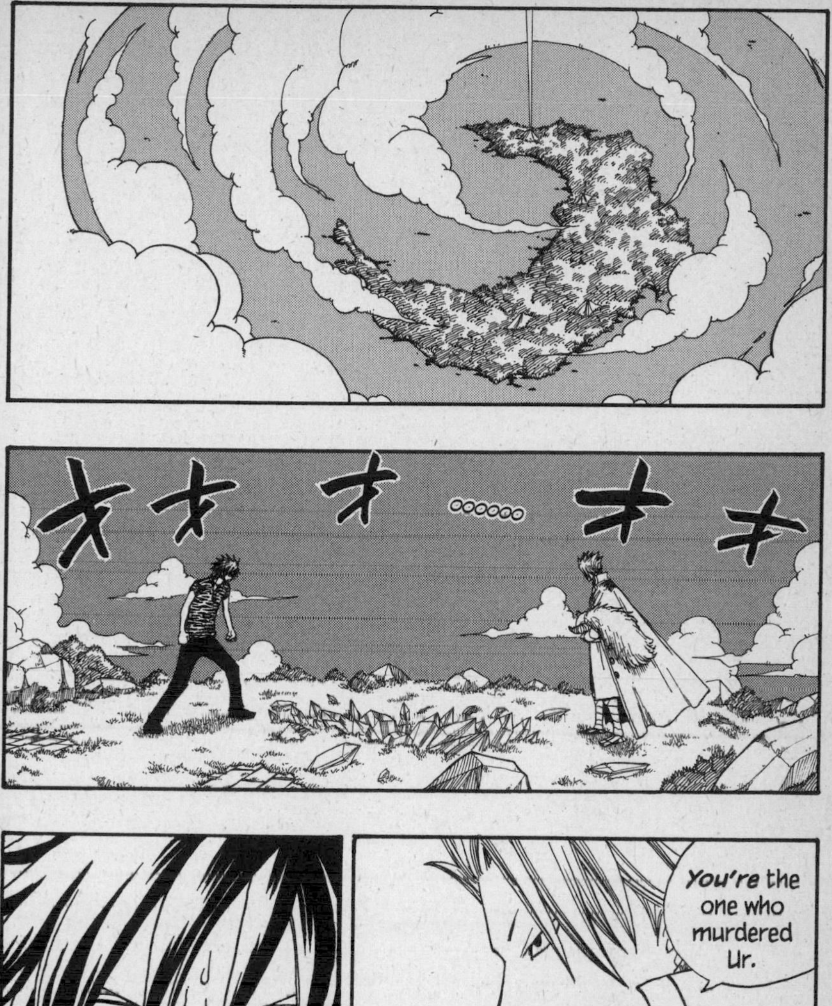
オオオ……オオ
You're the one who murdered Ur.
Gray!!

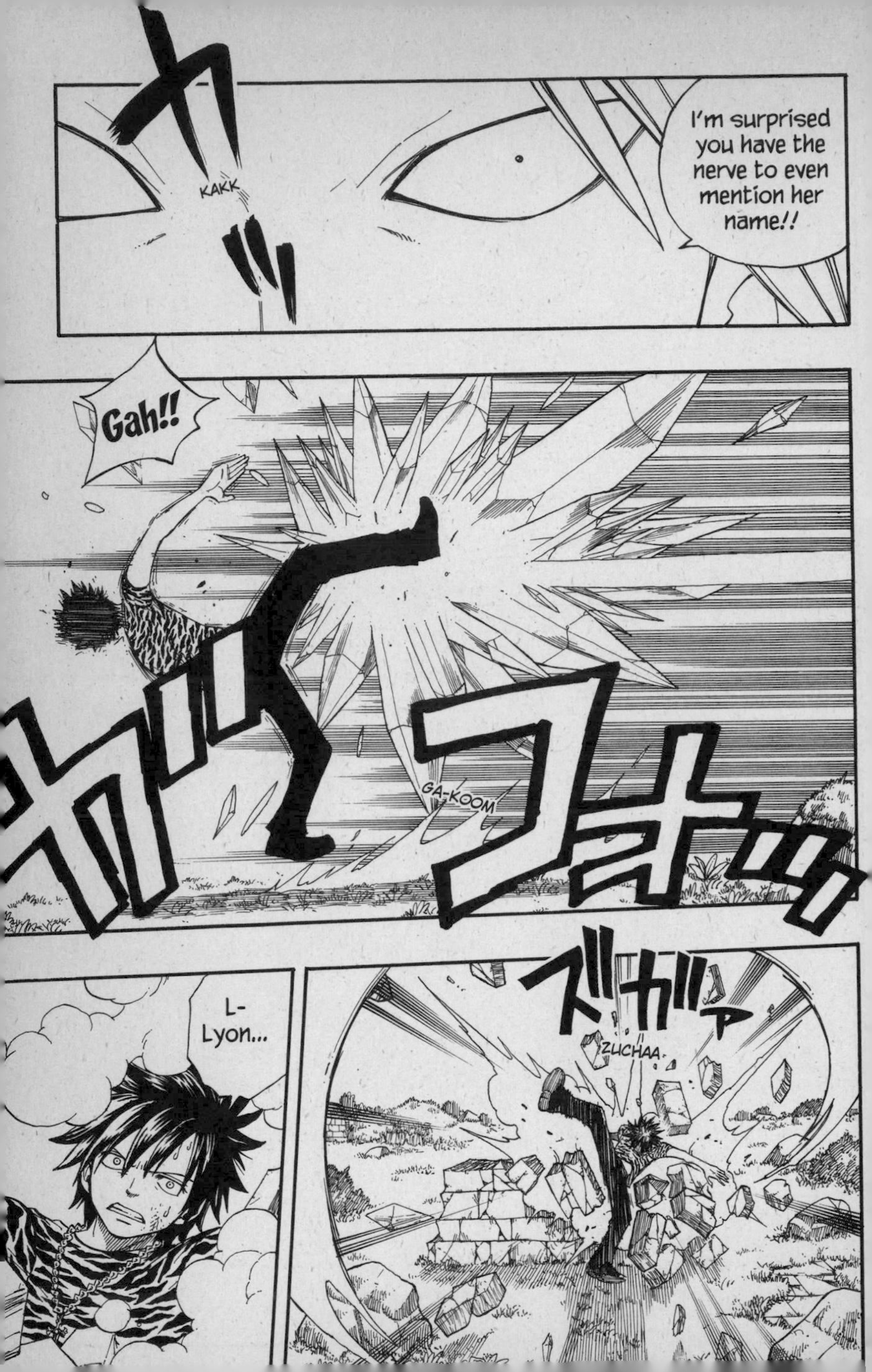
I'm surprised you have the nerve to even mention her name!!
KAKK
Gah!!
GA-KOOM
ZUCHAA
L- Lyon...

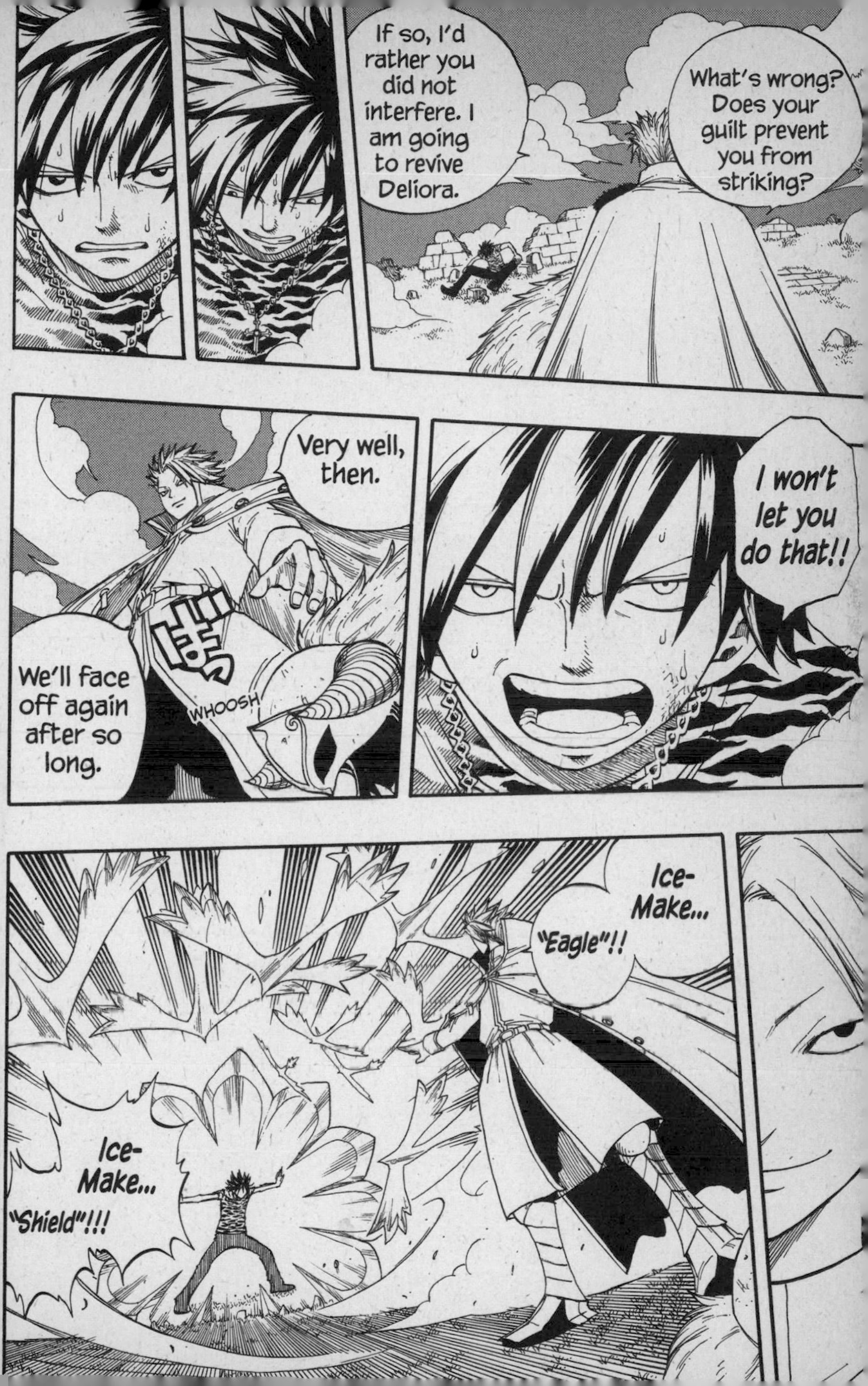
What's wrong? Does your guilt prevent you from striking?
If so, I'd rather you did not interfere. I am going to revive Deliora.
I won't let you do that!!
Very well, then.
We'll face off again after so long.
WHOOSH
Ice-Make...
"Eagle"!!
Ice-Make...
"Shield"!!!

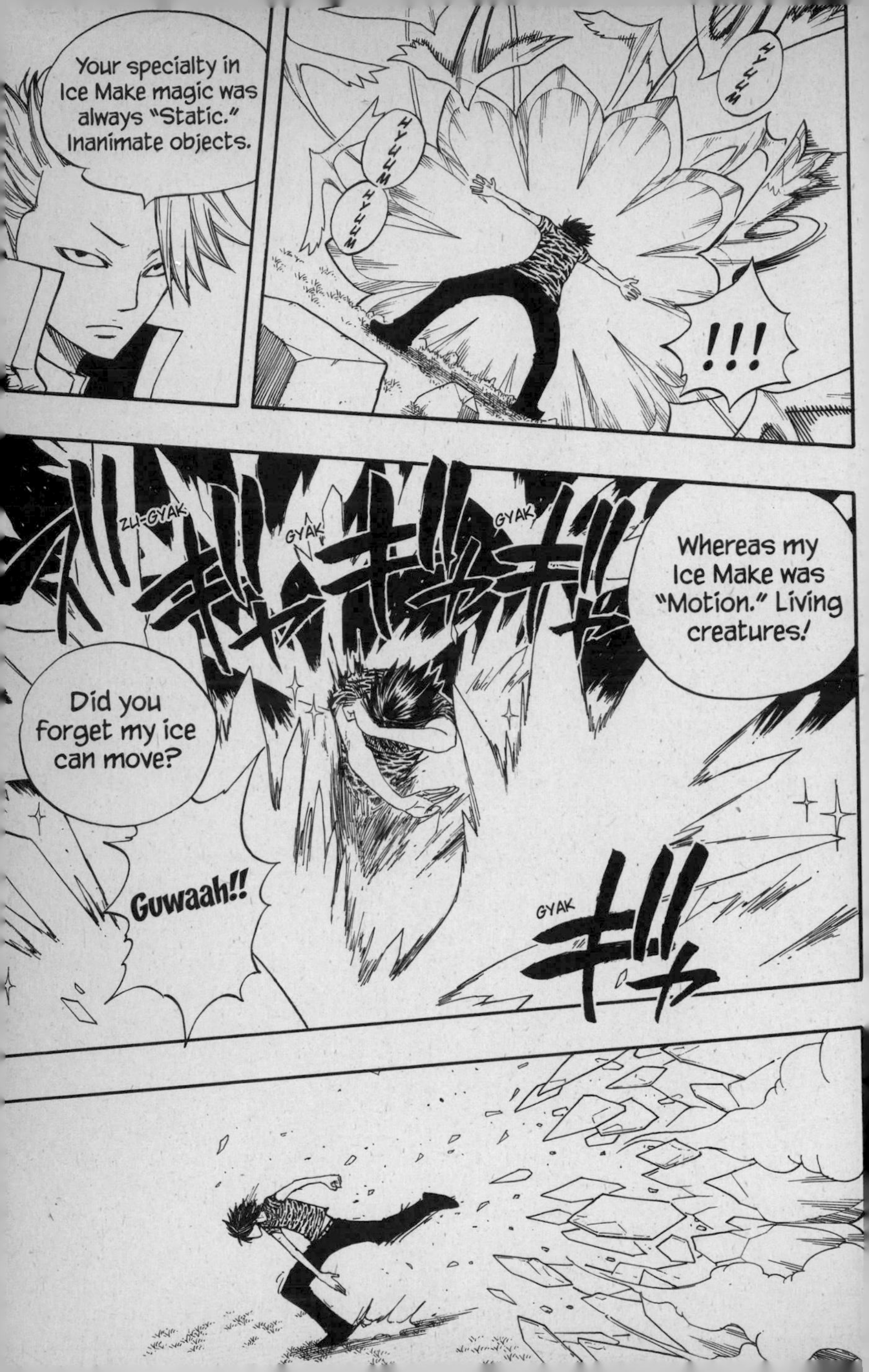
HYUUM
HYUUM
HYUUM
!!!
Your specialty in Ice Make magic was always "Static." Inanimate objects.
Whereas my Ice Make was "Motion." Living creatures!
GYAK
GYAK
ZU-GYAK
Did you forget my ice can move?
GYAK
Guwaah!!

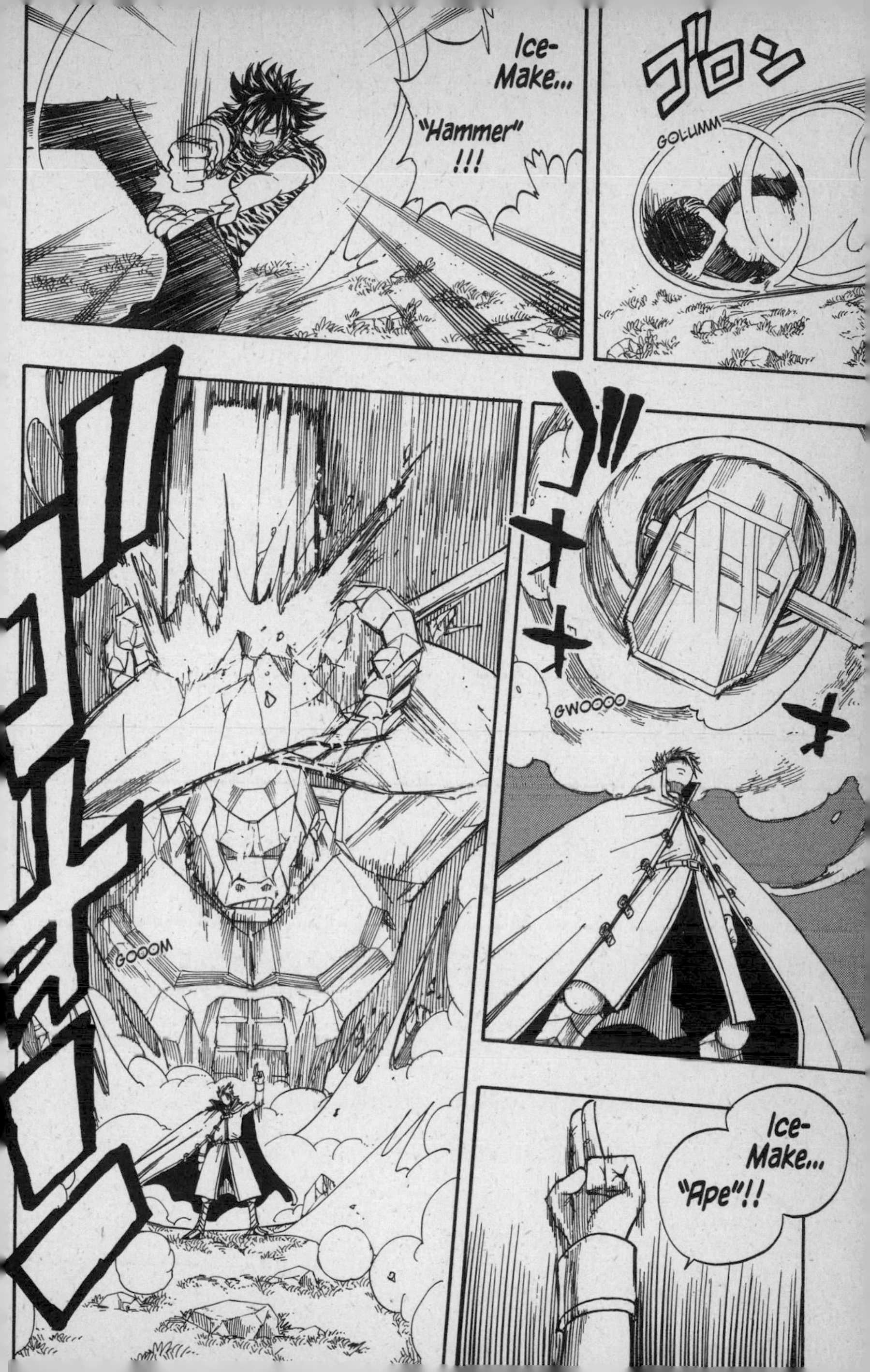
ゴロン
GOL-UMM
Ice-Make...
"Hammer"!!!
GWOOOO
Ice-Make...
"Ape"!!
GOOOM

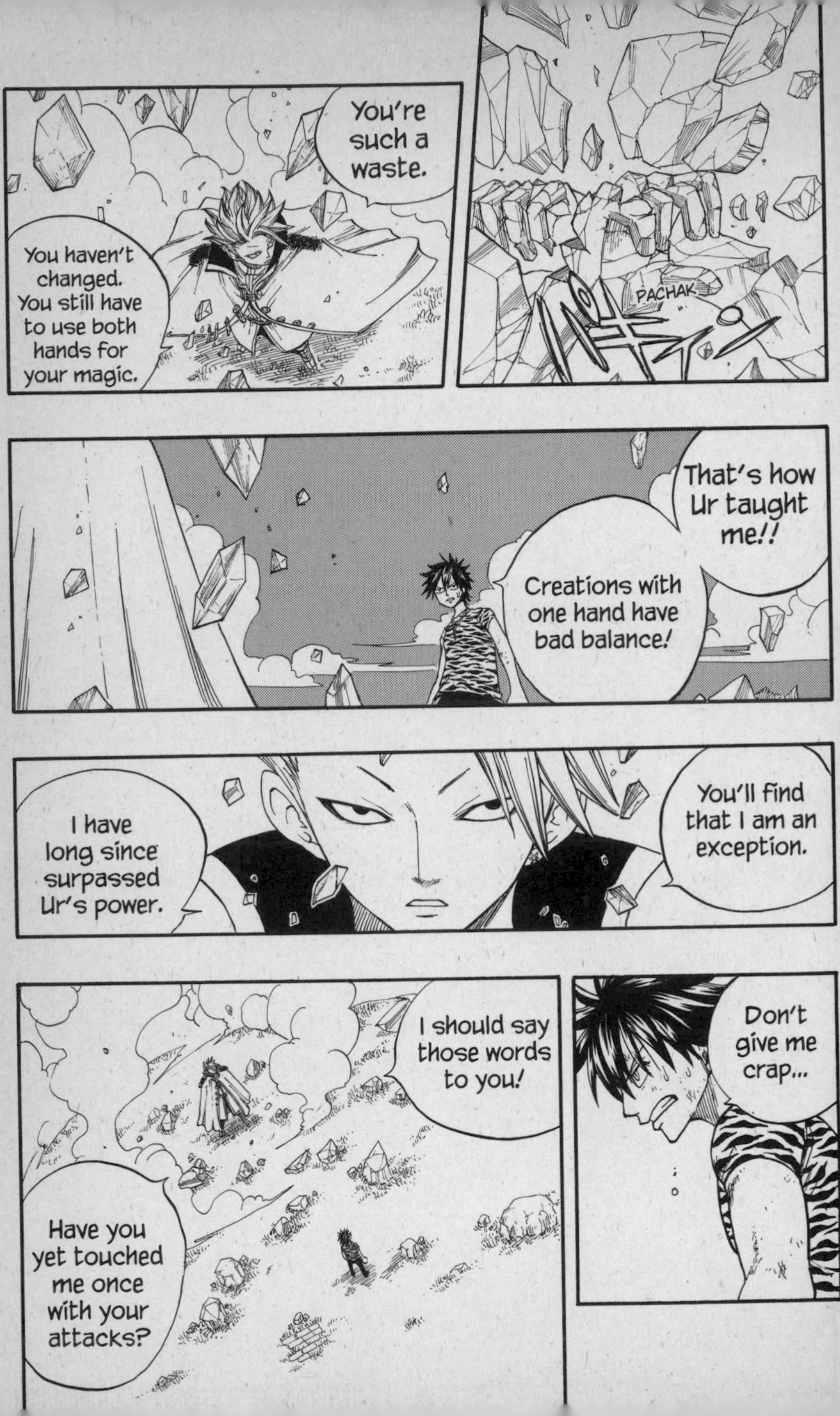
PACHAK
You're such a waste.
You haven't changed. You still have to use both hands for your magic.
That's how Ur taught me!!
Creations with one hand have bad balance!
You'll find that I am an exception.
I have long since surpassed Ur's power.
Don't give me crap...
I should say those words to you!
Have you yet touched me once with your attacks?

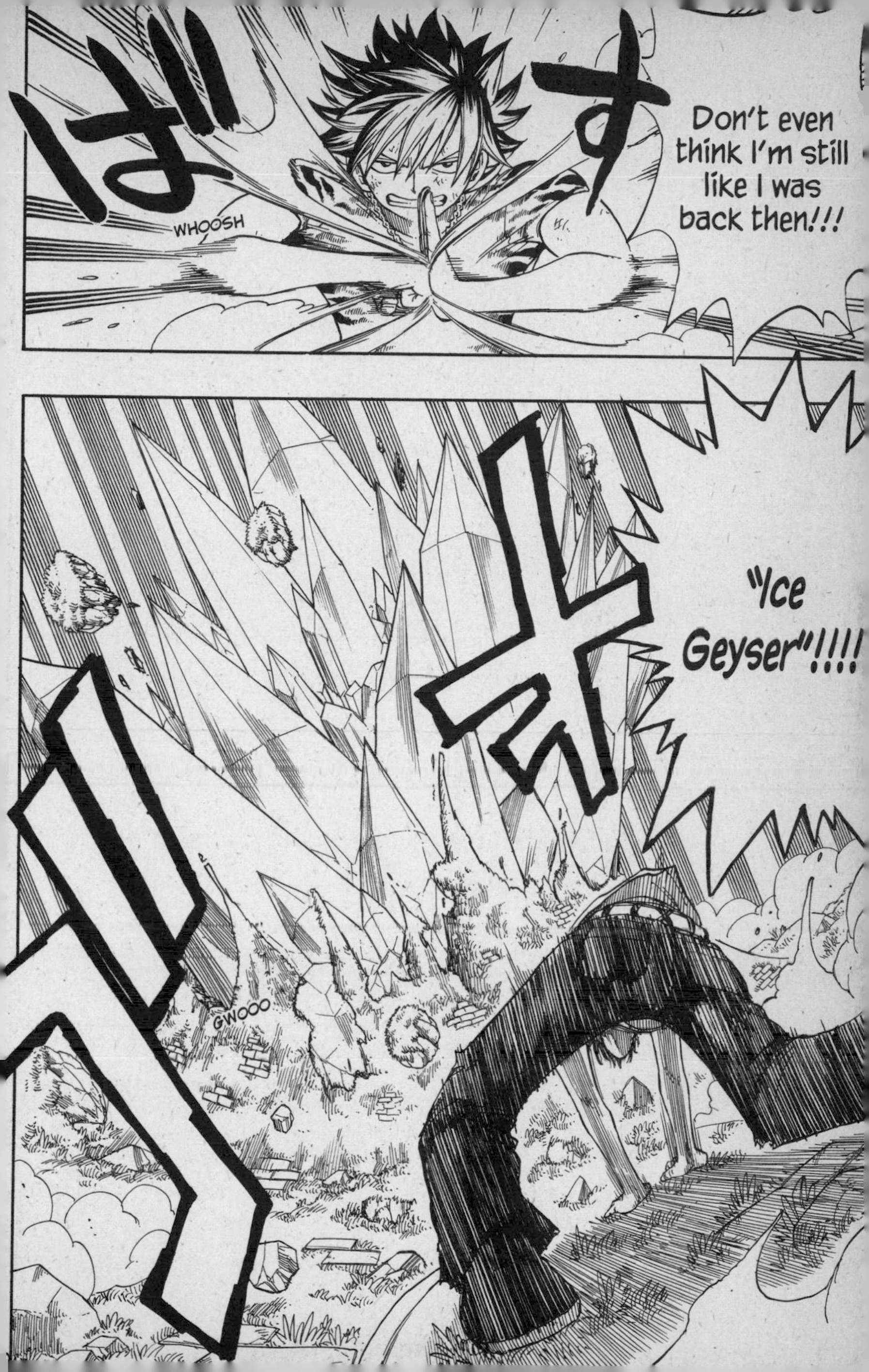
Don't even think I'm still like I was back then!!!
WHOOSH
"Ice Geyser"!!!!
GWOOO

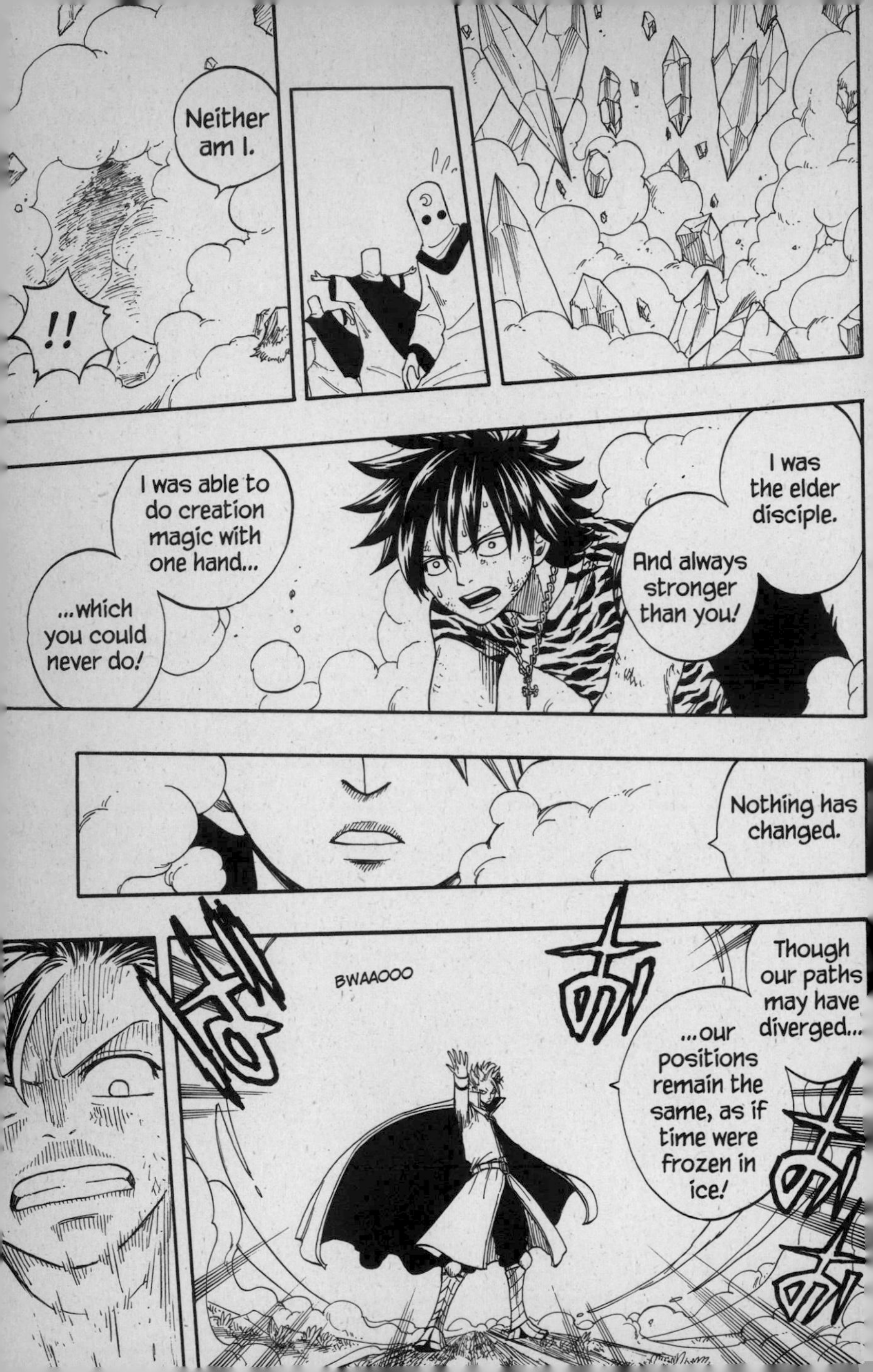
Neither am I.
!!
I was the elder disciple.
And always stronger than you!
I was able to do creation magic with one hand...
...which you could never do!
Nothing has changed.
Though our paths may have diverged...
...our positions remain the same, as if time were frozen in ice!
BWAAOOO

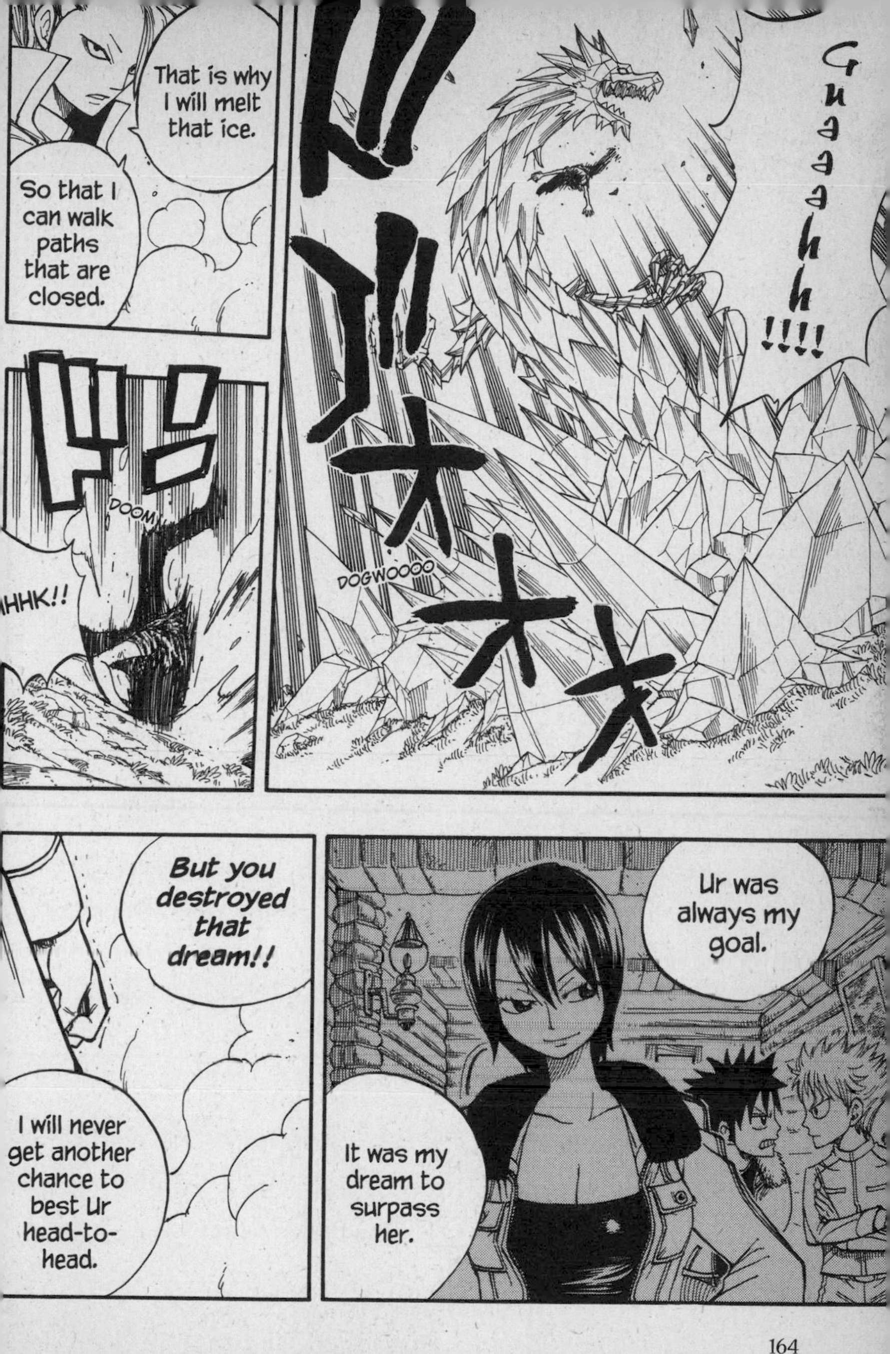

Guaaaahh!!!!
DOGWOOOO
That is why I will melt that ice.
So that I can walk paths that are closed.
DOOM
HHK!!
Ur was always my goal.
It was my dream to surpass her.
But you destroyed that dream!!
I will never get another chance to best Ur head-to-head.

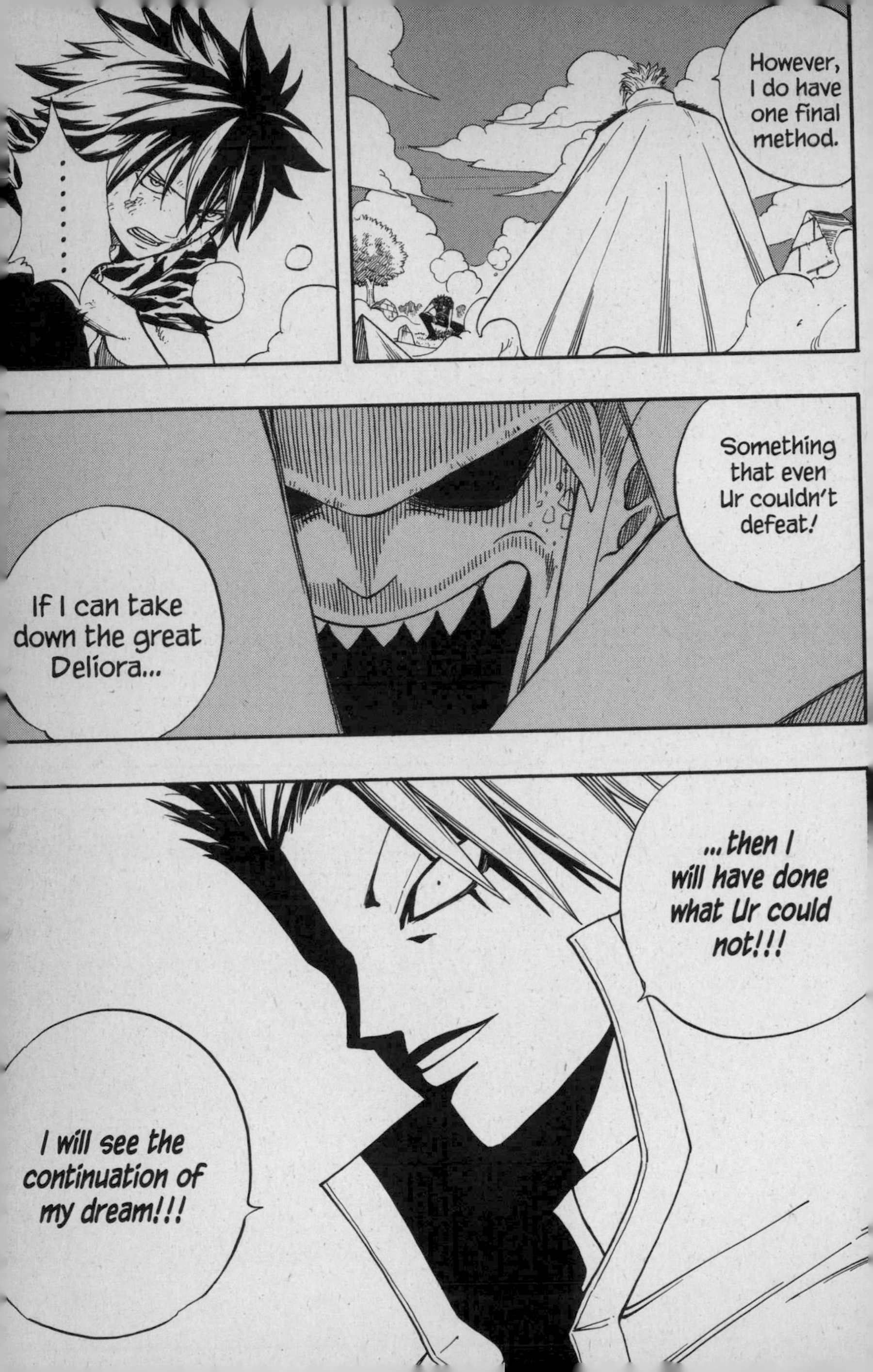
However, I do have one final method.
Something that even Ur couldn't defeat!
If I can take down the great Deliora...
...then I will have done what Ur could not!!!
I will see the continuation of my dream!!!

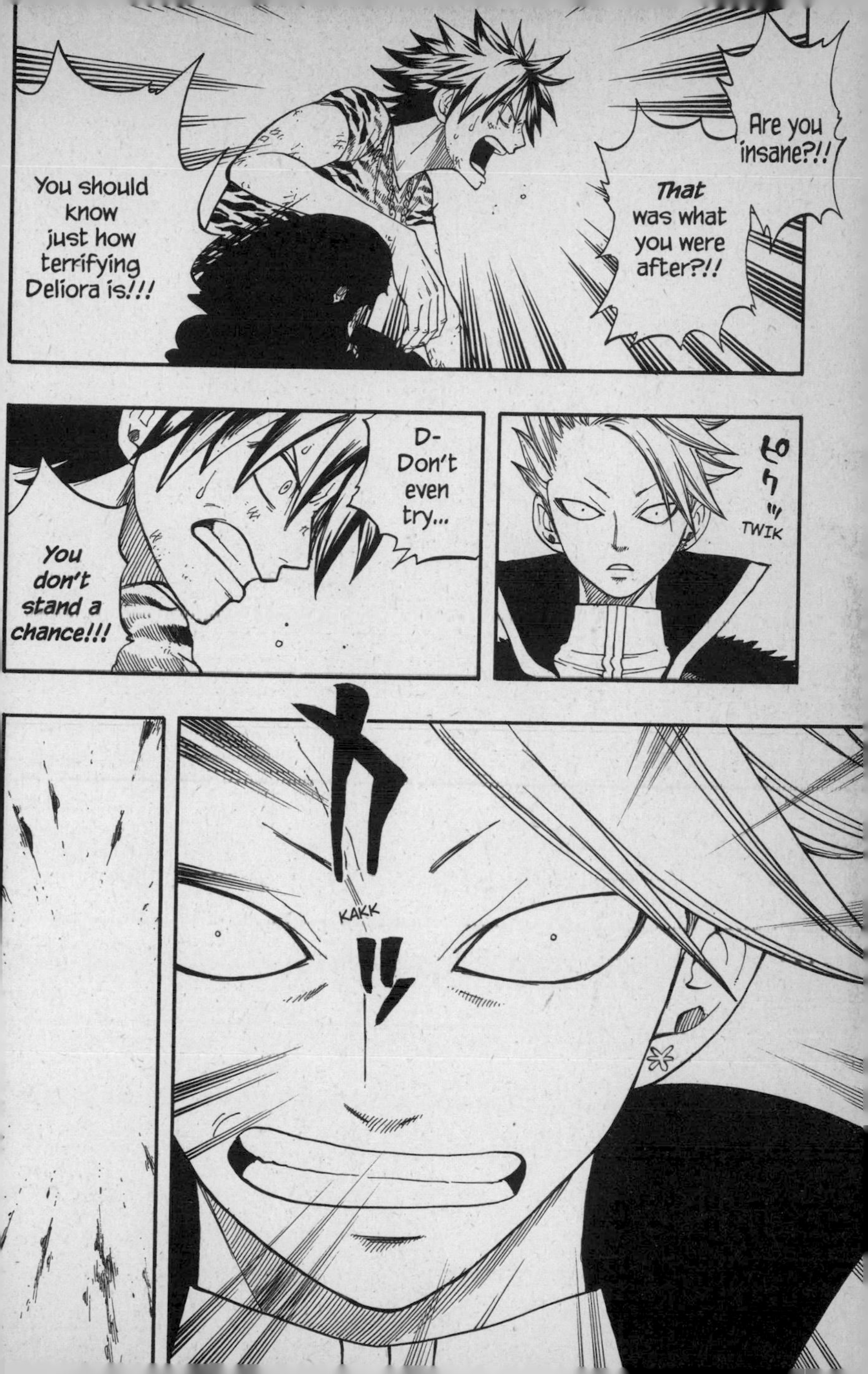
Are you insane?!!
That was what you were after?!!
You should know just how terrifying Deliora is!!!
TWIK
D- Don't even try...
You don't stand a chance!!!
KAKK

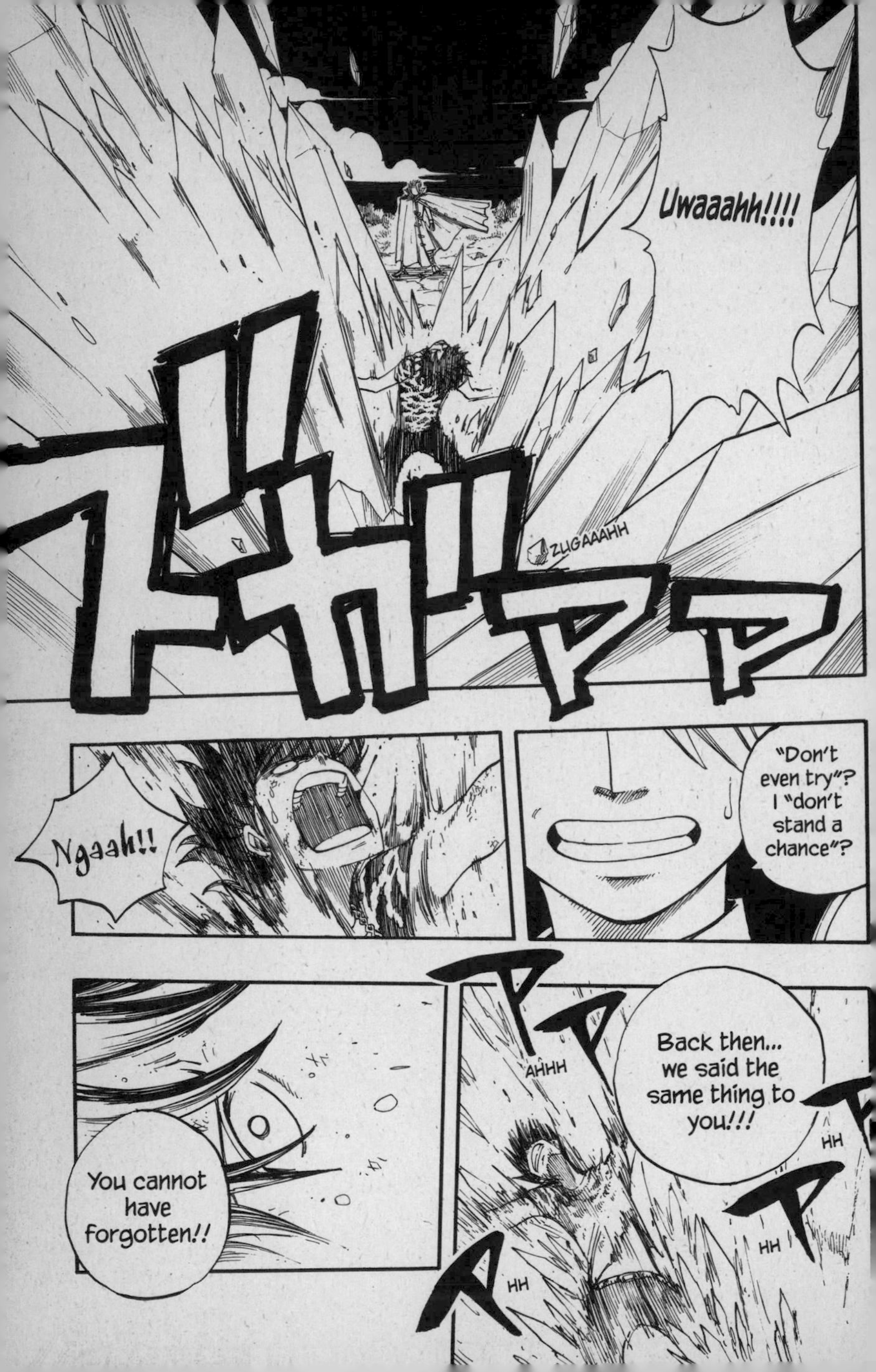
Uwaaahh!!!!
ZUGAAAHH
"Don't even try"? I "don't stand a chance"?
Ngaah!!
Back then... we said the same thing to you!!!
AHHH
HH
HH
HH
You cannot have forgotten!!

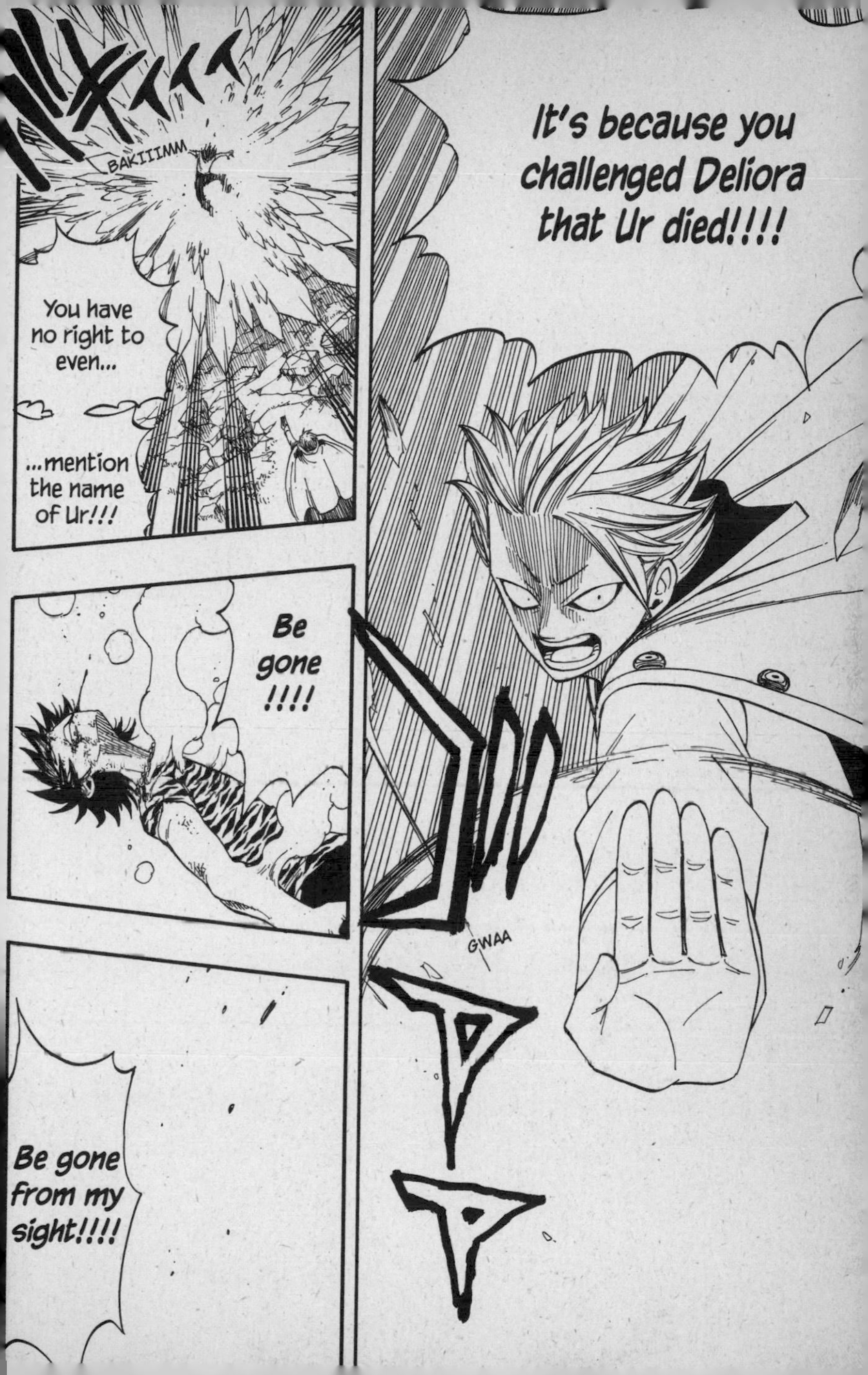

It's because you challenged Deliora that Ur died!!!!
GWAA
BAKIIIMM
You have no right to even...
...mention the name of Ur!!!
Be gone!!!!
Be gone from my sight!!!!

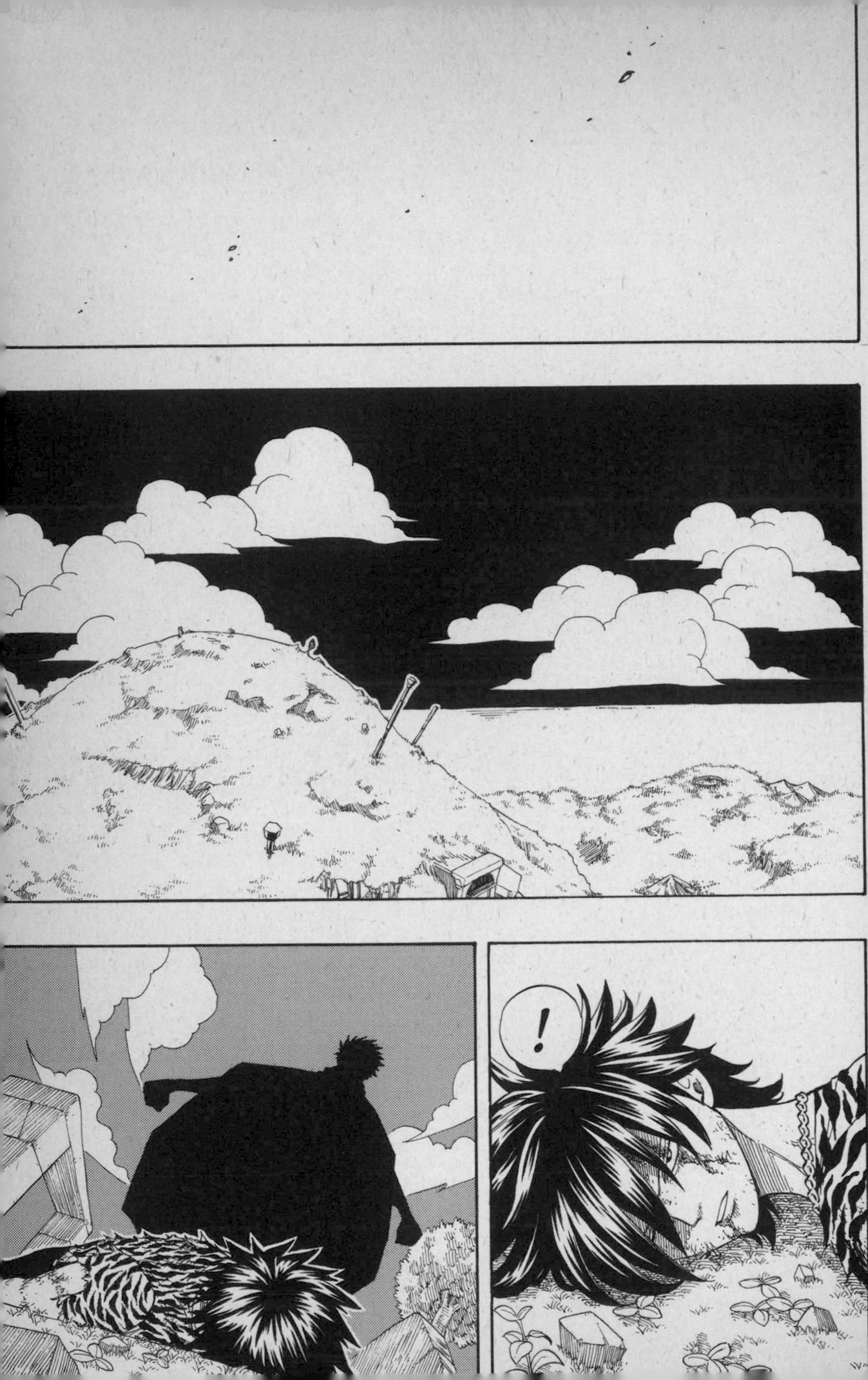
!

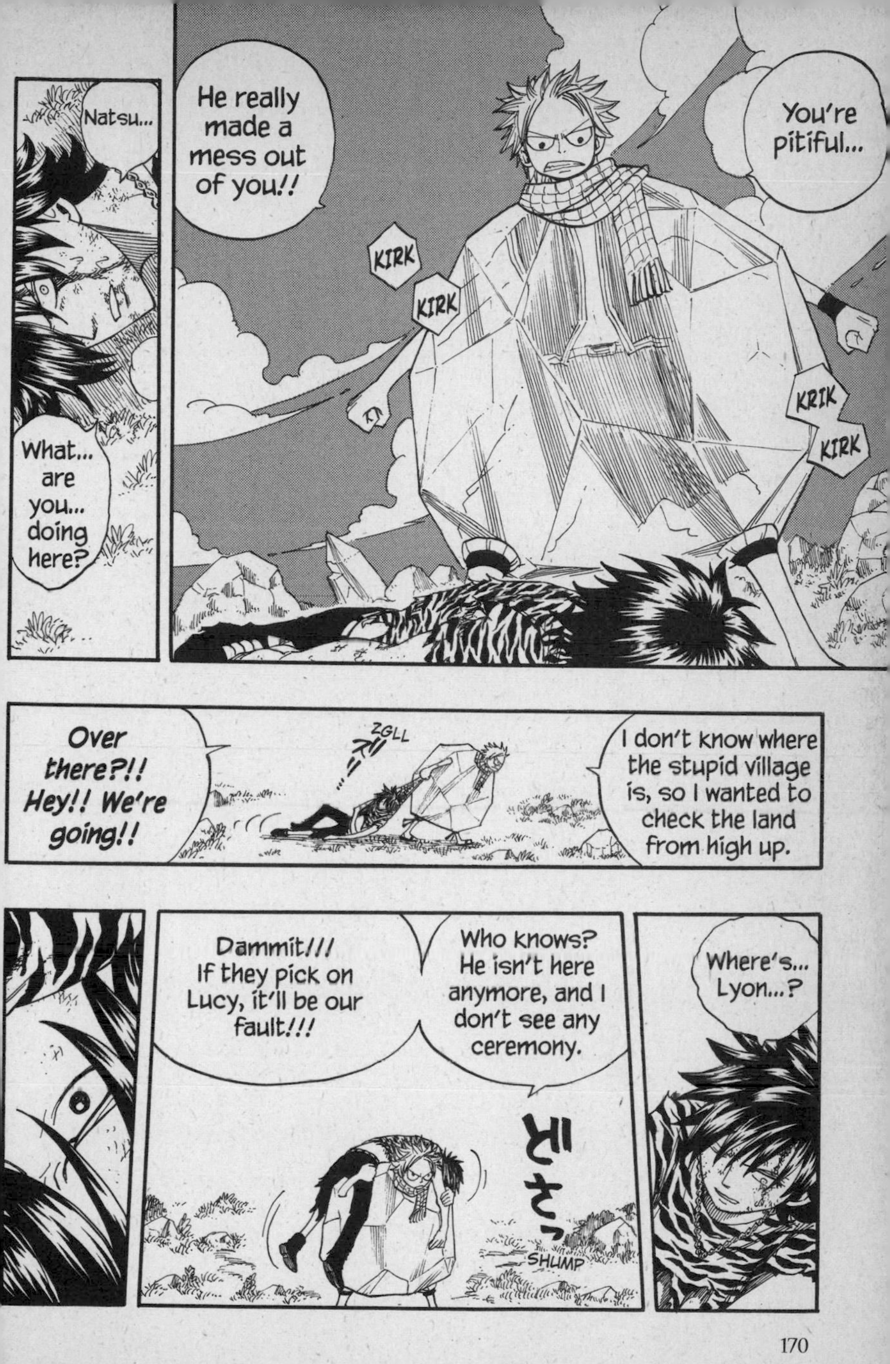
You're pitiful...
He really made a mess out of you!!
KIRK
KIRK
KRIK
KIRK
Natsu...
What... are you... doing here?
I don't know where the stupid village is, so I wanted to check the land from high up.
ZGLL
Over there?!! Hey!! We're going!!
Where's... Lyon...?
Who knows? He isn't here anymore, and I don't see any ceremony.
Dammit/// If they pick on Lucy, it'll be our fault!!!
どさっ
SHUMP

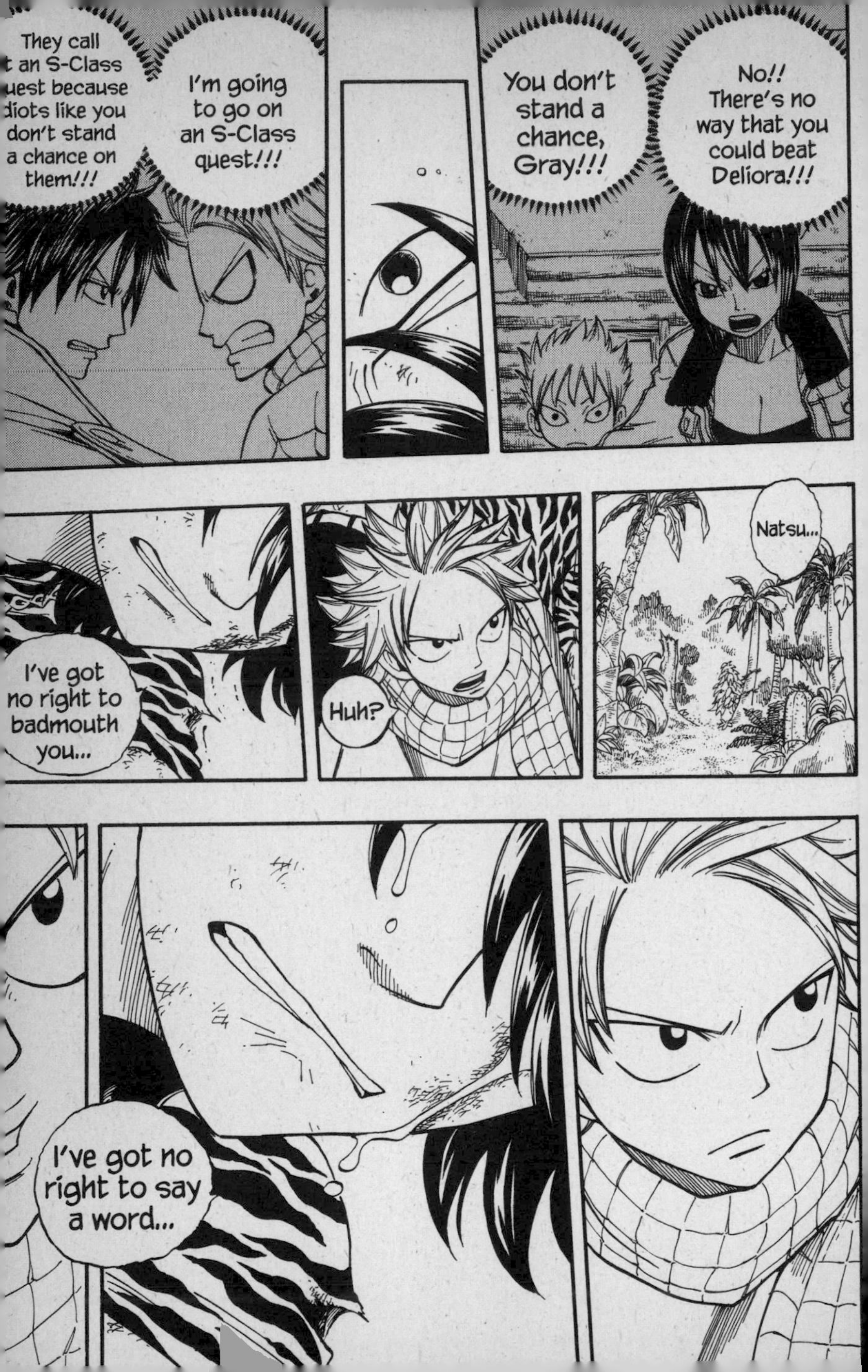
No!! There's no way that you could beat Deliora!!!
You don't stand a chance, Gray!!!
I'm going to go on an S-Class quest!!!
They call t an S-Class uest because diots like you don't stand a chance on them!!!
Natsu...
Huh?
I've got no right to badmouth you...
I've got no right to say a word...

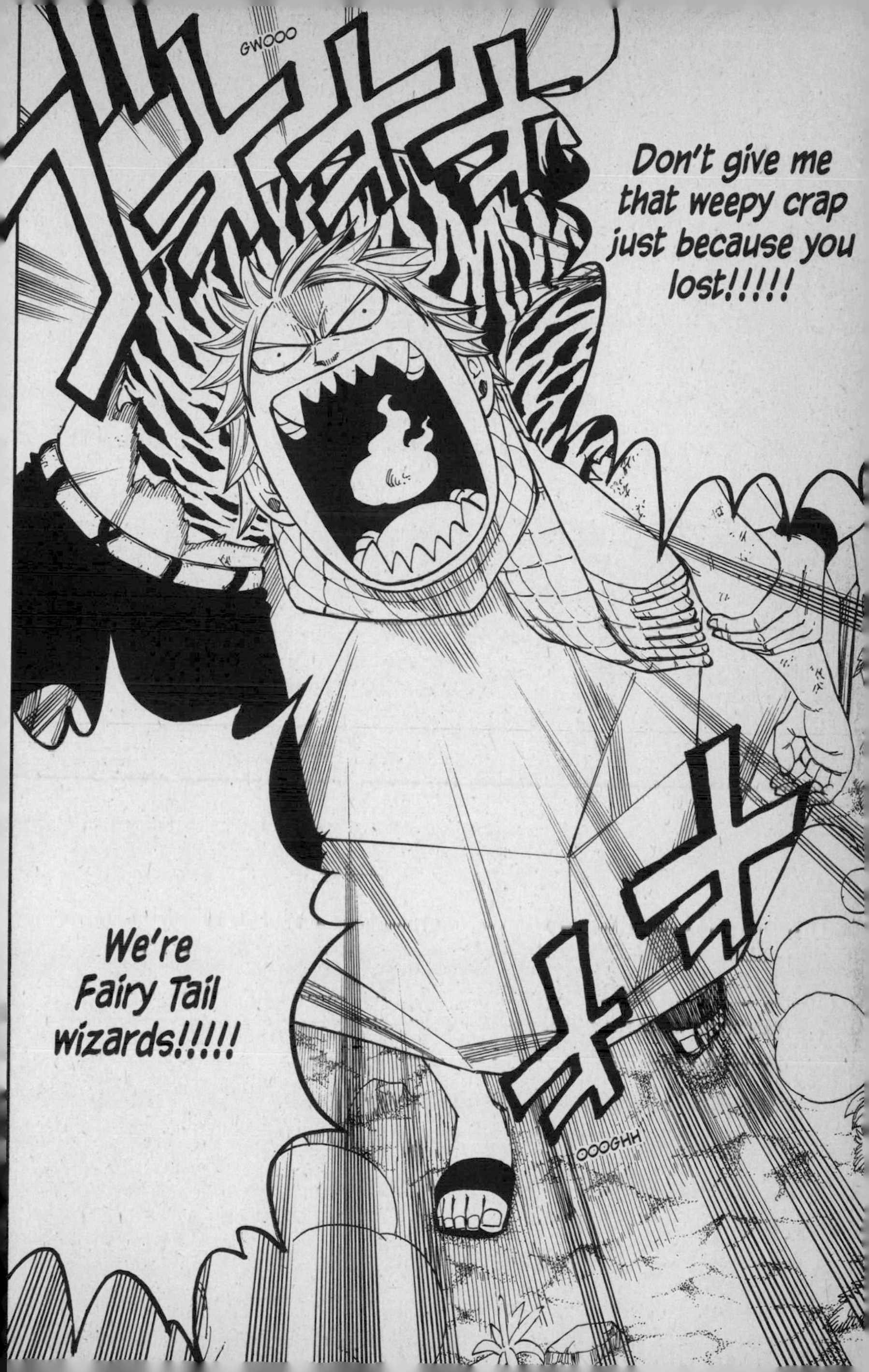
GWOOO
Don't give me that weepy crap just because you lost!!!!!
We're Fairy Tail wizards!!!!!
OOOGHH

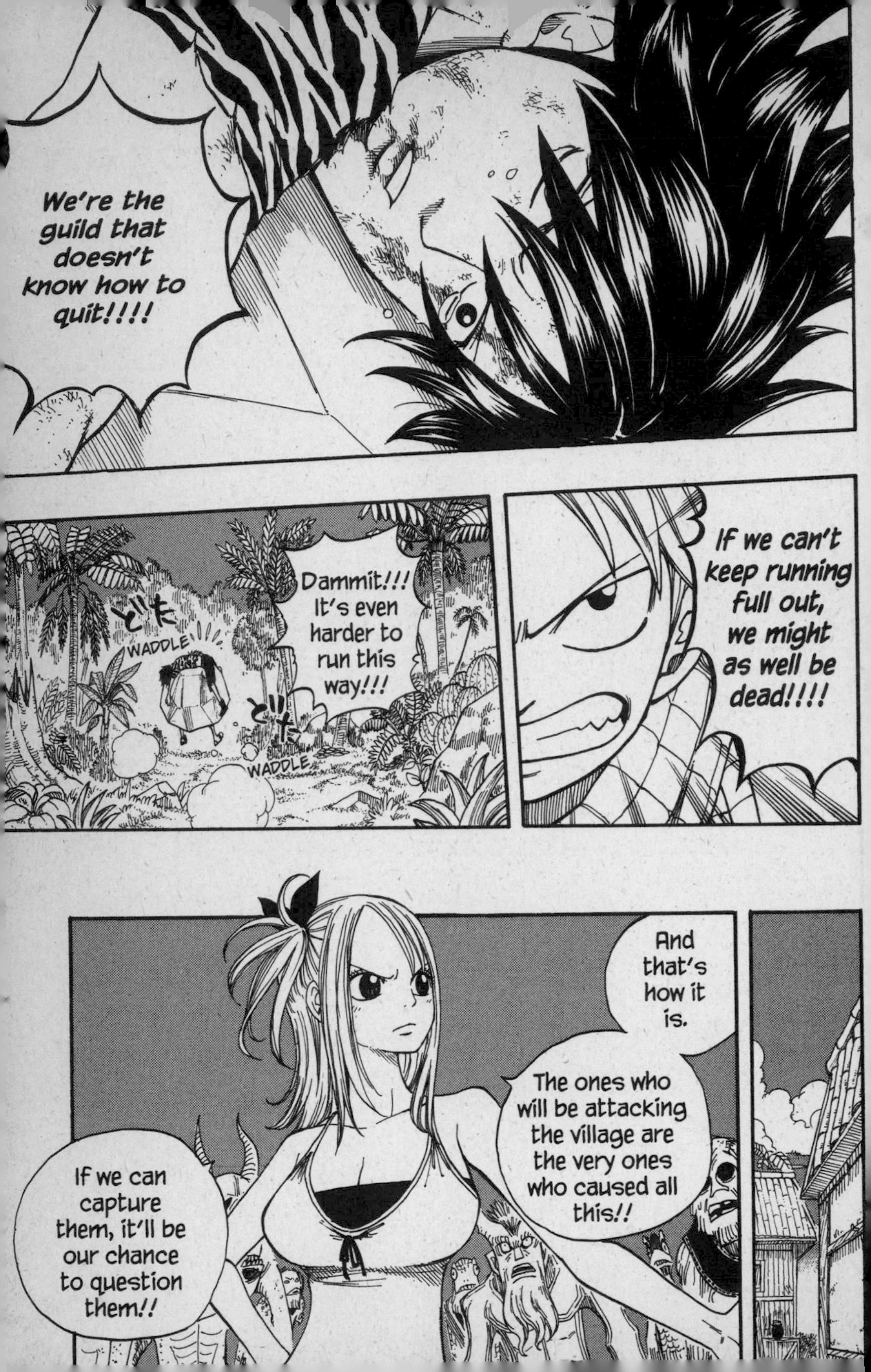
We're the guild that doesn't know how to quit!!!!
If we can't keep running full out, we might as well be dead!!!!
Dammit!!! It's even harder to run this way!!!
WADDLE
WADDLE
And that's how it is.
The ones who will be attacking the village are the very ones who caused all this!!
If we can capture them, it'll be our chance to question them!!

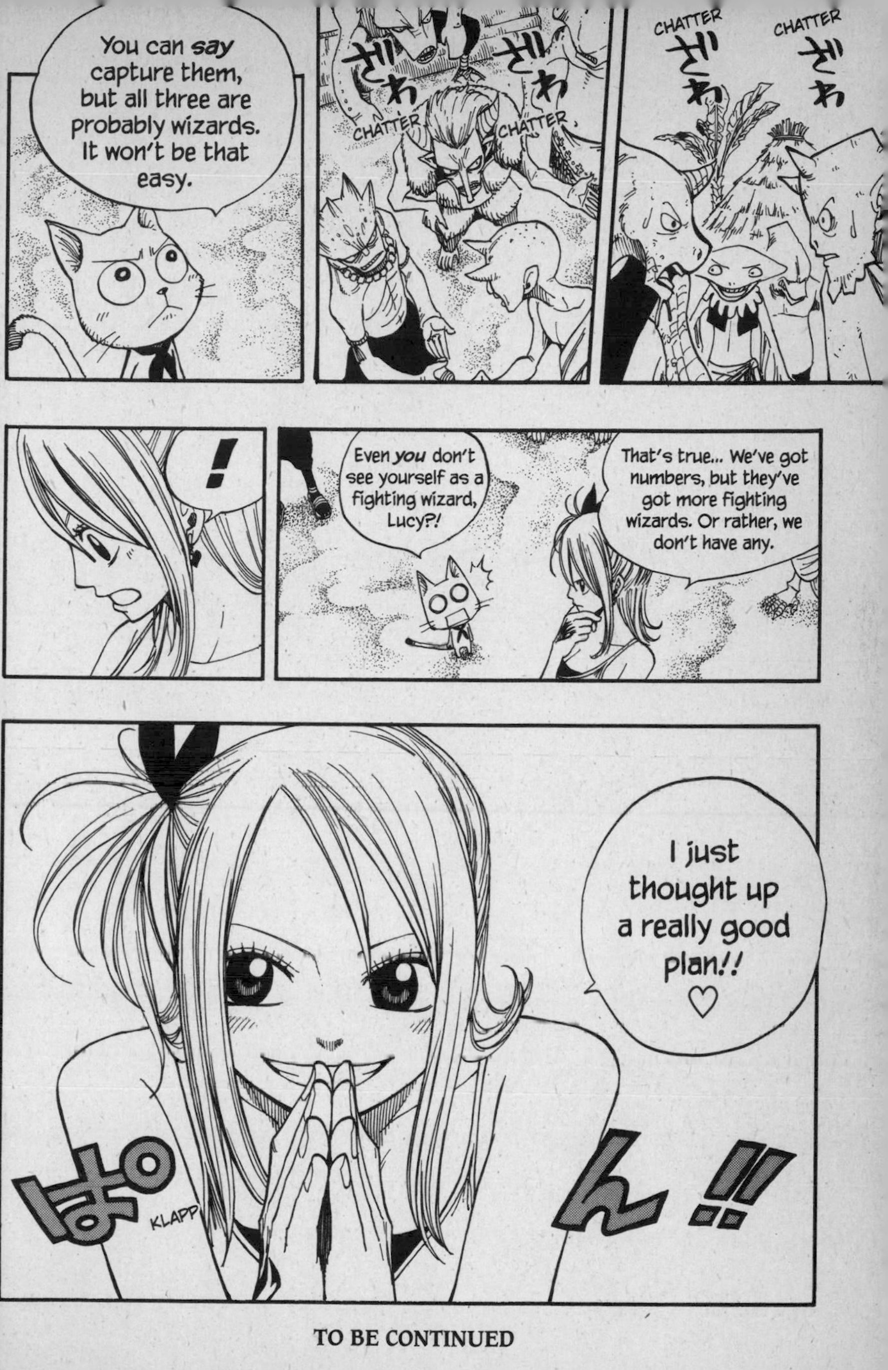
CHATTER
ざわ
CHATTER
ざわ
CHATTER
ざわ
CHATTER
ざわ
You can *say* capture them, but all three are probably wizards. It won't be that easy.
That's true... We've got numbers, but they've got more fighting wizards. Or rather, we don't have any.
Even *you* don't see yourself as a fighting wizard, Lucy?!
!
I just thought up a really good plan!! ♡
ぱん!!
KLAPP

TO BE CONTINUED

FAIRY TAIL

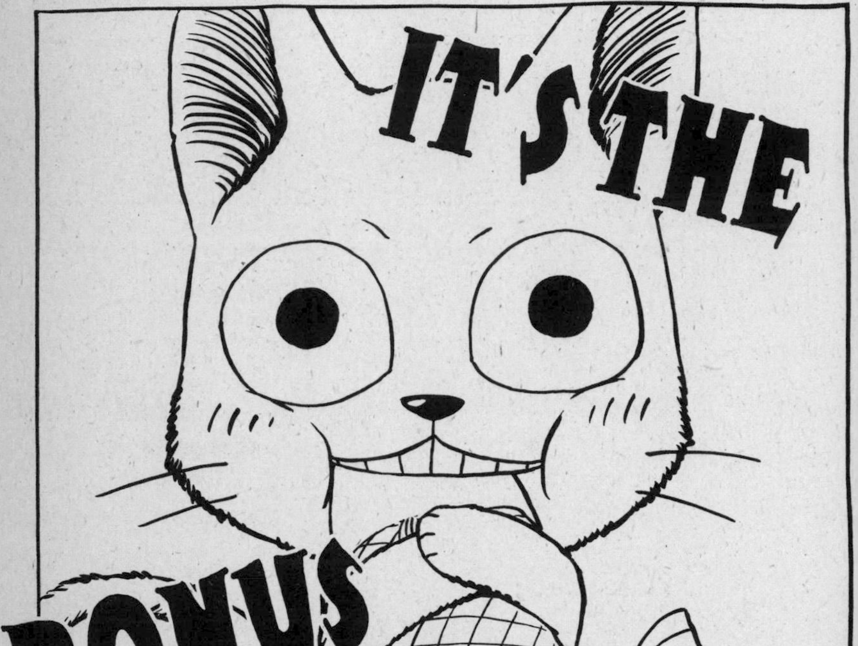
IT'S THE
BONUS
PAGES

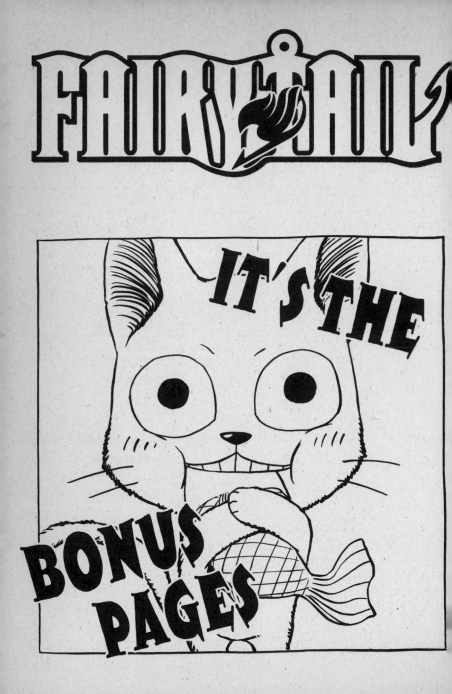

• A Rejected Splash Page •

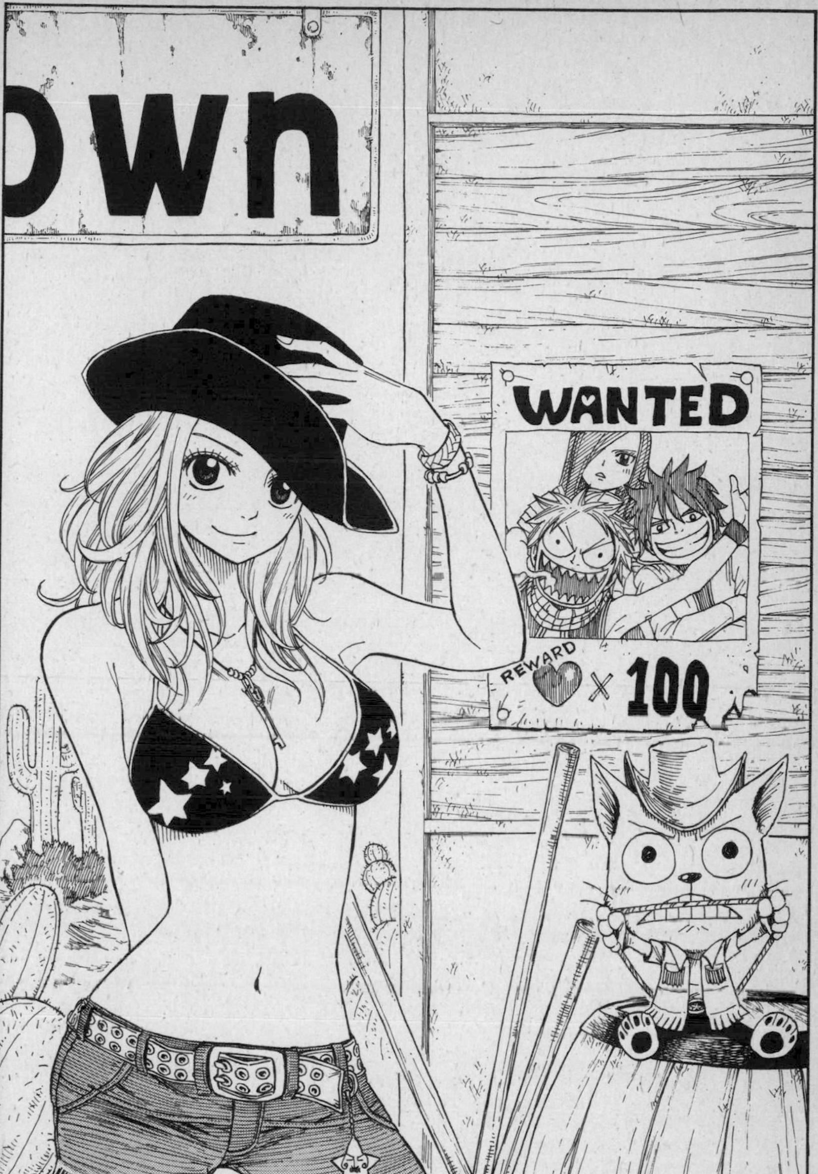
OWN
WANTED
REWARD
× 100

I guess I had drawn so many splash pages
with Lucy that this one got shelved.

Introducing a Brand-New Four-Wheeled Magic Rental Vehicle!!

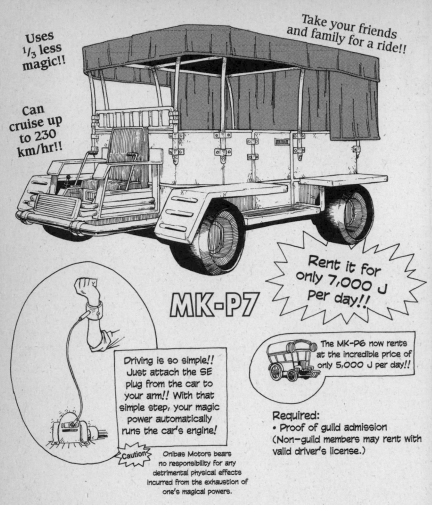

Uses 1/3 less magic!!

Take your friends and family for a ride!!

Can cruise up to 230 km/hr!!

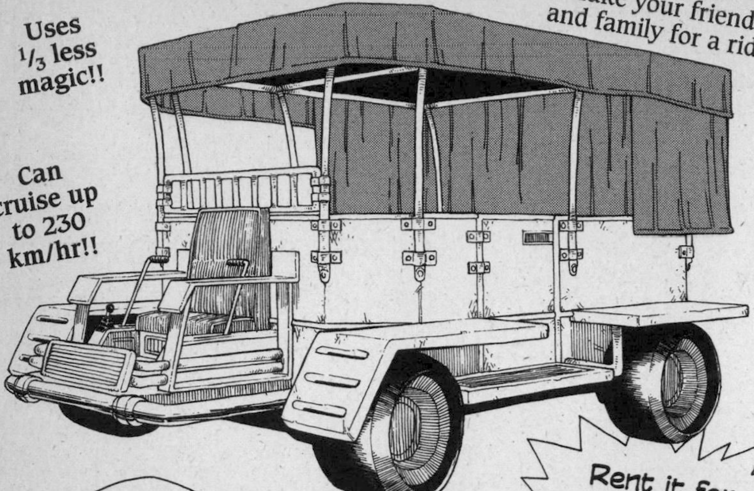

Rent it for only 7,000 J per day!!

MK-P7

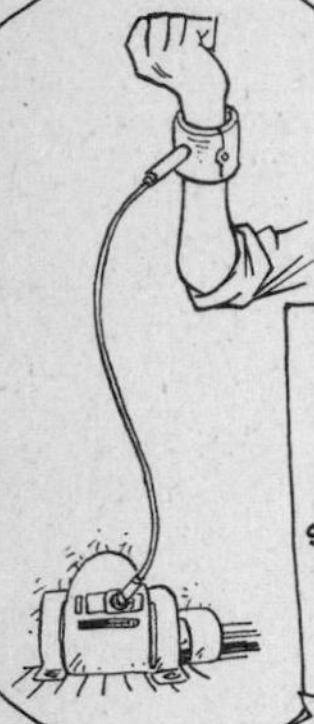

Driving is so simple!! Just attach the SE plug from the car to your arm!! With that simple step, your magic power automatically runs the car's engine!

Caution: Onibas Motors bears no responsibility for any detrimental physical effects incurred from the exhaustion of one's magical powers.

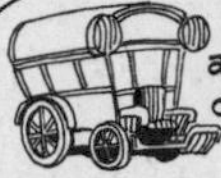

The MK-P6 now rents at the incredible price of only 5,000 J per day!!

Required:

- Proof of guild admission (Non-guild members may rent with valid driver's license.)

A Message to Drivers

Four-wheeled magic vehicles will soon be available for purchase!!!

Up till now, they've only been available for rental, but we've heard the demands from customers who dream of owning their own vehicles!! Now our advancements in magic technology will make that dream possible!! The bottleneck presently preventing personal vehicle ownership is the problems caused by magic-power exhaustion. But Onibas Motors is developing a groundbreaking system that will solve that issue!! Buyers, your dreams will soon be fulfilled!!

—Onibas Motors

Early Preproduction Illustration

I drew this to illustrate the feeling of a guild. Since it was still very early in the conceptual stage, Happy-like cats have wings for arms. And there are two of them! That's Mirajane on the guitar, and I think that's supposed to be Natsu behind her, but both their hairstyles have changed. By the way, at the time of this drawing, the first chapter had a scene of Mirajane singing. I worked very hard on the lyrics, but the entire scene was cut. Well… still… it's allowed my lack of talent for creating lyrics to remain a closely kept secret.

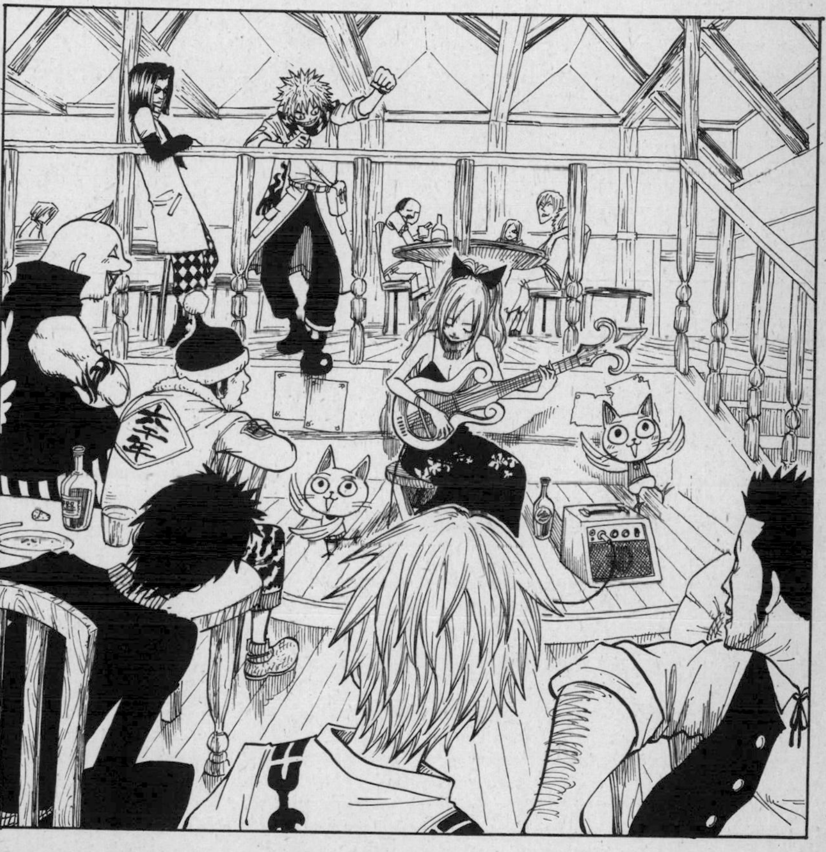

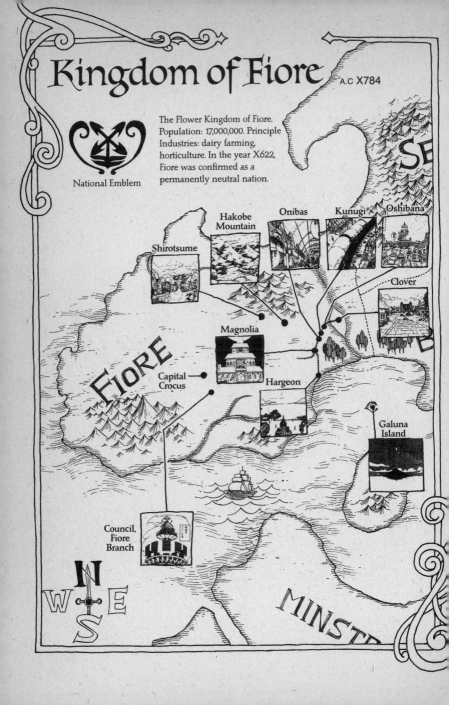

Kingdom of Fiore

A.C X784

The Flower Kingdom of Fiore. Population: 17,000,000. Principle Industries: dairy farming, horticulture. In the year X622, Fiore was confirmed as a permanently neutral nation.

National Emblem

Shirotsume

Hakobe Mountain

Onibas

Kunugi

Oshibana

Clover

Magnolia

FIORE

Capital Crocus

Hargeon

Galuna Island

Council, Fiore Branch

SE

MINST

N
W
S
E

Erza's Magic Armor Collection

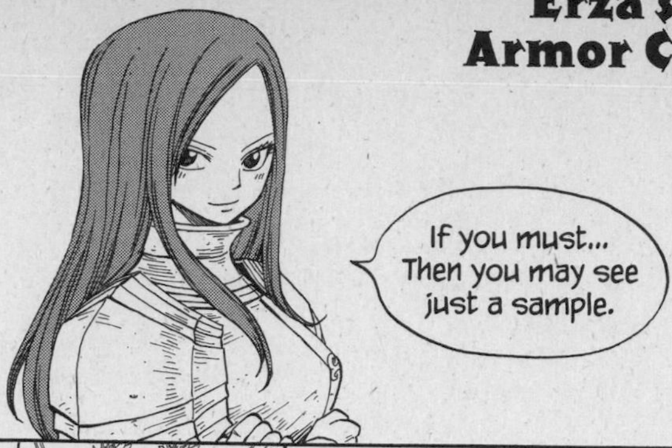
If you must...
Then you may see
just a sample.

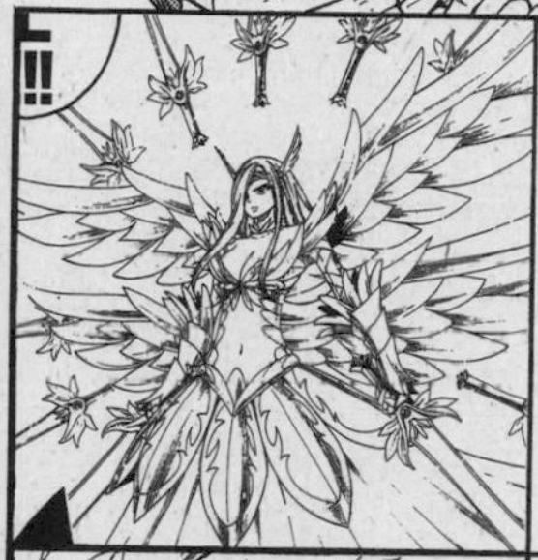

Heaven's Wheel Armor

An armor that allows her to wield a large number of weapons at once.

Attack Strength ☆☆☆★★
Defense Strength ☆☆☆★★
Speed ☆☆★★★
Range ☆☆☆☆☆

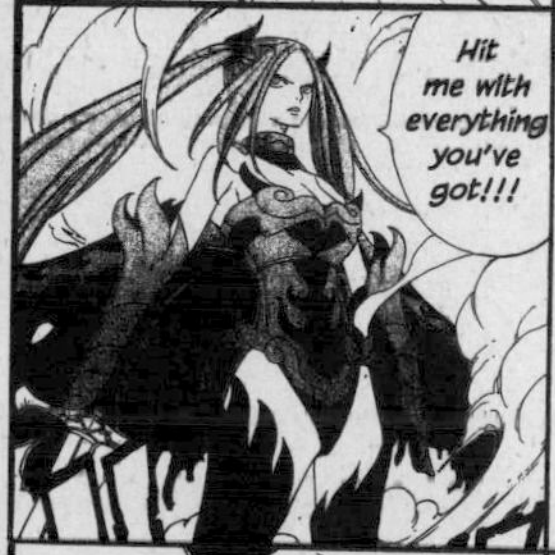
Hit me with everything you've got!!!

Fire Empress Armor

Anti-fire armor. Apparently it can halve Natsu's fire attacks.

Attack Strength ☆☆★★★
Defense Strength ☆☆☆☆★
Speed ☆☆☆★★
Range ☆☆★★★

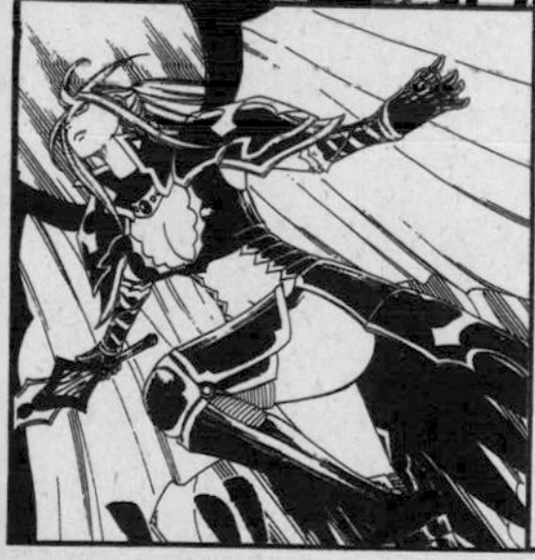

Black Wing Armor

Armor that greatly increases the power of a single attack. It also enhances one's jumping ability.

Attack Strength ☆☆☆☆☆
Defense Strength ☆★★★★
Speed ☆☆☆★★
Range ☆★★★★

Celestial Spirit Data

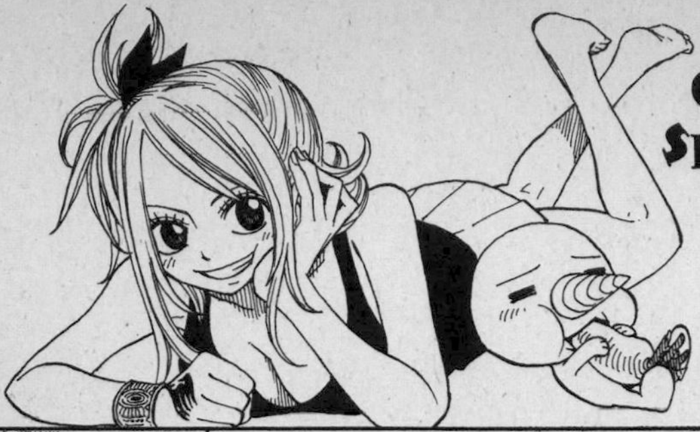

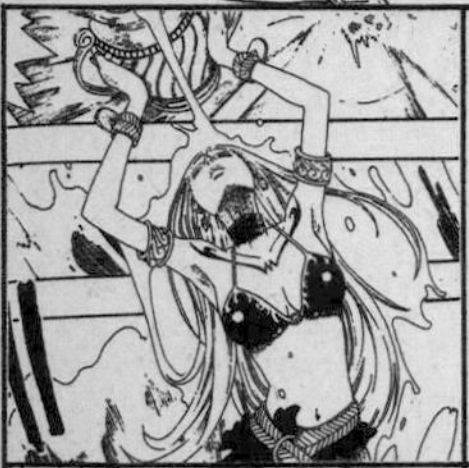

Aquarius of the Water Bearer Palace

One of the Twelve Golden Gates. Can create tidal waves that do not distinguish between friend and foe. Has great power, but is difficult to control. Can only be called in the presence of water.

Physical Power: 250
Attack Power: 388
Defensive Power: 275
Magic Power Expended: 100
Shift: Only on Wednesdays.

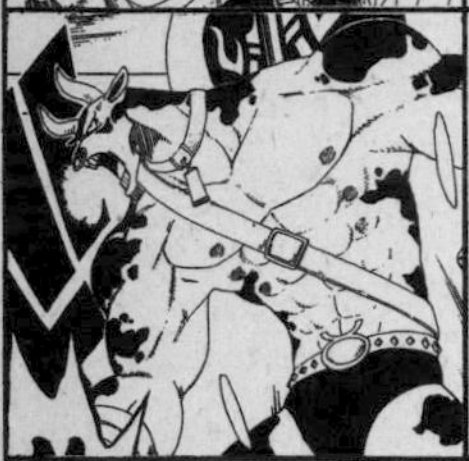

Taurus of the Golden Bovine Palace

One of the Twelve Golden Gates. Possesses Herculean strength, but tends toward sexual harassment with a fixation on breasts.

Physical Power: 160
Attack Power: 200
Defensive Power: 154
Magic Power Expended: 52
Shift: Monday, Wednesday, Friday, Saturday.

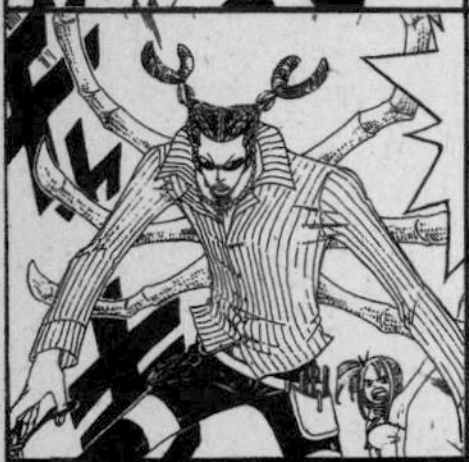

Cancer of the Great Crab Palace

One of the Twelve Golden Gates. His distinctive features are the inability to size up the situation and tacking on "-ebi" to the end of his sentences. He is in charge of Lucy's hair and makeup.

Physical Power: 147
Attack Power: 176
Defensive Power: 179
Magic Power Expended: 51
Shift: Wednesday, Thursday, Saturday, Sunday.

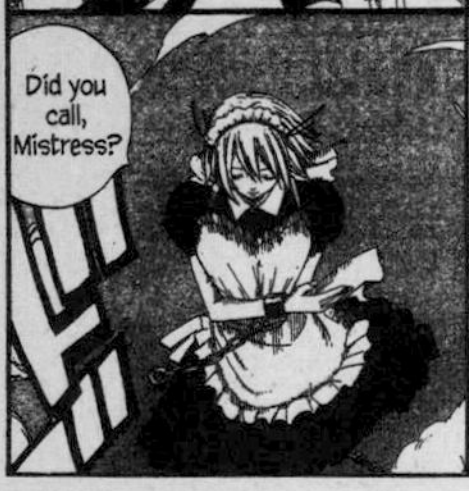
Did you call, Mistress?

Virgo of the Virgin Palace

One of the Twelve Golden Gates. Originally was under contract to Count Everlue but has switched to Lucy. She is especially good at digging holes.

Physical Power: 121
Attack Power: 164
Defensive Power: 84
Magic Power Expended: 43
Shift: Monday through Saturday.

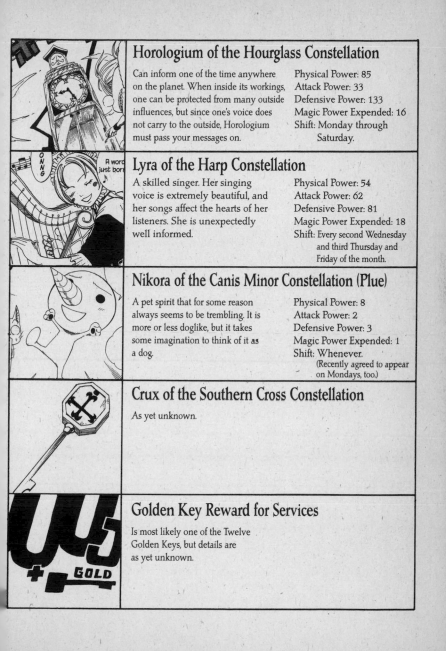

Horologium of the Hourglass Constellation

Can inform one of the time anywhere on the planet. When inside its workings, one can be protected from many outside influences, but since one's voice does not carry to the outside, Horologium must pass your messages on.

Physical Power: 85
Attack Power: 33
Defensive Power: 133
Magic Power Expended: 16
Shift: Monday through Saturday.

ONNG
A word
just bor

Lyra of the Harp Constellation

A skilled singer. Her singing voice is extremely beautiful, and her songs affect the hearts of her listeners. She is unexpectedly well informed.

Physical Power: 54
Attack Power: 62
Defensive Power: 81
Magic Power Expended: 18
Shift: Every second Wednesday and third Thursday and Friday of the month.

Nikora of the Canis Minor Constellation (Plue)

A pet spirit that for some reason always seems to be trembling. It is more or less doglike, but it takes some imagination to think of it as a dog.

Physical Power: 8
Attack Power: 2
Defensive Power: 3
Magic Power Expended: 1
Shift: Whenever. (Recently agreed to appear on Mondays, too.)

Crux of the Southern Cross Constellation

As yet unknown.

GOLD

Golden Key Reward for Services

Is most likely one of the Twelve Golden Keys, but details are as yet unknown.

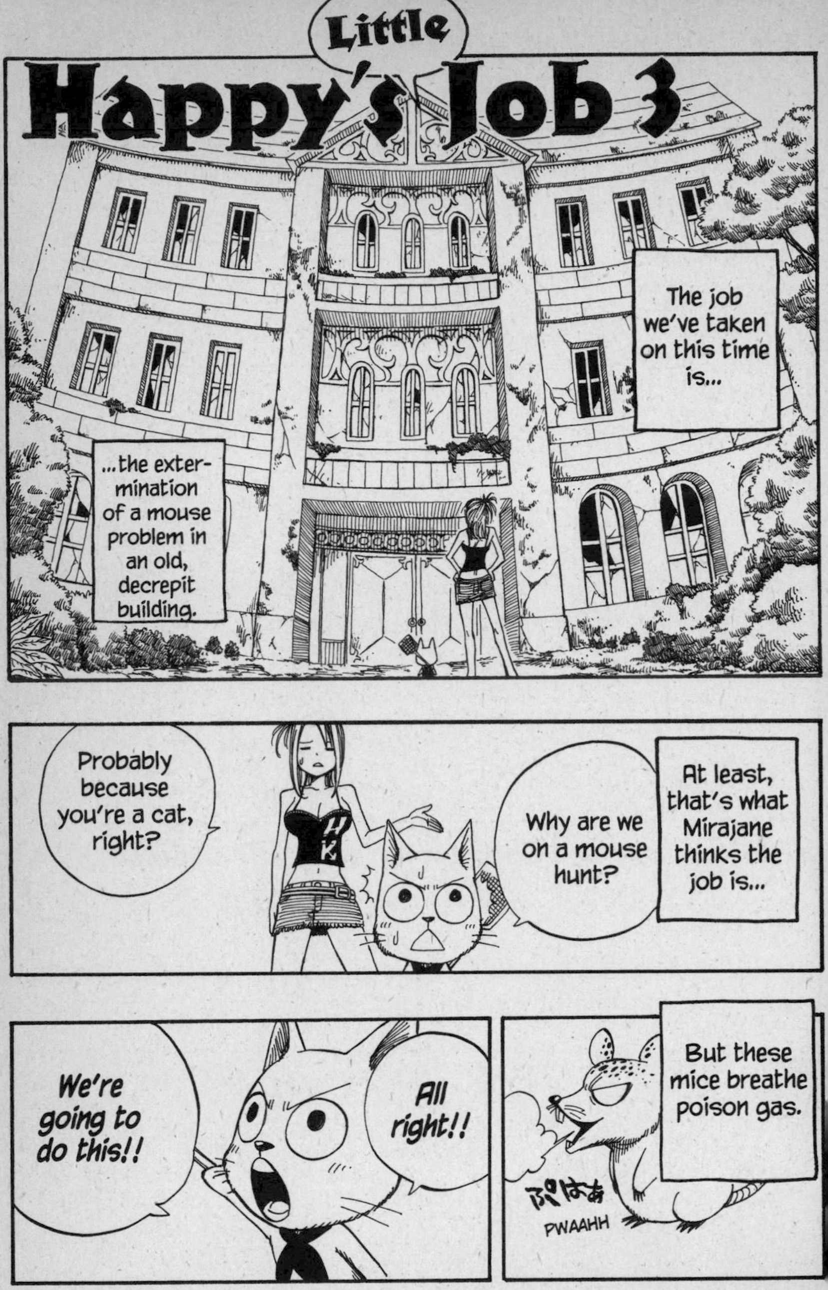
Little Happy's Job 3
The job we've taken on this time is...
...the extermination of a mouse problem in an old, decrepit building.
At least, that's what Mirajane thinks the job is...
Why are we on a mouse hunt?
Probably because you're a cat, right?
But these mice breathe poison gas.
ぷはぁ
PWAAHH
All right!!
We're going to do this!!

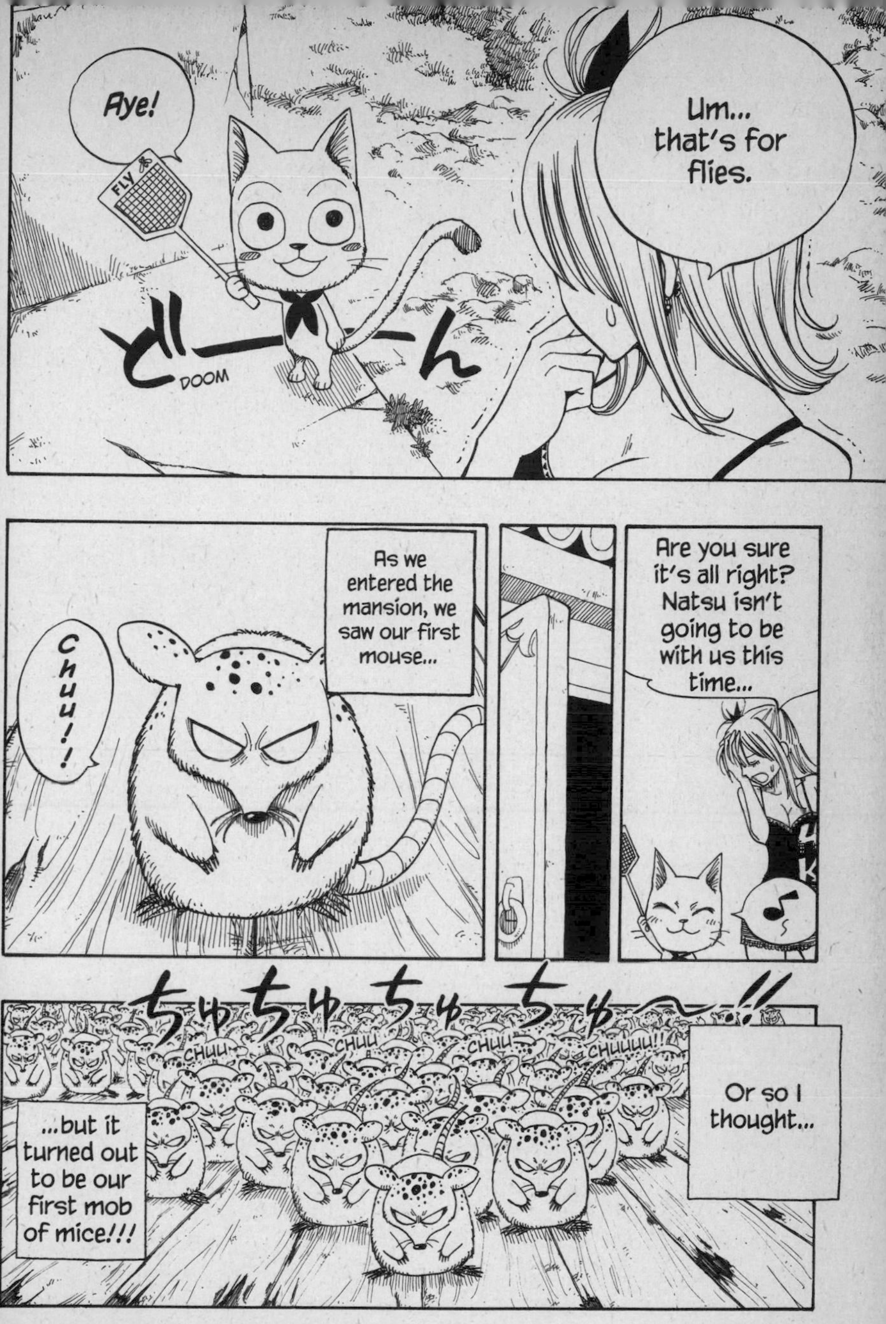
Um... that's for flies.
Aye!
FLY
DOOM
Are you sure it's all right? Natsu isn't going to be with us this time...
As we entered the mansion, we saw our first mouse...
Chuu!!
Or so I thought...
CHUUUUU!!
CHUU
CHUU
CHUU
...but it turned out to be our first mob of mice!!!

Happy, your fly swatter!!
What about you, Lucy?!! Your celestial spirits!!!
TMP
TMP
TMP
TMP
TMP
TMP
TMP
TMP
Open...
......
!!!
CHRING
In the end, it's me doing all the work!!!
Oops! I think that I forgot my keys!!
Aah!! What an absent-minded kid!!!
"Absent-minded kid"?!!

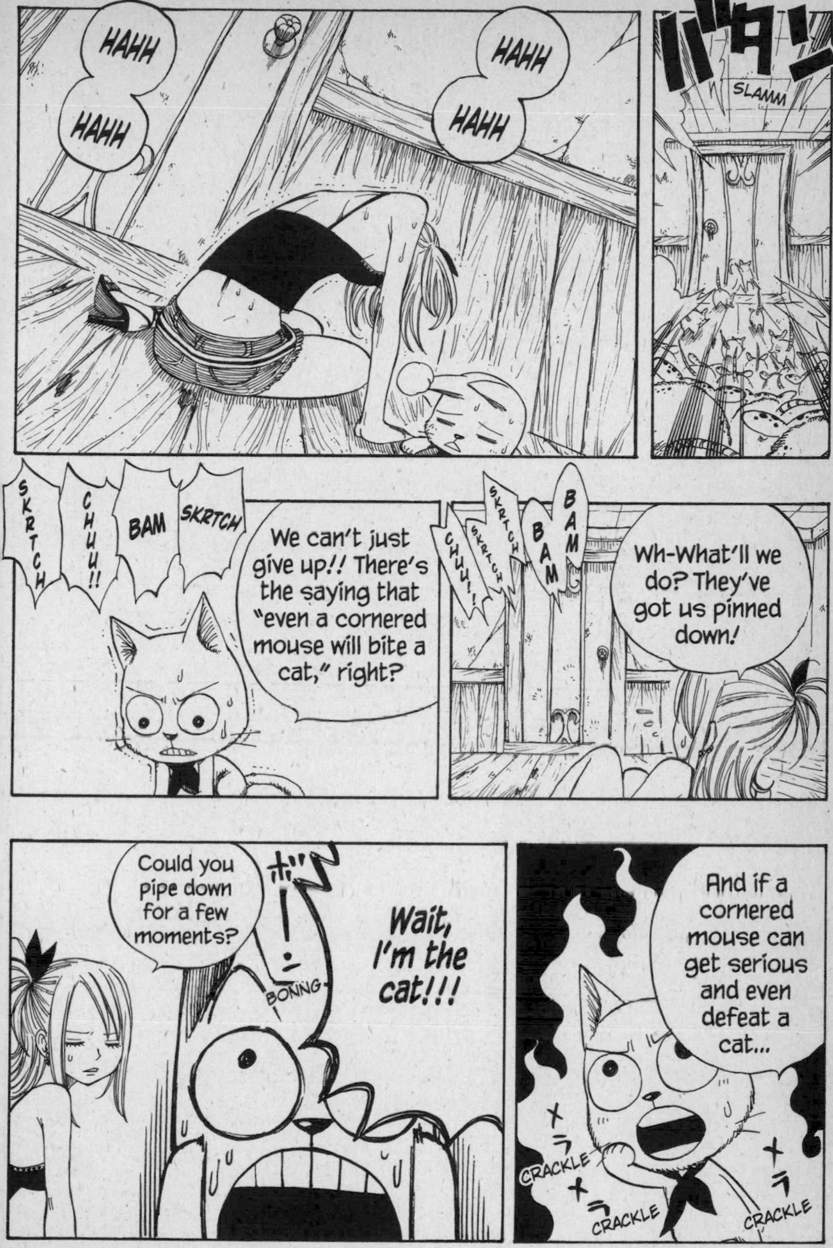
SLAMM
HAHH HAHH
HAHH HAHH
BAM BAM
SKRTCH
SKRTCH
CHUU!!
Wh-What'll we do? They've got us pinned down!
SKRTCH
BAM
CHUU!!
SKRTCH
We can't just give up!! There's the saying that "even a cornered mouse will bite a cat," right?
And if a cornered mouse can get serious and even defeat a cat...
CRACKLE
CRACKLE
CRACKLE
Wait, I'm the cat!!!
BONNG
Could you pipe down for a few moments?

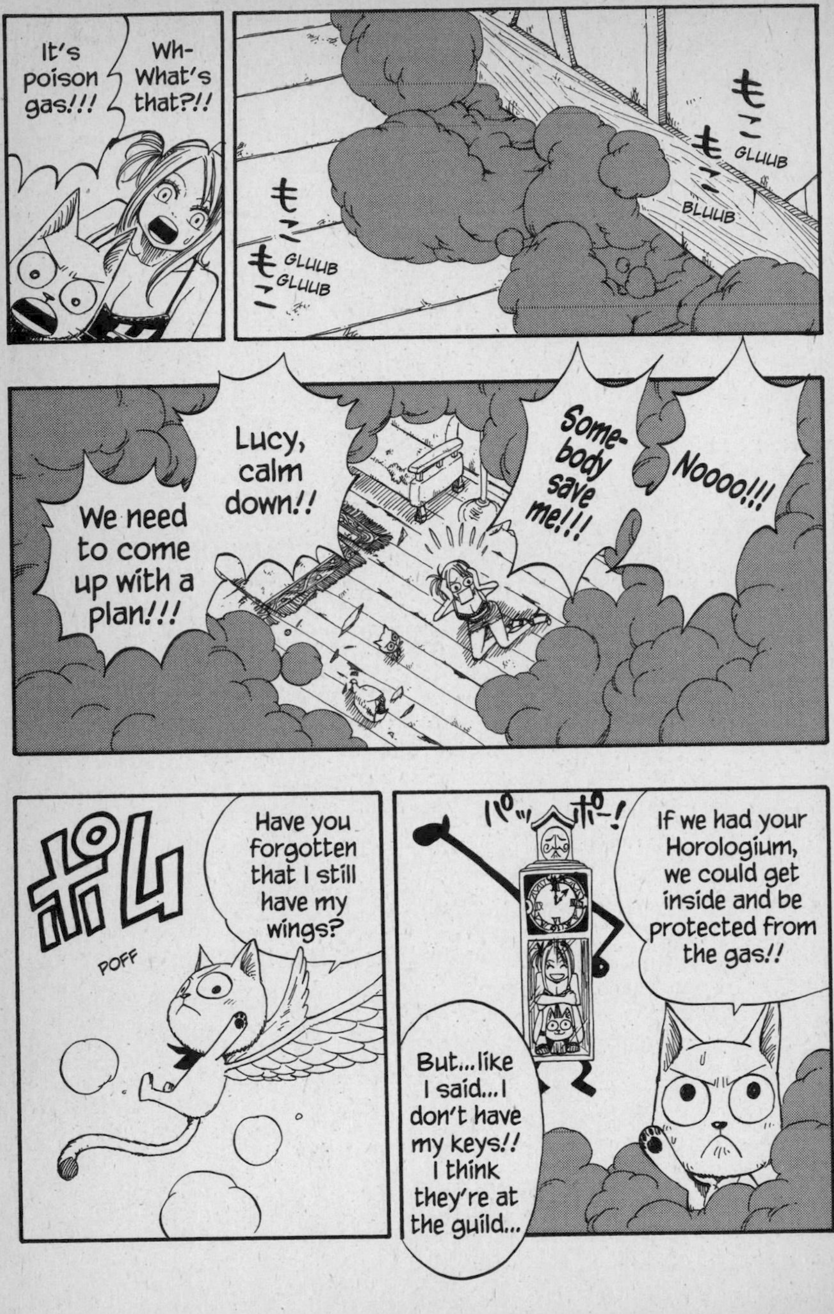

もこ
もこ
GLUUB
BLUUB
もこ
もこ
GLUUB
GLUUB
Wh- What's that?!!
It's poison gas!!!
Noooo!!!
Some-body save me!!!
Lucy, calm down!!
We need to come up with a plan!!!
パッポー!
If we had your Horologium, we could get inside and be protected from the gas!!
But...like I said...I don't have my keys!! I think they're at the guild...
ポム
POFF
Have you forgotten that I still have my wings?

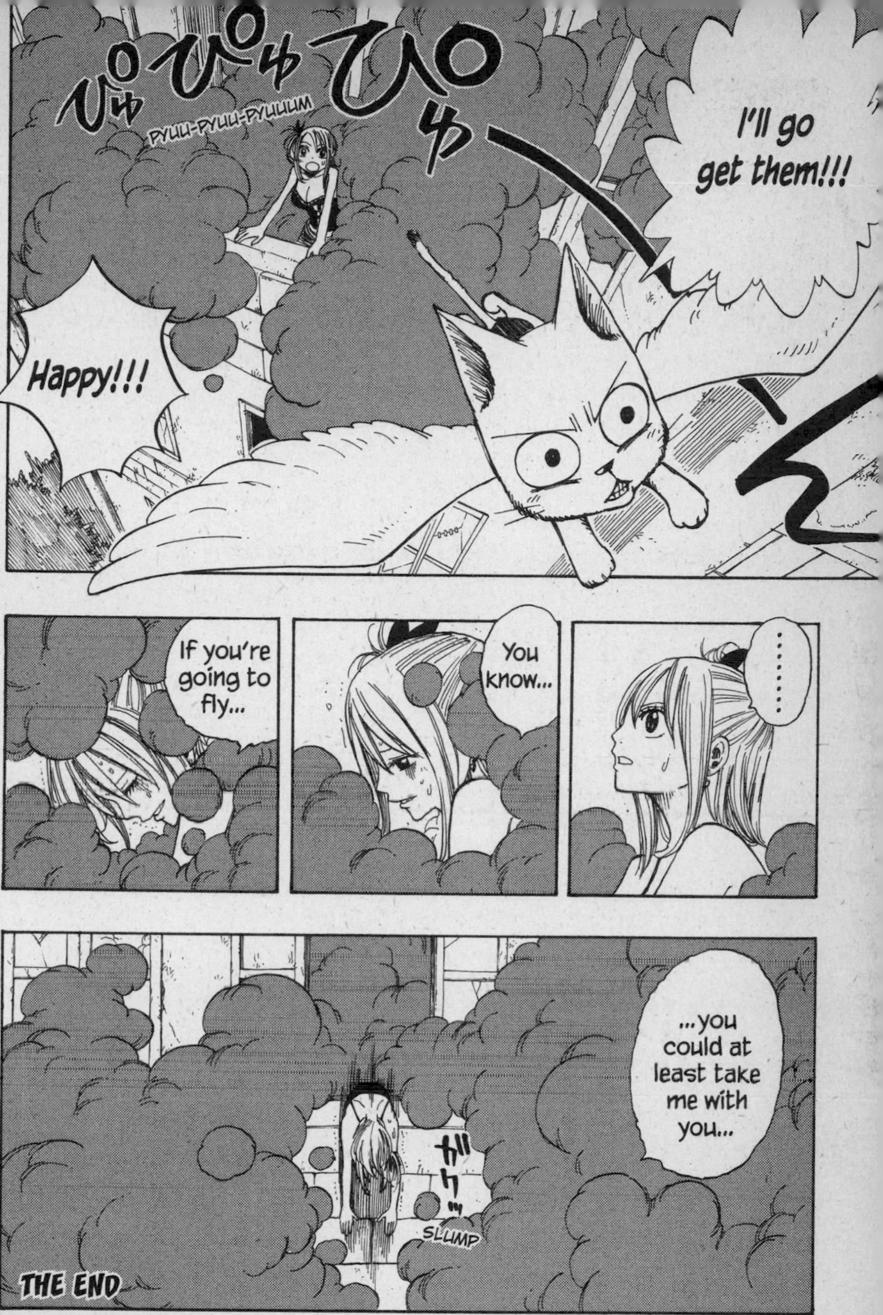
PYUU-PYUU-PYUUUM
I'll go get them!!!
Happy!!!
......
You know...
If you're going to fly...
...you could at least take me with you...
SLUMP
THE END

AFTERWORD

I introduced the "Guild de Art" illustration corner in the last volume, and I got a huge load of postcards for it!! We're still putting together presents for those selected, so we'll publish them in the next volume — which means we're still accepting entries!!!* Below you'll find some rules we'd like you to follow when sending in your postcards.

1 • Only use standard postcard size. (Entries too big or too small will not be published.)

2 • Draw only with black pen. (Colored pens and pencil marks don't print very well.)

3 • Don't forget your name and address. (For those using a penname, include your real name as well.)

*This refers to the original publication in Japan in May 2007.

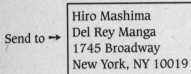

Send to →

Hiro Mashima
Del Rey Manga
1745 Broadway
New York, NY 10019

While Del Rey Manga will make its best efforts to get your letters to Mashima-sensei, we cannot guarantee a reply.

Now to change the subject to this volume, S-Class quests! What does the S in S-Class mean? Well, it means Super. It means Special. It means *Soreya yabai-zo!!* (That's gotta be dangerous!!) Anyway, it means that there are a lot of amazing jobs! And Natsu and his group went and grabbed one of these high-level jobs without permission!! What's going to happen with them?! That's what this part of the series is all about! And the story is all wound up in Gray's past. **Why Gray?!** Well... Let's not think too much about that. I-It's got nothing to do with me seeing a lot of female fans out there!! Or rather, I don't really see many, so I hope to pick up more female fans.... Hopefully, that's the effect. Actually, Mirajane mentioned it a while back, but Fairy Tail's members have something in their pasts. Erza, Loke, and Elfman... I want to get their stories into the manga little by little. I'd like the readers to get the sense that every character has a deeper side. At least, that's what I want to attempt.

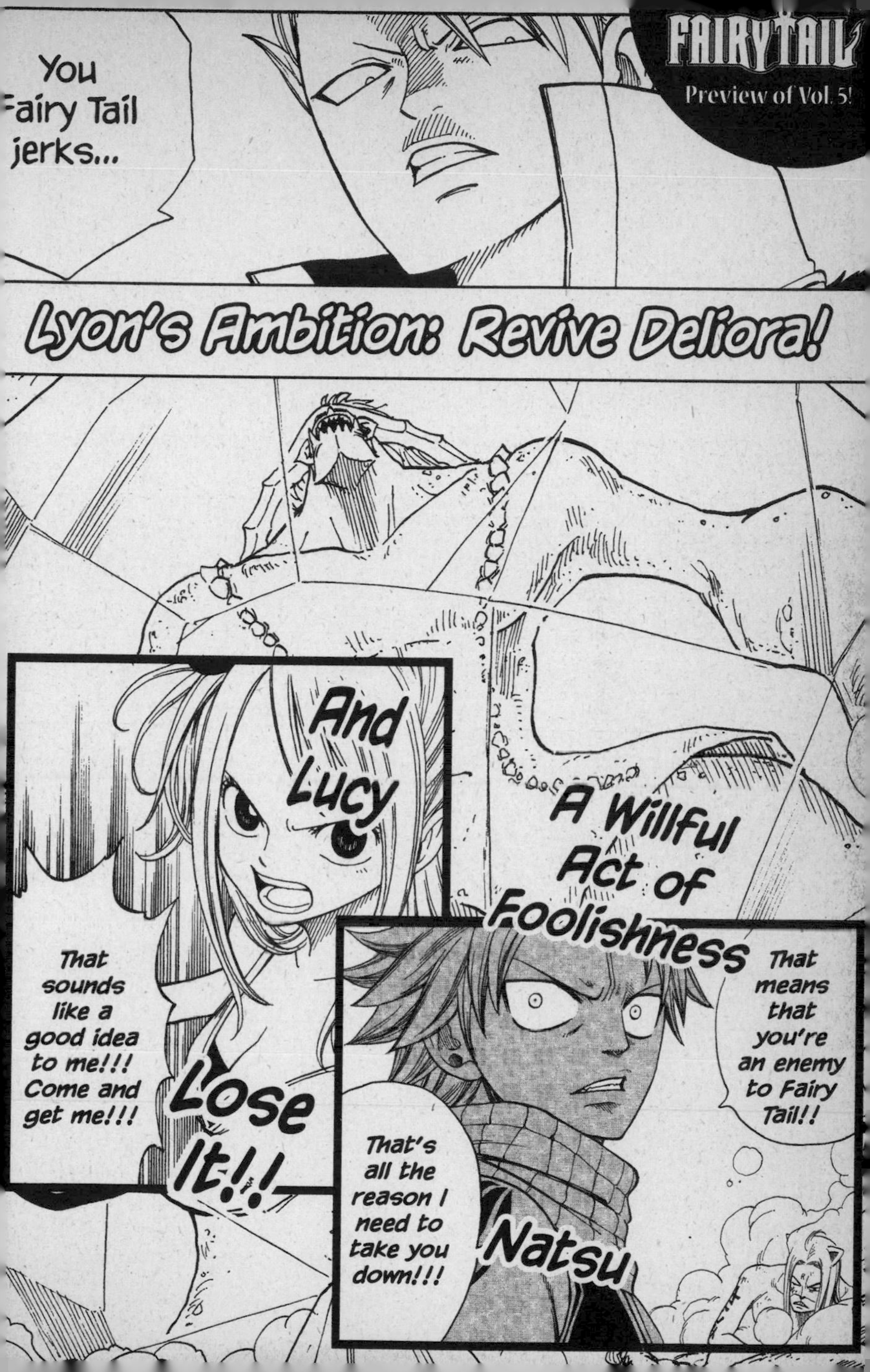
FAIRY TAIL
Preview of Vol. 5!
You Fairy Tail jerks...
Lyon's Ambition: Revive Deliora!
A Willful Act of Foolishness
That means that you're an enemy to Fairy Tail!!
That's all the reason I need to take you down!!!
Natsu
And Lucy
That sounds like a good idea to me!!! Come and get me!!!
Lose It!!!

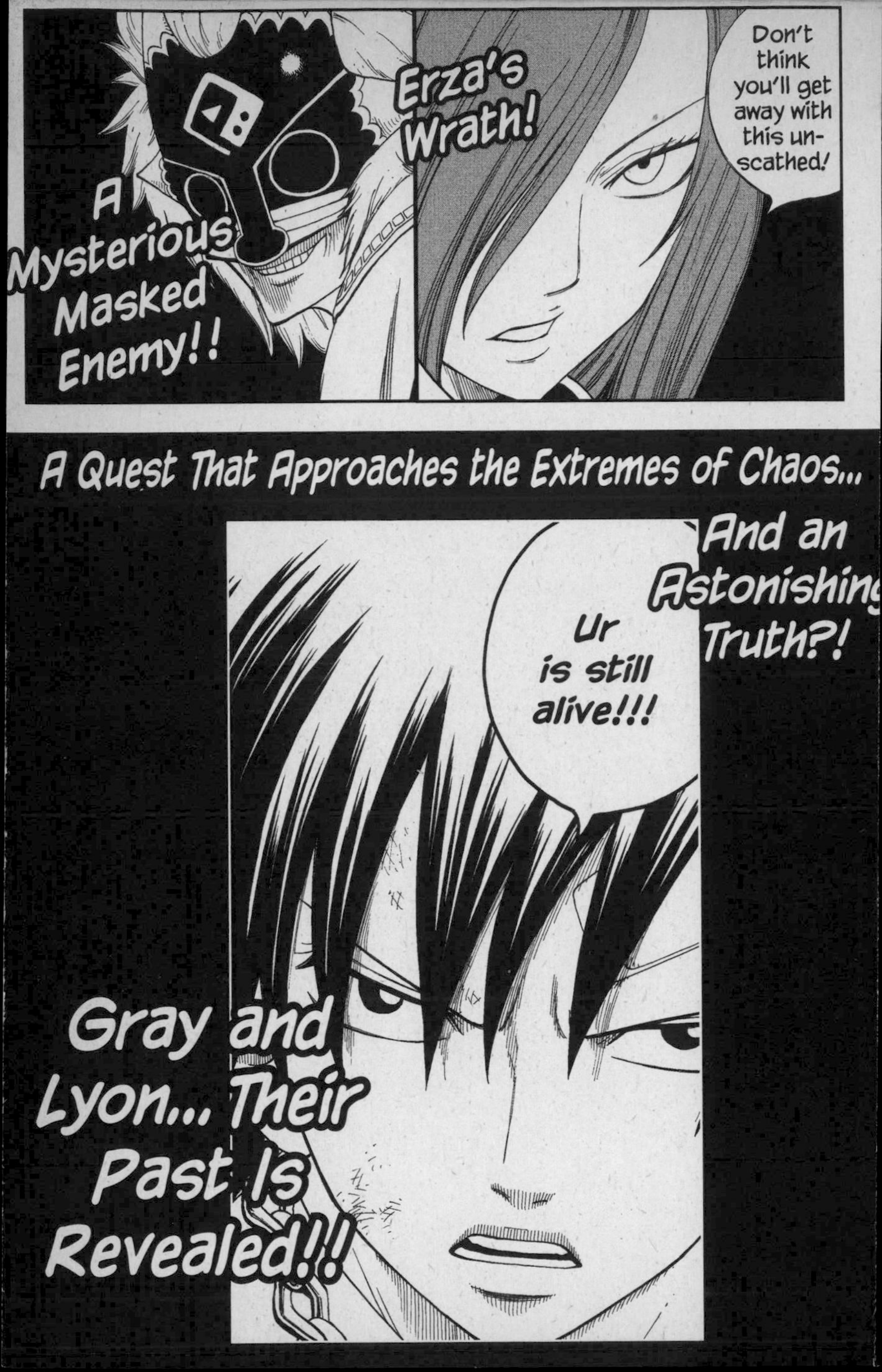
Don't think you'll get away with this unscathed!
Erza's Wrath!
A Mysterious Masked Enemy!!
A Quest That Approaches the Extremes of Chaos...
And an Astonishing Truth?!
Ur is still alive!!!
Gray and Lyon... Their Past Is Revealed!!!

About the Creator

HIRO MASHIMA was born May 3, 1977, in the Nagano prefecture. His series *Rave Master* has made him one of the most popular manga artists in America. *Fairy Tail*, currently being serialized in *Weekly Shonen Magazine*, is his latest creation.

Translation Notes

Japanese is a tricky language for most Westerners, and translation is often more art than science. For your edification and reading pleasure, here are notes on some of the places where we could have gone in a different direction in our translation of the work, or where a Japanese cultural reference is used.

General Notes:
Wizard

In the original Japanese version of *Fairy Tail*, you'll find panels in which the English word "wizard" is part of the original illustration. So this translation has taken that as its inspiration and translated the word *madôshi* as "wizard." But *madôshi*'s meaning is similar to certain Japanese words that have been borrowed by the English language, such as judo (the soft way) and kendo (the way of the sword). *Madô* is the way of magic, and *madôshi* are those who follow the way of magic. So although the word "wizard" is used in the original dialogue, a Japanese reader would be likely to think not of traditional Western wizards such as Merlin or Gandalf, but of martial artists.

Names

Hiro Mashima has graciously agreed to provide official English spellings for just about all of the characters in *Fairy Tail*. Because this version of *Fairy Tail* is the first publication of most of these spellings, there will inevitably be differences between these spellings and some of the fan interpretations that may have spread throughout the Web or in other fan circles. Rest assured that the spellings contained in this book are the spellings that Mashima-sensei wanted for *Fairy Tail*.

Freedom!! page 24

Natsu shouts the English word here. American action movies are very popular in Japan, so the cry of "Freedom!!" from the movie *Braveheart* would certainly be remembered. However, on the popular stand-up comedy TV show *God of Entertainment*, the final act in every show features a young "blues singer" who sings new verses of his ironic "Freedom Blues" song each week, refreshing the meaning of the English word "freedom" in Japanese minds.

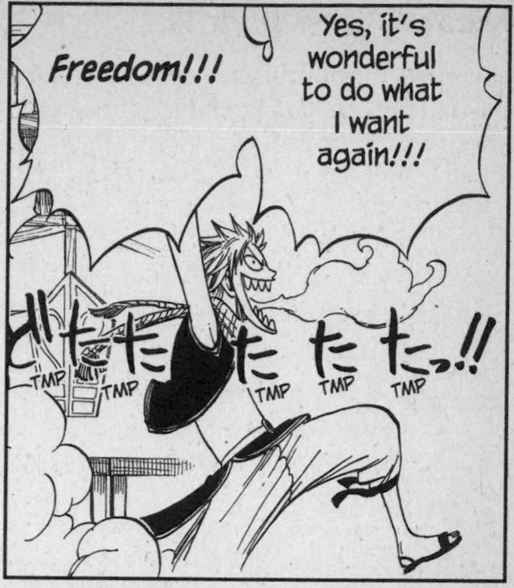
Yes, it's wonderful to do what I want again!!!
Freedom!!!
TMP TMP TMP TMP TMP

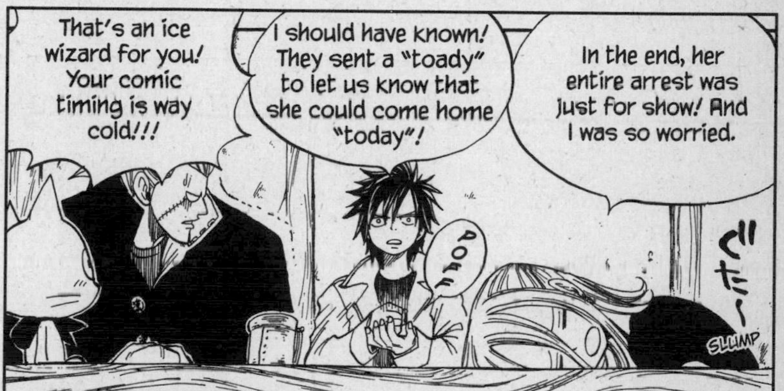
In the end, her entire arrest was just for show! And I was so worried.
I should have known! They sent a "toady" to let us know that she could come home "today"!
That's an ice wizard for you! Your comic timing is way cold!!!
SLUMP

Toady and cold, page 25

The Japanese version of Gray's pun was that the "frog" (*kaeru*) servant was a secret message that Erza would "come back" (also pronounced *kaeru*) very soon. Elfman's response that Gray, being an ice wizard, was "cold" played on the idea in Japan that a bad pun gives one the shivers. Fortunately there were handy puns in English that didn't change the meaning very much from the original.

Number kanji, page 31

The kanji for numbers used on this page are number kanji that were used in prewar Japan. They give a slightly archaic feel to Mystogan's countdown.

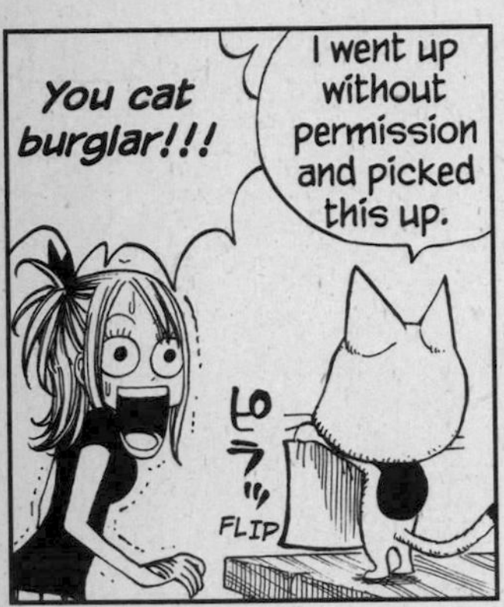
I went up without permission and picked this up.
You cat burglar!!!
FLIP

Cat burglar, page 44

The Japanese words translate directly to "cat thief" or "cat burglar."

Ahem, ahem, page 74

In the original text, the onomatopoeia used was *hoga hoga*, which is the sound old men make when opening and closing their mouths trying to get their false teeth back in alignment. I couldn't come up with a sound that would convey that sentiment very well in English, so I went with the words "ahem, ahem"—the sound of clearing one's throat before a speech. Fortunately it fit the character of a village headman pretty well.

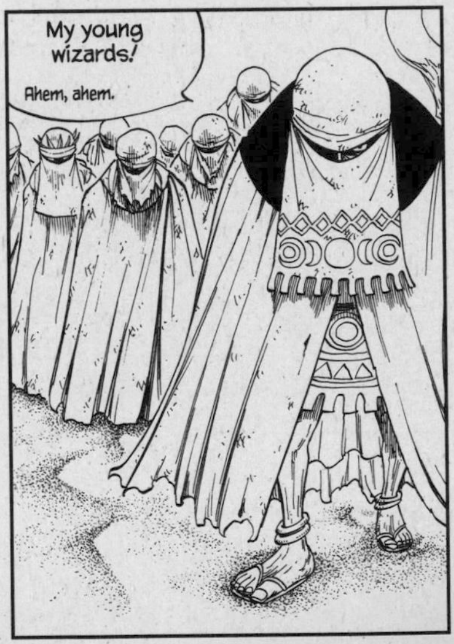
My young wizards!
Ahem, ahem.

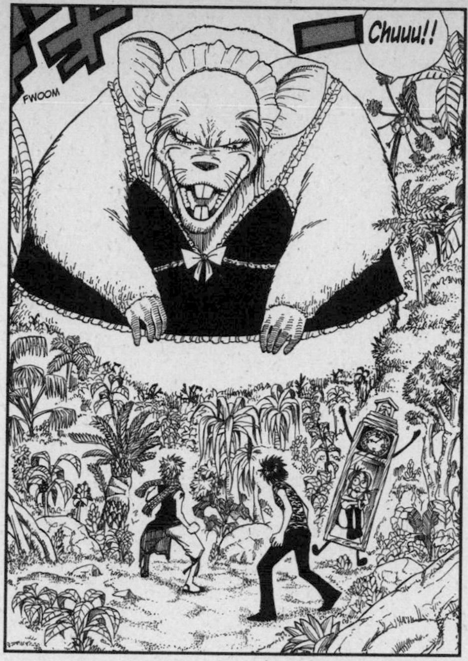
Chuuu!!
FWOOM

Chuu, page 92

The sound mice and rats make, as the Japanese hear it, is *chuu*. (Much like English speakers seem to hear mice and rats say, "Squeek.") There are many puns one can make using the sound, so this translation used the Japanese onomatopoeia on this page and at the back of the book in case Mashima wants to make comic use of the sound later in the series.

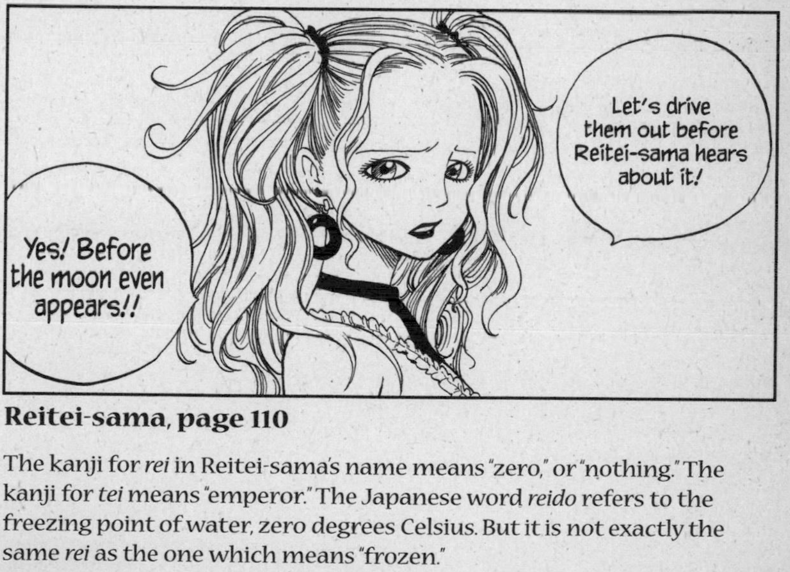
Let's drive them out before Reitei-sama hears about it!
Yes! Before the moon even appears!!

Reitei-sama, page 110

The kanji for *rei* in Reitei-sama's name means "zero," or "nothing." The kanji for *tei* means "emperor." The Japanese word *reido* refers to the freezing point of water, zero degrees Celsius. But it is not exactly the same *rei* as the one which means "frozen."

Lyra's lyrics, page 124

This translation makes no attempt to make the lyrics of Lyra's song rhyme. What's important here is the content: a direct translation of the lyrics best conveys why Lyra's song had such a profound effect on Gray.

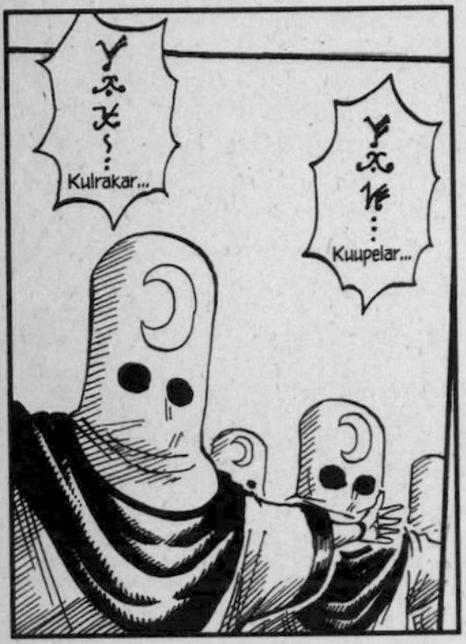
Kuupelar...
Kulrakar...

Chanting, page 128

The strange characters in this panel are not Japanese—they're a fictional language. In the original Japanese, an approximate Japanese pronunciation for each word was provided; here, we've provided the English approximation.

Splash page, page 176

In American comics terms, a splash page is the first page of a comic in which the entire page is taken up with one dynamic scene. Japanese usually have a splash page at the beginning of every chapter, called the *tobira peeji* ("door page"). Since they serve pretty much the same function, this translation interprets *tobira peeji* as "splash page."

Preview of Volume 5

We're pleased to present you with a preview from volume 5. Please check our website (www.delreymanga.com) to see when this volume will be available in English. For now you'll have to make do with Japanese!

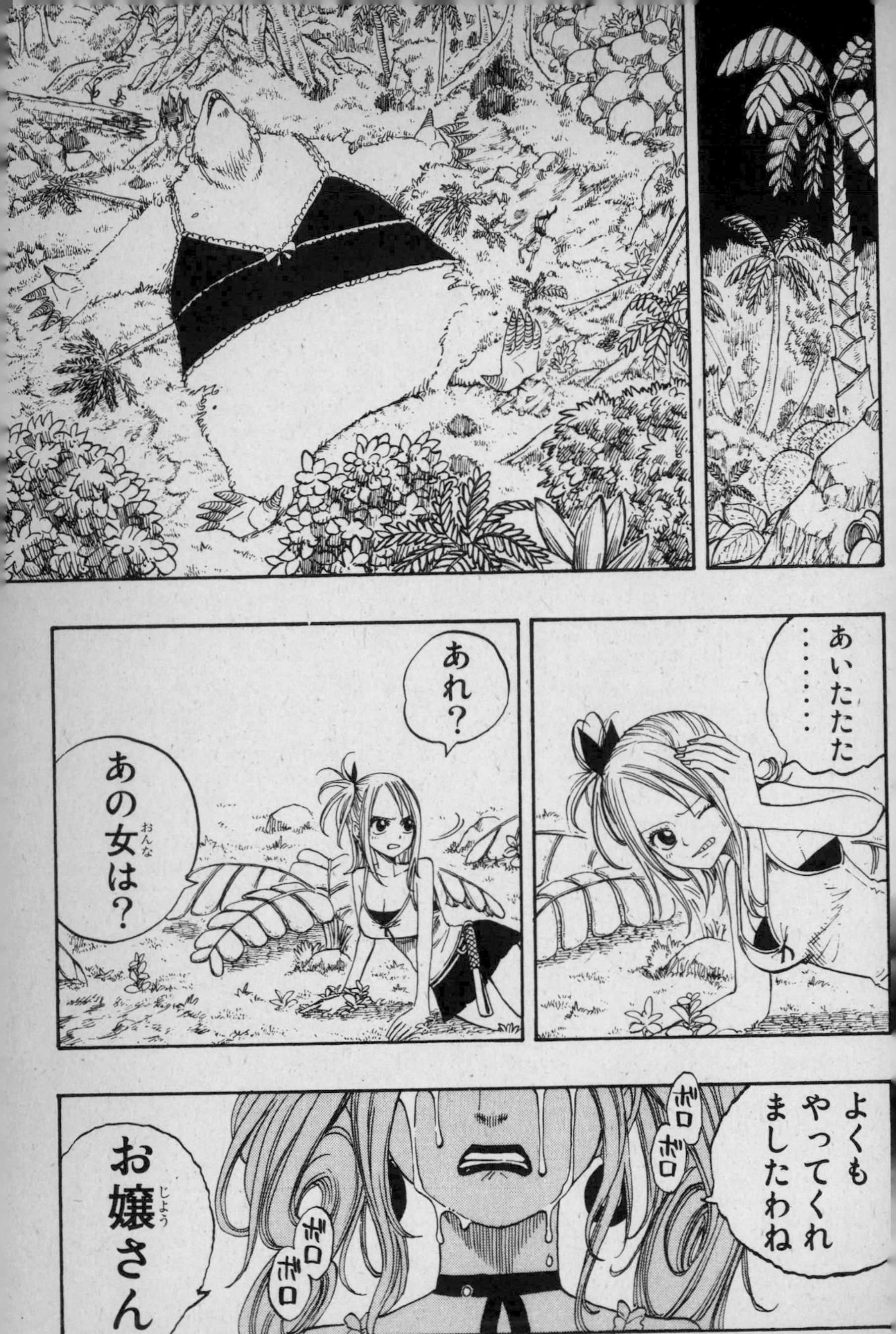
あいたたた……
あれ？
あの女は？
よくもやってくれましたわね
ボロボロ
ボロボロ
お嬢さん

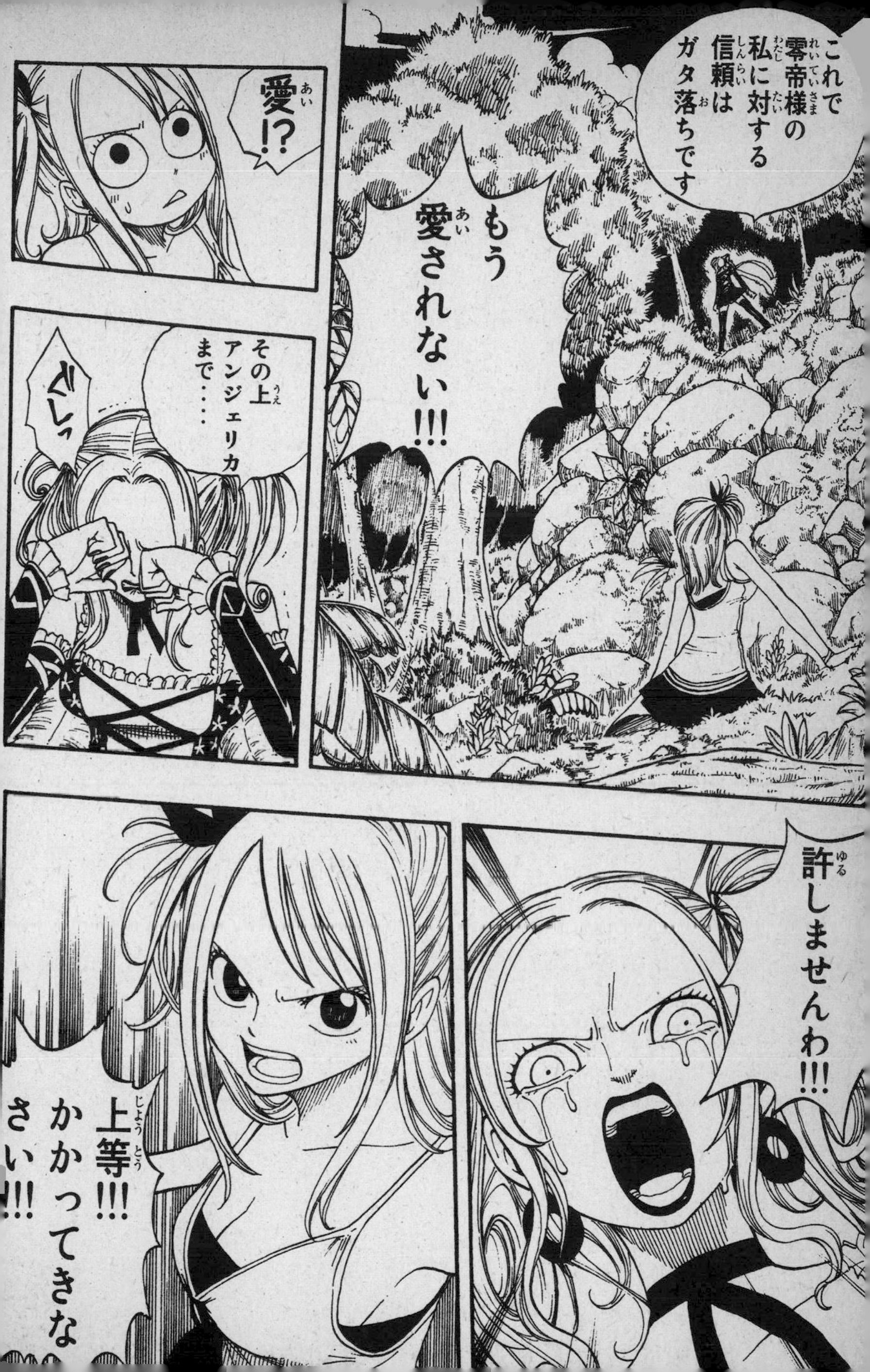

これで零帝様の私に対する信頼はガタ落ちです
もう愛されない!!!
愛!?
その上アンジェリカまで‥‥
ぐしっ
許しませんわ!!!
上等!!! かかってきなさい!!!

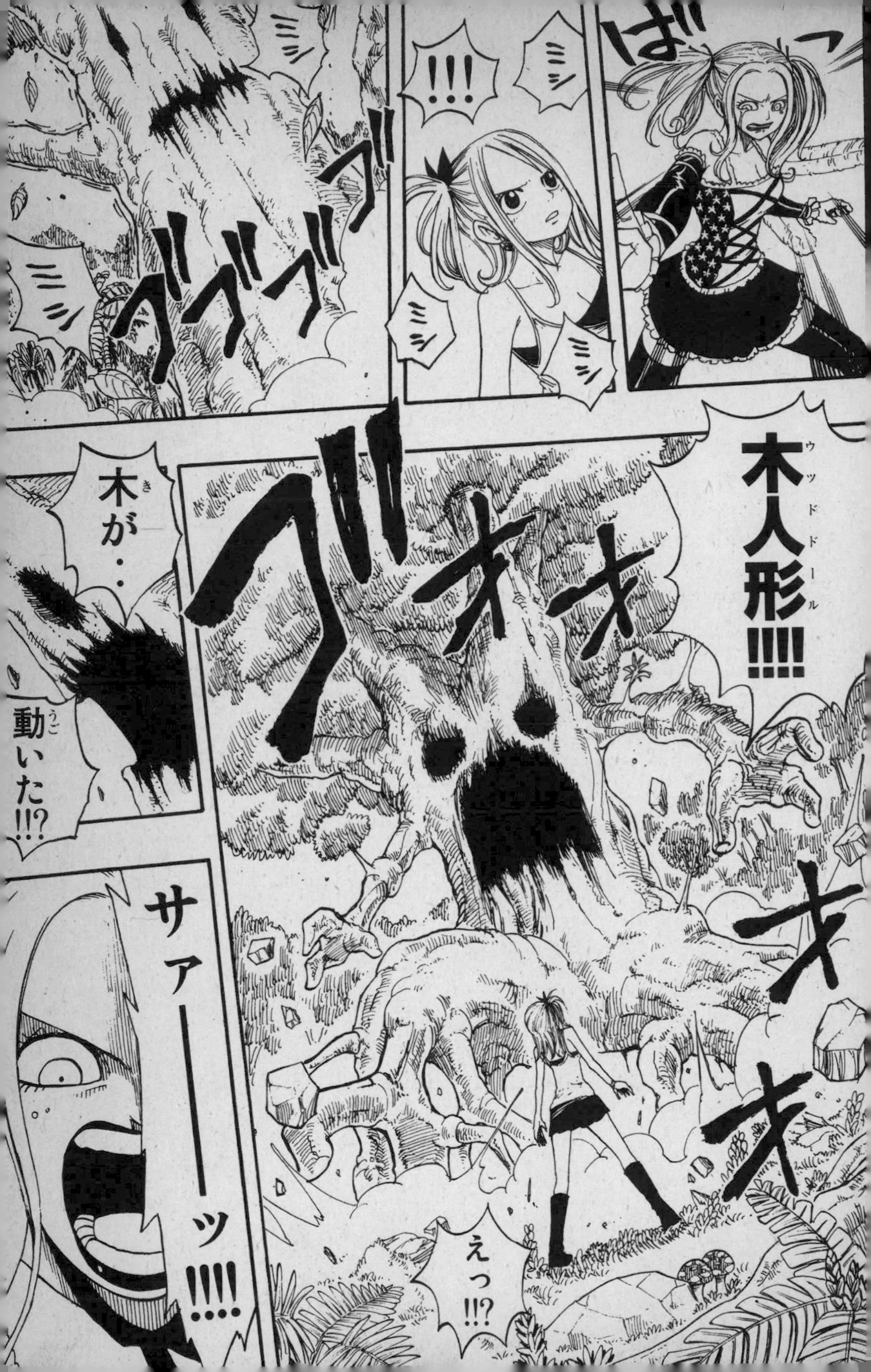
ばっ
ミシ
!!!
ミシ
ミシ
ミシ
ゴゴゴゴ
ミシ
木人形(ウッドドール)!!!!
ゴオォォォオ
えっ!!?
木(き)が・・・
動(うご)いた!!?
サアーーーッ!!!!

TOMARE!

止まれ

[STOP!]

You're going the wrong way!

Manga is a completely different type of reading experience.

To start at the *beginning*, go to the *end*!

That's right! Authentic manga is read the traditional Japanese way—from right to left, exactly the opposite of how American books are read. It's easy to follow: Just go to the other end of the book and read each page—and each panel—from right side to left side, starting at the top right. Now you're experiencing manga as it was meant to be!